VMware vSphere 6.x Datacenter Design Cookbook

Second Edition

Over 75 practical recipes to confidently design an efficient
virtual datacenter with VMware vSphere 6.x

Hersey Cartwright

[PACKT] enterprise 88
PUBLISHING   professional expertise distilled

BIRMINGHAM - MUMBAI

VMware vSphere 6.x Datacenter Design Cookbook

Second Edition

Copyright © 2016 Packt Publishing

First published: January 2014

Second published: June 2016

Production reference: 1220616

Published by Packt Publishing Ltd.
Livery Place
35 Livery Street
Birmingham B3 2PB, UK.

ISBN 978-1-78528-346-8

www.packtpub.com

Credits

Author

Hersey Cartwright

Reviewer

Kim Bottu

Commissioning Editor

Pratik Shah

Acquisition Editor

Vinay Argekar

Content Development Editor

Viranchi Shetty

Technical Editor

Dhiraj Chandanshive

Copy Editor

Stuti Srivastava

Project Coordinator

Izzat Contractor

Proofreader

Safis Editing

Indexer

Mariammal Chettiyar

Graphics

Jason Monteiro

Kirk D'Penha

Production Coordinator

Melwyn Dsa

Cover Work

Melwyn Dsa

About the Author

Hersey Cartwright has worked in the technology industry since 1996 in many roles, from help desk support to IT management. He first started working with VMware technologies in 2006. He is currently a solutions architect for SimpliVity, where he designs, sells, and supports VMware vSphere enterprise environments running on the SimpliVity **Hyperconverged Infrastructure (HCI)** platform. He has experience of working with a wide variety of server and storage platforms.

In 2012, he began preparing to submit a design to defend for his VMware Certified Design Expert. In February 2013, he successfully completed his defense and obtained VCDX. His VCDX number is #128.

Since January 2011, he has been an instructor with the VMware IT Academy at Tidewater Community college where he teaches vSphere 5 and vSphere 6 classes. He designed and implemented the lab environment that is used by students in the virtualization and security programs offered at the Chesapeake Campus of Tidewater Community College. He enjoys teaching and learns a lot from teaching others about the benefits of virtualization.

He actively participates in the VMware community, and he has been awarded the vExpert title every year since 2012. He has presented multiple ProfessionalVMware.com vBrownBags on vSphere administration, vSphere design, and vSphere disaster recovery. He regularly blogs about virtualization and other technologies at `http://www.vhersey.com/`.

I want to thank my family, especially my wife Sandy, for putting up with the long hours I work, listening to the noisy lab gear in the closet, and supporting everything I do. You guys are my everything, and your support and encouragement means the world to me.

I also want to thank the great VMware community. There are a lot of great folks there that are always willing to help out. A special thanks to the #vCoffee crew on Twitter: Shane, Susan, Matt, and Todd.

About the Reviewer

Kim Bottu is a virtualization engineer in the EMEA region for an international Biglaw firm, where he focuses on virtual datacenter operations, optimization, and design. In his current role, he takes care of the consolidated virtual datacenters in Asia and Europe, and he is the SME for the EMEA Litigation virtual datacenters.

He holds the following certifications and honors: VCA-NV, VCP5-DCV, VCP6-DCV, and VCAP5-DCD, and has been named vExpert 2016.

Kim currently lives in Belgium and is a proud dad of his daughter named Zoey. In his spare time you might find him playing with his daughter, reading books, or riding his mountain bike.

He can be reached at www.vMusketeers.com.

www.PacktPub.com

eBooks, discount offers, and more

Did you know that Packt offers eBook versions of every book published, with PDF and ePub files available? You can upgrade to the eBook version at www.PacktPub.com and as a print book customer, you are entitled to a discount on the eBook copy. Get in touch with us at customercare@packtpub.com for more details.

At www.PacktPub.com, you can also read a collection of free technical articles, sign up for a range of free newsletters and receive exclusive discounts and offers on Packt books and eBooks.

https://www2.packtpub.com/books/subscription/packtlib

Do you need instant solutions to your IT questions? PacktLib is Packt's online digital book library. Here, you can search, access, and read Packt's entire library of books.

Why subscribe?

- ▶ Fully searchable across every book published by Packt
- ▶ Copy and paste, print, and bookmark content
- ▶ On demand and accessible via a web browser

Instant updates on new Packt books

Get notified! Find out when new books are published by following @PacktEnterprise on Twitter or the *Packt Enterprise* Facebook page.

Table of Contents

Preface

VMware is the industry leader for datacenter virtualization. This second edition of the Datacenter Design Cookbook covers VMware's vSphere 6.x suite of products, which provide a robust and resilient platform to virtualize server and application workloads. The features available in vSphere 6.x simplify management, increase availability, provide security, and guarantee the performance of workloads deployed in the virtualized datacenter.

The *VMware vSphere 6.x Datacenter Design Cookbook Second Edition* provides recipes to create a virtual datacenter design using the features of vSphere 6.x. It does this by guiding you through the process of identifying the design factors and applying them to the logical and physical design process.

This book steps through the design process from beginning to end, from the discovery process, to creating the conceptual design, to calculating the resource requirements of the logical storage, compute, and network design, to mapping the logical requirements to a physical design, and finally creating the design documentation.

This book's recipes provide guidance for making design decisions to ensure the successful creation, and ultimately the successful implementation, of a VMware vSphere 6.x virtual datacenter design.

What this book covers

Chapter 1, The Virtual Datacenter, provides an introduction to the benefits of the virtual datacenter, VMware vSphere products, and basic virtualization concepts. This chapter identifies the differences between a datacenter administrator and a datacenter architect. An overview of the **VMware Certified Advanced Professional Datacenter Design** (**VCAP-DCD**) certification is also covered.

Chapter 2, The Discovery Process, explains how to identify stakeholders, conduct stakeholder interviews, and perform technical assessments in order to discover the business and technical goals of a virtualization project. This chapter covers how to use tools, VMware Capacity Planner, Windows Performance Monitor, and vRealize Operations Manager to collect resource information during the discovery process.

Chapter 3, The Design Factors, explains how to identify and document the design requirements, constraints, assumptions, and risks. This chapter details how to use the design factors to create the conceptual design.

Chapter 4, vSphere Management Design, describes the vCenter Server components and their dependencies. This chapter contains recipes to determine the vCenter Server deployment option, the Windows server or virtual appliance that you need to use, and determine the type of database that you need to use, based on the deployment size.

Chapter 5, vSphere Storage Design, covers logical storage design. Recipes are included to calculate the storage capacity and performance requirements for the logical storage design. This chapter covers the details of selecting the correct RAID level and storage connectivity to support a design. Recipes for VSAN and VVOLs are provided in this chapter.

Chapter 6, vSphere Network Design, provides details on logical network design. This chapter explains how to calculate bandwidth requirements to support a vSphere design. Details on selecting a virtual switch topology, designing for network availability, and the network requirements to support vMotion and IP connected storage are also covered.

Chapter 7, vSphere Compute Design, provides recipes to calculate the CPU and memory requirements to create the logical compute design. This chapter also covers cluster design considerations for **High Availability** (**HA**) and the **Distributed Resource Scheduler** (**DRS**).

Chapter 8, vSphere Physical Design, explains how to satisfy the design factors by mapping the logical management, storage, network, and compute designs to hardware to create the physical vSphere design. The chapter also provides details of creating a custom installation ISO to install ESXi and the best practices for host BIOS configurations.

Chapter 9, Virtual Machine Design, looks at the design of virtual machines and application workloads running in the virtual datacenter. Recipes are provided to right-size virtual machine resources, enable the ability to add virtual machine resources, and create virtual machine templates. This chapter details the use of affinity and anti-affinity rules to improve application efficiency and availability. Converting or migrating physical servers to virtual machines is also covered in this chapter.

Chapter 10, vSphere Security Design, provides an overview of vSphere features available to provide security in the virtual datacenter. Recipes covering authentication, access controls, and security hardening that must be incorporated into the datacenter design to secure the vSphere environment.

Chapter 11, Disaster Recovery and Business Continuity, covers options for backup, recovery, and continued operations in the event of system failure. This chapter covers how to create backups of vSphere configurations so that they can be quickly restored. The protection of virtual machines using VMware products for backup and replication is also covered in this chapter.

Chapter 12, Design Documentation, covers documenting a vSphere design. Documentation includes the Architecture Design Document, the Implementation Plan, the Installation Guide, the Validation and Test Plan, and the Operational Procedures. This chapter also provides tips to present the design to stakeholders and using the design documentation to implement the design.

What you need for this book

The following are the software requirements for this book:

- ▶ VMware vSphere ESXi 6.x
- ▶ VMware vCenter Server 6.x
- ▶ VMware PowerCLI 6.x
- ▶ VMware vCLI 6.x

Who this book is for

If you are an administrator or consultant interested in designing virtualized datacenter environments using VMware vSphere 5.x and the supporting components, then this book is for you. This book will help both new and experienced architects deliver professional VMware vSphere virtual datacenter designs.

Sections

In this book, you will find several headings that appear frequently (Getting ready, How to do it, How it works, There's more, and See also).

To give clear instructions on how to complete a recipe, we use these sections as follows:

Getting ready

This section tells you what to expect in the recipe, and describes how to set up any software or any preliminary settings required for the recipe.

How to do it...

This section contains the steps required to follow the recipe.

How it works...

This section usually consists of a detailed explanation of what happened in the previous section.

There's more...

This section consists of additional information about the recipe in order to make the reader more knowledgeable about the recipe.

See also

This section provides helpful links to other useful information for the recipe.

Conventions

In this book, you will find a number of text styles that distinguish between different kinds of information. Here are some examples of these styles and an explanation of their meaning.

Code words in text, database table names, folder names, filenames, file extensions, pathnames, dummy URLs, user input, and Twitter handles are shown as follows: "VIB files have the .vib file extension."

Any command-line input or output is written as follows:

```
ESX1 # esxcli network ip netstack add -N "Name_of_Stack"
```

New terms and **important words** are shown in bold. Words that you see on the screen, in menus or dialog boxes for example, appear in the text like this: "The **Send a notification email** or **Send a notification trap** action can be configured in the alarm **Actions** section."

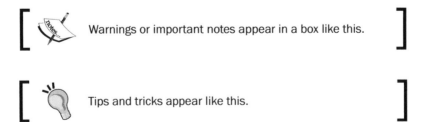

> Warnings or important notes appear in a box like this.

> Tips and tricks appear like this.

Reader feedback

Feedback from our readers is always welcome. Let us know what you think about this book—what you liked or disliked. Reader feedback is important for us as it helps us develop titles that you will really get the most out of.

To send us general feedback, simply e-mail `feedback@packtpub.com`, and mention the book's title in the subject of your message.

If there is a topic that you have expertise in and you are interested in either writing or contributing to a book, see our author guide at `www.packtpub.com/authors`.

Customer support

Now that you are the proud owner of a Packt book, we have a number of things to help you to get the most from your purchase.

Downloading the color images of this book

We also provide you with a PDF file that has color images of the screenshots/diagrams used in this book. The color images will help you better understand the changes in the output. You can download this file from `http://www.packtpub.com/sites/default/files/downloads/VMwarevSphere6xDatacenterDesignCookbookSecondEdition_ColorImages.pdf`.

Errata

Although we have taken every care to ensure the accuracy of our content, mistakes do happen. If you find a mistake in one of our books—maybe a mistake in the text or the code—we would be grateful if you could report this to us. By doing so, you can save other readers from frustration and help us improve subsequent versions of this book. If you find any errata, please report them by visiting `http://www.packtpub.com/submit-errata`, selecting your book, clicking on the **Errata Submission Form** link, and entering the details of your errata. Once your errata are verified, your submission will be accepted and the errata will be uploaded to our website or added to any list of existing errata under the Errata section of that title.

To view the previously submitted errata, go to `https://www.packtpub.com/books/content/support` and enter the name of the book in the search field. The required information will appear under the **Errata** section.

Piracy

Piracy of copyrighted material on the Internet is an ongoing problem across all media. At Packt, we take the protection of our copyright and licenses very seriously. If you come across any illegal copies of our works in any form on the Internet, please provide us with the location address or website name immediately so that we can pursue a remedy.

Please contact us at `copyright@packtpub.com` with a link to the suspected pirated material.

We appreciate your help in protecting our authors and our ability to bring you valuable content.

Questions

If you have a problem with any aspect of this book, you can contact us at `questions@packtpub.com`, and we will do our best to address the problem.

1

The Virtual Datacenter

In this chapter, we will cover the following topics:

- ► Becoming a virtual datacenter architect
- ► Using a holistic approach to datacenter design
- ► Passing the VMware VCAP-DCV Design exam
- ► Identifying what's new in vSphere 6
- ► Planning a vSphere 6 upgrade

Introduction

This chapter focuses on many of the basic concepts and benefits of virtualization. It provides a quick overview of VMware virtualization, introduces the virtual datacenter architect, and lays some of the groundwork necessary to create and implement a successful virtual datacenter design using VMware vSphere 6.x.

We will also explore the **VMware Certified Advanced Professional-Datacenter Virtualization (VCAP6-DCV)** design exam and the new **VMware Certified Implementation Expert-Datacenter Virtualization (VCIX6-DCV)** certification, including a few tips that should help you prepare to successfully complete the exam and certification.

Then, we will look at some of the new features of vSphere 6. This section will include where to find the current release notes and the latest vSphere product documentation.

Finally, we will take a high-level look at the process of planning an upgrade to an existing vSphere deployment to vSphere 6.

If you are already familiar with virtualization, this chapter will provide a review of many of the benefits and technologies of virtualization.

Since the focus of this book is on design, we will not go into great detail discussing the specifics of how to configure resources in a virtual datacenter. Most of you probably already have a good understanding of VMware's virtualization architecture. So, this section will provide just a basic overview of the key VMware components that are the building blocks to the virtual datacenter.

Virtualization creates a layer of abstraction between the physical hardware and the virtual machines that run on it. Virtual hardware is presented to the virtual machine, granting access to the underlying physical hardware, which is scheduled by the hypervisor's kernel. The hypervisor separates the physical hardware from the virtual machine, as shown in the following diagram:

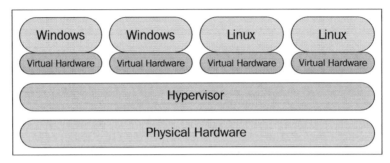

The hypervisor separates the physical hardware from the virtual machine

The new release of vSphere 6 does not change the design process or the design methodologies. The new functions and features of the release provide an architect with more tools to satisfy design requirements.

The hypervisor

At the core of any virtualization platform is the hypervisor. The VMware hypervisor is named vSphere ESXi, simply referred to as ESXi. ESXi is a Type 1 or bare-metal hypervisor. This means it runs directly on the host's hardware to present virtual hardware to the virtual machines. In turn, the hypervisor schedules access to the physical hardware of the hosts.

ESXi allows multiple virtual machines with a variety of operating systems to run simultaneously, sharing the resources of the underlying physical hardware. Access to physical resources, such as memory, CPU, storage, and network, used by the virtual machines is managed by the scheduler or the **Virtual Machine Monitor** (**VMM**) provided by ESXi. The resources presented to the virtual machines can be overcommitted. This means more resources than are available can be allocated to the virtual machines on the physical hardware. Advanced memory sharing and reclamation techniques, such as **Transparent Page Sharing** (**TPS**) and ballooning, along with CPU scheduling, allow for overcommitment of these resources, resulting in greater virtual to physical consolidation ratios.

ESXi 6 is a 64-bit hypervisor that must be run on a 64-bit hardware. An ESXi 6 installation requires at least 1 GB of disk space for installation. It can be installed on a hard disk locally, on a USB device, on a **Logical Unit Number** (**LUN**), on a **Storage Area Network** (**SAN**), or can be deployed stateless on hosts with no storage using Auto Deploy. The small footprint of an ESXi installation provides a reduction in the management overhead associated with patching and security hardening.

With the release of vSphere 5.0, VMware retired the ESX hypervisor. ESX had a separate Linux-based service console for the management interface of the hypervisor. Management functions were provided by agents running in the service console. The service console has since been removed from ESXi, and agents now run directly on ESXi's VMkernel.

To manage a standalone host running ESXi, a **Direct Console User Interface** (**DCUI**) is provided for basic configuration and troubleshooting. A shell is available that can either be accessed locally from the console or remotely using **Secure Shell** (**SSH**). esxcli and other commands can be used in the shell to provide advanced configuration options.

An ESXi host can also be accessed directly using the vSphere client. The ESXi DCUI is shown in the following screenshot:

ESXi's DCUI

The DCUI can be accessed remotely using SSH by typing the `dcui` command in the prompt. Press *Ctrl* + *C* to exit the remote DCUI session.

Virtual machines

A virtual machine is a software computer that runs a guest operating system. Virtual machines comprise a set of configuration files and data files stored on local or remote storage. These configuration files contain information about the virtual hardware presented to the virtual machine. This virtual hardware includes the CPU, RAM, disk controllers, removable devices, and so on. It emulates the same functionality as the physical hardware. The following screenshot depicts the virtual machine files that are stored on a shared **Network File System** (**NFS**) data store:

Virtual machine files stored on a shared NFS data store displayed using the vSphere web client

The files that make up a virtual machine are typically stored in a directory set aside for the particular virtual machine they represent. These files include the configuration file, virtual disk files, NVRAM file, and virtual machine log files.

The following table lists the common virtual machine file extensions along with a description of each:

File extension	Description
.vmx	This is a virtual machine configuration file. It contains the configurations of the virtual hardware that is presented to the virtual machine.
.vmdk	This is a virtual disk descriptor file. It contains a header and other information pertaining to the virtual disk.
-flat.vmdk	This is a preallocated virtual disk. It contains the content or data on the disk used by the virtual machine.
.nvram	This is a file that stores the state of a virtual machine's **Basic Input Output System (BIOS)** or **Extensible Firmware Interface (EFI)** configurations.
.vswp	This is a virtual machine swap file. It gets created when a virtual machine is powered on. The size of this file is equal to the amount of memory allocated minus any memory reservations.
.log	This is a virtual machine logfile.
.vmsd	This is a virtual machine file used with snapshots to store data about each snapshot active on a virtual machine.
.vmsn	This is a virtual machine snapshot data file.

Virtual machines can be deployed using a variety of methods as follows:

- Using the **New Virtual Machine** wizard in the vSphere client or vSphere web client
- By getting converted from a physical machine using the VMware converter
- By getting imported from an **Open Virtualization Format (OVF)** or **Open Virtualization Archive (OVA)**
- By getting cloned from an existing virtual machine
- By getting deployed from a virtual machine template

When a new virtual machine is created, a guest operating system can be installed on the virtual machine. VMware vSphere 6 supports more than 80 different guest operating systems. These include many versions of the Windows server and desktop operating systems, many distributions and versions of Linux and Unix operating systems, and Apple Mac OS operating systems.

Virtual appliances are preconfigured virtual machines that can be imported to the virtual environment. A virtual appliance can comprise a single virtual machine or a group of virtual machines with all the components required to support an application. The virtual machines in a virtual appliance are preloaded with guest operating systems, and the applications they run are normally preconfigured and optimized to run in a virtual environment.

Since virtual machines are just a collection of files on a disk, they become portable. Virtual machines can be easily moved from one location to another by simply moving or copying the associated files. Using VMware vSphere features such as vMotion, Enhanced vMotion, or Storage vMotion, virtual machines can be migrated from host to host or data store to data store while they are running. Virtual machines can also be exported to an OVF or OVA to be imported into another VMware vSphere environment.

Virtual infrastructure management

VMware vCenter Server provides a centralized management interface to manage and configure groups of ESXi hosts in the virtualized datacenter. The vCenter Server is required to configure and control many advanced features, such as the **Distributed Resource Scheduler** (**DRS**), Storage DRS, and VMware **High Availability** (**HA**). The vCenter Server is accessed using either the Windows vSphere client or the vSphere web client. Many vendors provide plugins that can be installed to allow third-party storage, network, and compute resources to be managed using the vSphere client or vSphere web client.

> The C#, or Windows vSphere client, is still available in vSphere 6. Since the release of vSphere 5.5, access to, and the configuration of, new features is only available using the vSphere web client. The vSphere web client can be accessed at `https://FQDN_or_IP_of_vCenter_Server:9443/`.

The vCenter Server can be installed on a 64-bit Windows server. It can be run on dedicated physical hardware or as a virtual machine. When the vCenter Server is deployed on the Windows server, it requires either the embedded vPostgres database, a Microsoft SQL database, or an Oracle database to store configuration and performance information. IBM DB2 databases are supported with vSphere 5.1, but this support was removed in vSphere 5.5.

With the release of vCenter 6, the Microsoft SQL Express database is no longer used as the embedded database. vPostgres is now used as the embedded database for small deployments. The vPostgres database on a Windows server can be used to support environments of fewer than 20 hosts and 200 virtual machines. When upgrading to vCenter 6, if the previous version was using the Microsoft SQL Express database, the database will be converted to the embedded vPostgres database as part of the upgrade.

Another option to deploy the vCenter Server is the **vCenter Server Appliance** (**VCSA**). The VCSA is a preconfigured, Linux-based virtual machine, preinstalled with the vCenter Server components. The appliance includes an embedded vPostgres database that supports up to 1,000 hosts and 10,000 virtual machines. The embedded vPostgres database is suitable for almost all deployments, using an external Oracle database is also supported.

Several other management and automation tools are available to aid the day-to-day administration of a vSphere environment. One of them is the **vSphere Command-Line Interface** (**vCLI**). Another one is the vSphere PowerCLI, which provides a Windows PowerShell interface. The vRealize Orchestrator can be used to automate tasks, and the **vSphere Management Assistant** (**vMA**) is a Linux-based virtual appliance that is used to run management and automation scripts against hosts. These tools allow an administrator to use command-line utilities to manage hosts from remote workstations.

VMware provides a suite of other products that benefits the virtualized datacenter. These datacenter products, such as VMware **vRealize Operations** (**vROps**), VMware **Site Recovery Manager** (**SRM**), and VMware **vRealize Automation** (**vRA**), can each be leveraged in the virtual datacenter to meet specific requirements related to management, disaster recovery, and cloud services. At the core of these products is vSphere suite, which includes ESXi, the vCenter Server, and the core supporting components.

Understanding the benefits of virtualization

The following table provides a matrix of some of the core VMware technologies and the benefits that can be realized using them. This is not meant to be an exhaustive list of all VMware technologies and features, but it provides an insight into many of the technologies commonly deployed in the enterprise virtual datacenter:

VMware technology	Primary benefits	Description
vSphere ESXi	Server consolidation Resource efficiency	ESXi is VMware's bare-metal hypervisor that hosts virtual machines, also known as guests, and schedules virtual hardware access to physical resources.
vSphere HA	Increased availability	HA restarts virtual machines in the event of a host failure. It also monitors and restarts the virtual machines in the event of a guest operating system failure.
vMotion and vSphere DRS	Resource efficiency Increased availability	vMotion allows virtual machines to be live-migrated between hosts in a virtual datacenter. DRS determines the initial placement of the virtual machine on the host resources within a cluster and makes recommendations, or automatically migrates the virtual machines to balance resources across all hosts in a cluster.

VMware technology	Primary benefits	Description
Resource pools	Resource efficiency	These are used to guarantee, reserve, or limit the virtual machine's CPU, memory, and disk resources.
VMware **Fault Tolerance** (**FT**)	Increased availability	FT provides 100 percent uptime for a virtual machine in the event of a host hardware failure. It creates a secondary virtual machine that mirrors all the operations of the primary. In the event of a hardware failure, the secondary virtual machine becomes the primary and a new secondary is created.
Thin provisioning	Resource efficiency	This allows for storage to be overprovisioned by presenting the configured space to a virtual machine but only consuming the space on the disk that the guest actually requires.
Hot add CPU and memory	Resource efficiency Scalability	This allows for the addition of CPU and memory resources to a virtual machine while the virtual machine is running.
Storage vMotion	Resource efficiency	This moves virtual machine configuration files and disks between storage locations that have been presented to a host.
vSphere Data Protection (**VDP**)	Disaster recovery	This provides agentless image-level backup and recovery of virtual machines.
vSphere Replication	Disaster recovery	This features provides the ability to replicate virtual machines between sites.
vCenter Server	Simplified management	This provides a single management interface to configure and monitor the resources available to virtual datacenters.

VMware technology	Primary benefits	Description
vCenter Server Linked Mode	Simplified management	This links multiple vCenter Servers together to allow them to be managed from a single client.
Host Profiles	Simplified management	This maintains consistent configuration and configuration compliance across all the hosts in the environment.

There are many others, and each technology or feature may also have its own set of requirements that must be met in order to be implemented. The purpose here is to show how features or technologies can be mapped to benefits, which can then be mapped to requirements and ultimately mapped into a design. This is helpful in ensuring that the benefits and technologies provided by virtualization satisfy the design requirements.

Identifying when not to virtualize

Not all applications or server workloads are good candidates for virtualization. It is important that these workloads are identified early on in the design process.

There are a number of reasons a server or application may not be suitable for virtualization. Some of these include the following:

- ▶ Vendor support
- ▶ Licensing issues
- ▶ Specialized hardware dependencies
- ▶ High resource demand
- ▶ Lack of knowledge or skill set

A common reason to not virtualize an application or workload is the reluctance of a vendor to support their application in a virtual environment. As virtualization has become more common in the enterprise datacenter, this has become uncommon. However, there are still application vendors that will not support their products once virtualized.

Software and operating systems licensing in a virtual environment can also be a challenge, especially when it comes to conversions from physical server to virtual machine. Many physical servers are purchased with **Original Equipment Manufacturer** (**OEM**) licenses, and these licenses, in most cases, cannot be transferred to a virtual environment. Also, many licenses are tied to hardware-specific information, such as interface MAC addresses or drive signatures. Licensing issues can usually be overcome. Many times, the primary risk becomes the cost of upgrading or acquiring new licensing. As with other potential design risks, it is important that any issues and the potential impact of licensing on the design be identified early on in the design process.

Some applications may require the use of specialized hardware. Fax boards, serial ports, and security dongles are common examples. There are ways to provide solutions for many of these. However, often, with the risks associated with the ability to support the application or with the loss of one or more of the potential benefits of virtualizing the application, the better solution may be to leave the application on dedicated physical hardware. Again, it is important that these types of applications be identified very early on in the design process.

Physical servers configured with a large amount of CPU and memory resources where applications are consuming a large amount of these resources may not be good candidates for virtualization. This also holds true for applications with high network utilization and large storage I/O requirements. vSphere 6.0 supports virtual machines configured with up to 128 **Virtual CPUs** (**vCPUs**) and 4 TB of memory, but the high utilization of these configured resources can have a negative impact on other workloads in the virtual environment. These high-utilization workloads will also require more resources to be reserved for failover. The benefits of virtualizing resource-intensive applications must be weighed against the impact placed on the environment. In some cases, it may be better to leave these applications on dedicated physical hardware.

Many administrators may lack knowledge of the benefits or skills to manage a virtualized datacenter. The administrator of a virtual environment must be well-versed with storage, networking, and virtualization in order to successfully configure, maintain, and monitor a virtual environment. Though this may not necessarily be a reason not to leverage the benefits of a virtualized environment, it can be a substantial risk to the acceptance of a design and its implementation. This is especially true with smaller IT departments where the roles of the server, application, storage, and network administrators are combined.

Each of these can introduce risks in the design. We will discuss how risk impacts the design process in much more detail in *Chapter 2, The Discovery Process*, and *Chapter 3, The Design Factors*.

Becoming a virtual datacenter architect

The virtual datacenter architect, or simply the architect, is someone who identifies requirements, designs a virtualization solution to meet those requirements, and then oversees the implementation of the solution. Sounds easy enough, right?

How to do it...

The primary role of the architect is to provide solutions that meet customer requirements. At times, this can be difficult since the architect may not always be part of the complete sales process. Many times, customers may purchase hardware from other vendors and look to us to help them "make it all work". In such situations, the purchased hardware becomes a constraint on the design. Identifying and dealing with constraints and other design factors will be discussed in more detail in *Chapter 2, The DiscoveryProcess*, and *Chapter 3, The Design Factors*.

The architect must also be able to identify requirements, both business and technical, by conducting stakeholder interviews and analyzing current configurations. Once the requirements have been identified, the architect must then map the requirements into a solution by creating a design. This design is then presented to the stakeholders and if approved, it is implemented. During the implementation phase, the architect ensures that configurations are done to meet the design requirements, and the work done stays within the scope of the design.

The architect must also understand best practice. Not just best practice to configure the hypervisor, but for management, storage, security, and networking. Understanding best practice is the key. The architect not only knows best practice but understands why it is considered best practice. It is also important to understand when to deviate from what is considered best practice.

There's more...

The large part of an architect's work is "customer-facing". This includes conducting interviews with stakeholders to identify requirements and ultimately presenting the design to decision makers. Besides creating a solid solution to match the customer's requirements, it is important that the architect gains and maintains the trust of the project stakeholders. A professional appearance and, more importantly, a professional attitude are both helpful in building this relationship.

Using a holistic approach to datacenter design

The virtual datacenter architect must be able to take a holistic approach to datacenter design. This means that, for every decision made, the architect must understand how the environment, as a whole, will be impacted.

An architect is required to be, at the very least, familiar with all aspects of the datacenter. They must understand how the different components of a datacenter, such as storage, networking, computing, security, and management, are interconnected, as shown in the following diagram:

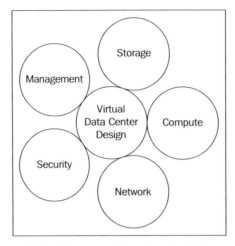

The holistic approach to datacenter design

It has become very important to understand how any decision or change will impact the rest of the design. Identifying dependencies becomes an important part of the design process. If a change is made to the network, how are computing, management, and storage resources affected? What other dependencies will this introduce in the design? Failing to take a holistic approach to design can result in unnecessary complications during the design process and potentially costly fixes after the design is implemented.

How to do it...

You have been engaged to design a virtualization solution for a financial organization. The solution you are proposing is using 10 GB **Converged Network Adapters** (**CNA**) to provide connectivity to the organization's network in three 1U rackmount servers. The organization needs to separate a **Virtual Local Area Network** (**VLAN**) that is currently configured to be delivered over the CNA onto a physically separate network to satisfy a new compliance requirement. A 1 GB network will provide sufficient bandwidth for this network, and the network should be highly available. Single points of failure should be minimized.

To support this compliance requirement, you, the architect, must take a holistic approach to the design by answering a number of questions about each design decision. Some questions are as follows:

> ▸ Are there available network ports in the current rackmount servers, or will a network card need to be added? If a card must be added, are there available **Peripheral Component Interconnect** (**PCI**) slots?

> ▸ Will a dual port network card provide sufficient redundancy, or will the network need to be separated across physical cards? Are there onboard network ports available that can be used with a PCI network card to provide in-box redundancy?

> ▸ Has the physically separate switch's hardware been obtained? If not, how long before the equipment is received and deployed? Will this have an impact on the implementation schedule?

> ▸ How will the virtual switch need to be configured to provide the connectivity and redundancy required?

How it works...

The impact can be fairly significant, depending on some of the answers. For example, let's say that the 1U rackmount server will not support the required network adapters needed to satisfy the requirement, and a different 2U rackmount server must be used. This then raises more questions, such as: "Is there sufficient space in the rackmount to support the new server footprint?"

What if the requirement had been that the applications connected to this network be virtualized on separate physical server hardware and storage? What parts of the design would have to change? The architect must be able to understand the dependencies of each part of the design and how a change in one place may affect other areas of the design.

As you think through these questions, you should be able to see how a change to a requirement can have a deep impact on many other areas of the design. It becomes very important to identify requirements early on in the design process.

Passing the VMware VCAP6-DCV Design exam

For vSphere 5 and vSphere 6, VMware released advanced exams, testing the ability of a person to deploy, administer, and design complex virtual environments. The exams for vSphere 6 are the **VMware Certified Advanced Professional 6-Datacenter Virtualization Deployment** (**VCAP6-DCV Deployment**) exam, which focuses on deploying and administering a VMware vSphere environment, and the **VMware Certified Advanced Professional 6-Datacenter Virtualization Design** (**VCAP6-DCV Design**) exam, which focuses on designing an enterprise VMware vSphere environment. VMware has introduced a new certification, **VMware Certified Implementation Expert-Datacenter Virtualization** (**VCIX6-DCV**), which is obtained by passing both the VCAP6-DCV Deployment and VCAP6-DCV Design.

The current VMware Certification path is mapped out in the following flowchart:

VMware certification path for datacenter administrators and architects

The VCAP6-DCV Design exam tests your ability to design enterprise virtualized environments. To be successful, you must have an in-depth understanding of VMware's core components and the relationship they share with other components of the datacenter, such as storage, networking, and application services, along with a mastery of VMware's datacenter design methodologies and principles. All the exam objectives, including study resources, can be found in the exam blueprint. VMware exam roadmaps and the VCAP exam blueprints can be found on the VMware Certification portal page at `https://mylearn.vmware.com/portals/certification/`.

The final stop on the VMware certification path is the **VMware Certified Design Expert (VCDX)**. The VCDX certification requires you to create a VMware vSphere design, submitting the design to VMware for review, and then defending the design before a panel of VMware Design Experts.

Getting ready

Before you are eligible to take the VCAP6-DCV Design exam, you should have obtained the **VMware Certified Professional 6–Data Center Virtualization (VCP6-DCV)** certification. Besides the training required for the VCP6-DCV certification, there is no other required training that must be completed in order to sit for the VCAP6-DCV Design exam. When you are ready to schedule your VCAP6-DCV Design exam, you must submit an exam authorization request to VMware. When you submit the exam authorization request, VMware will verify that you have met the certification prerequisites and provide you with the access necessary to schedule the exam.

At the time of writing this book, the VCAP6-DCV Design exam is in beta, and the final version has not yet been released. The VCAP6-DCV Design beta exam consists of 31 questions with a time limit of 240 minutes. The scoring of the exam has yet to be determined. The beta exam questions are comprised of a mixture of multiple-choice, drag-and-drop, and design scenarios. The final release of the VCAP6-DCV Design exam will likely be very similar. For details, refer to the VMware Certification portal at `https://mylearn.vmware.com/portals/ certification/`.

How to do it...

The VCAP-DCD exam for vSphere 5 was one of the most challenging exams I have ever taken. Here are a few tips to help you prepare for and successfully sit the VCAP-DCD or VCAP6-DCV Design exam:

- **Study the material on the exam blueprint**: The exam blueprint lists all the objectives of the exam, along with links to documentation related to each exam objective.

- **Review the vSphere 6 release notes and product documentation**: The release notes and product documentation will provide an overview of the features available, the requirements that must be met to support implementation of the new features, and the best practices to implement features to support design requirements.

- **Schedule your exam**: Scheduling your exam sets a goal date for you to work towards. Setting the date can provide motivation to help you stay on track with your studying efforts.

- **Watch the APAC vBrownBag DCD5 series**: The APAC vBrownBag did a series of podcasts focusing on the VCAP-DCD exam for vSphere 5 exam objectives. Even though these podcasts focus on version 5 of the exam, many of the design methodologies and concepts are similar. These podcast are still relevant and provide a valuable study resource. The podcast can be found at `http://www. professionalvmware.com/brownbags`.

- **Get familiar with the exam design interface**: On VMware's VCAP Certification page for the DCD exam, there is a UI Demo that will help you get familiar with the design interface that is used in the exam.

- **Practice time management**: It is very important that you are aware of the amount of time you are taking on a question and how much time remains. If you get hung up on a multiple-choice question, take your best guess and move on. Conserve time for the more complex drag-and-drop and design scenario questions.

- **Answer every question**: A question left unanswered will be marked incorrect and will not benefit your score in any way. A guess has some chance of being correct.

- **Study the material on the exam blueprint**: I know this has already been mentioned once, but it is worth mentioning again. The exam blueprint contains all the testable objectives. Study it!

There's more...

For up-to-date information on the VCAP6-DCV Design certification, to download the exam blueprint, and to book the exam once it has been released, visit the VMware Certification portal page at `https://mylearn.vmware.com/portals/certification/`.

Identifying what's new in vSphere 6

vSphere 6 is the latest release of VMware's virtual datacenter platform. This release includes features that provide increased scalability, enhanced security, increased availability, and simplified management of the virtual datacenter infrastructure. A few of the new features and enhancements include:

- New vCenter Architecture to simplify deployment and management of authentication and SSL certificates

- Cluster scalability increased to 64 hosts and 8,000 VMs

- **Fault Tolerance** (**FT**) enhancements to support virtual machines with up to four vCPUs

- **Virtual Volumes** (**VVOL**) providing object-based policy managed virtual machine aware storage

- NFS v4.1 support for NFS authentication and multipath support

- vMotion enhanced to support migrations across vCenter Servers and over distances of up to 100 ms RTT

- Content library centralized storage and management of virtual machine templates, ISO, and scripts

- Network IO Control version 3 provides the ability to reserve bandwidth to a single virtual machine or an entire virtual port group

These are just a few of the new features and enhancements introduced with the release of vSphere 6. A new version of vSphere with the new features and enhancements does not directly change the design process or methodology. The enhancements and features provide an architect with more tools and options to meet requirements, but can also introduce complexity into the design.

How to do it...

It is important for the architect to understand all the new features and enhancements available. This is a simple but important process, which includes:

▸ Accessing the vSphere 6.0 release notes at `https://www.vmware.com/support/vsphere6/doc/vsphere-esxi-vcenter-server-60-release-notes.html`

▸ Accessing the vSphere 6 documentation sets found at `https://www.vmware.com/support/pubs/vsphere-esxi-vcenter-server-6-pubs.html`

How it works...

Reading the vSphere 6 release notes gives the architect a summary of the additional features, bug fixes, and known issues. There is also information on the upgrade process and workarounds for known issues.

Reviewing the vSphere documentation, including the *vSphere Installation and Setup Guide*, *vSphere Upgrade Guide*, and *vSphere Virtual Machine Administration Guide*, gives the architect a deeper understanding of new features and how to implement new functionality. The documentation also provides specific requirements that must be satisfied in order to enable a new feature or function. These documentation sets are available online or can be downloaded in the `.pdf`, `.epub`, or `.mobi` formats.

There's more...

In the VMware Communities, `https://communities.vmware.com/`, there are forums available to discuss topics such as *vSphere Upgrade & Install* at `https://communities.vmware.com/community/vmtn/vsphere/upgradecenter` and ESXi 6 located at `https://communities.vmware.com/community/vmtn/vsphere/esxi6`, along with other Communities dedicated to each vSphere product. In these forums, an architect or administrator can find real-world issues encountered by other vSphere administrators and architects. Questions and discussions can be posted related to features and issues related to all vSphere products. If you run into issues or have questions about a specific feature, there are people in the community who are always happy to help.

Planning a vSphere 6 upgrade

Upgrading an existing vSphere environment to vSphere 6 is a fairly simple process and can be completed with minimal impact to production with the proper planning.

In this recipe, we will look at the steps required to properly plan an upgrade to vSphere 6. We will not cover the specifics of upgrading vCenter Server, ESXi hosts, or any other component of the virtual datacenter. Specific recipes for upgrading vCenter Server and ESXi hosts have been included in *Chapter 4, vSphere Management Design*, and recipes for upgrading virtual machine to the latest hardware are included in *Chapter 9, Virtual Machine Design*.

How to do it...

The following tasks should be completed when planning a vSphere 6 upgrade:

▶ Verify that the existing hardware is on the VMware **Hardware Compatibility List** (**HCL**) at `https://www.vmware.com/go/hcl`

▶ Check for interoperability between VMware products using the VMware Product Interoperability Matrix at `http://partnerweb.vmware.com/comp_guide2/sim/interop_matrix.php`

▶ Determine interoperability and support between VMware vSphere 6 and third-party hardware and software products

▶ Determine the proper upgrade path and sequence

Completing these steps to properly plan a vSphere 6 upgrade will ensure that the upgrade can be completed successfully.

How it works...

With each release of vSphere, VMware adds support for new hardware and firmware for devices such as disk controllers, server platforms, **network interface cards** (**NIC**), and so on. VMware also removes support for older hardware and firmware. It is important to verify that the hardware is on the supported compatibility list prior to attempting an upgrade. Using the VMware Hardware Compatibility List is covered in more detail in *Chapter 8, vSphere Physical Design*. Failure to validate support for hardware on HCL can cause significant issues after the upgrade. Unsupported hardware may not be available for use or may cause instability in the environment. Replacing unsupported hardware or upgrading firmware on current hardware to a supported configuration may be required as part of the upgrade process.

Checking for interoperability between vSphere products will help ensure that there is minimal impact on functionality during and after the upgrade process. Just like the hardware and firmware, the interoperability between vSphere products changes with each version. New support is added for newer products and features, while support may be removed for older, products and features. Details on using the VMware Product Interoperability can be found in *Chapter 4, vSphere Management Design*.

The virtual datacenter may contain many third-party products that integrate with the vSphere environment. These products often include backup and recovery software, replication software, and management and monitoring applications. Before upgrading to vSphere 6, check with each third-party product vendor to validate support for vSphere 6 or to determine the requirements for vSphere 6 support. This is the step I see missed most often, typically due to not fully understanding dependencies with these products. It is critical to understand what products require integration with the vSphere environment and the impact that changes to the environment may have on these products. Again, this is where proper planning from the beginning ensures a successful vSphere 6 upgrade.

The final step is to determine the proper upgrade path. If validation of support and interoperability has been completed correctly, this step will likely be the easiest in the process. Once the hardware is validated and, VMware product and third-party product interoperability has been validated, a plan can be formulated for upgrading.

Details are important when it comes to the support of hardware and software in the virtual datacenter. Spending time to properly plan will ensure a successful upgrade to vSphere 6.

The Discovery Process

2

In this chapter, we will cover the following topics:

- ▶ Identifying the design factors
- ▶ Identifying stakeholders
- ▶ Conducting stakeholder interviews
- ▶ VMware Capacity Planner
- ▶ Using Windows Performance Monitor
- ▶ Conducting a VMware Optimization Assessment
- ▶ Identifying dependencies

Introduction

This chapter will introduce you to the design factors and focus on the discovery phase of the design process.

The following image displays the phases of the design process:

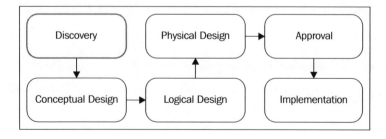

Discovery is the most important phase of the design process. It is also the most time-consuming. The discovery process includes a meeting with the stakeholders to determine business requirements that the design must meet. It also includes current state assessments to determine the technical requirements that the design must satisfy in order to meet the customer requirements, which in turn become the design requirements.

During the discovery process, an architect must interact with many different individuals in an organization to collect the necessary information that is needed to begin creating the conceptual design. Decision makers, strategic planners, facilities and maintenance providers, network administrators, storage administrators, application administrators, and application end users can, in some way, be impacted by or gain some benefit from a virtual datacenter design (some directly and others indirectly). Anyone who may be affected by the design should be identified to be included in the discovery process as early as possible.

The current state assessment is the process of collecting information about the physical resources currently supporting the environment, such as CPU, memory, and storage. Irrespective of whether the environment consists of physical servers, virtual servers, or a mix of virtual and physical servers, the current state assessment will identify the total resources available and the total resources actually in use.

There are a number of different tools available to perform a current state assessment of an environment. The tool used often depends on the size of the environment. VMware offers a **Capacity Planner** tool that provides a good way to automate this assessment. For a smaller environment of Windows servers, the Windows **Performance Monitor** (**PerfMon**) utility can be used to collect the current state information. For Linux systems, tools such as top, Kinfocenter, and Zabbix can be used to collect and analyze performance data. For environments that are already virtualized on vSphere, the **vSphere Optimization Assessment** (**VOA**) provides useful information on the current state of the environment.

Once the design factors have been identified and accepted, the design process continues with the logical and physical designs. The logical design maps the requirements to the resources required to satisfy the requirements. The physical design then maps the logical design onto the physical hardware that will provide these resources.

Identifying the design factors

The design factors are the primary considerations that influence the design. These factors define the function that the design must accomplish, how it should accomplish it, and what may prevent the design from accomplishing it.

How to do it...

The design factors encompass much more than just the physical resources, such as the CPU, memory, and storage, necessary to run workloads in a virtual environment.

You need the following requirements to identify the design factors:

- ▸ Functional and non-functional requirements
- ▸ Constraints
- ▸ Assumptions
- ▸ Risks

How it works...

Requirements define what a design must do and how it should do it. Requirements can be business or technical. There are two types of requirements: functional and nonfunctional. The requirements should be clearly defined. A good design requirement is verifiable, traceable, feasible, and specific.

Functional requirements specify a specific function of the design or simply what a design must do. Functional requirements can be business or technical requirements. The design must provide a capacity for 10 percent growth over the next 3 years; this is an example of a functional requirement.

Nonfunctional requirements specify how the design must perform or operate. While a functional requirement defines something that the design must do, a nonfunctional requirement defines how or how well it must be done. System response time is an example of a nonfunctional requirement. Nonfunctional requirements become constraints on the design.

Assumptions are considered valid until they have been proven otherwise. These factors are considered to be true, but further discovery is required to validate them. As part of the design process, assumptions should be documented and then proven or disproven. Sufficient bandwidth being available between different sites to support site-to-site replication is an example of an assumption, if the bandwidth available between the sites or the bandwidth required for replication has not yet been identified.

Constraints place limits on the design choices. Constraints can be business policies or technical limitations. Using a specific vendor for a server's hardware is an example of a technical constraint. The project's budget and deadlines are also common constraints. Nonfunctional requirements, since they specify how the design must perform or behave, will also become constraints on the design.

Risks may prevent the design from being successful. Risks should be clearly identified to minimize surprises that may prevent the successful implementation of the design. A good design will address and mitigate the risks.

Since the focus of this chapter is on design discovery, I felt it was important to provide this brief introduction to the design factors. We will dive much deeper into determining and defining the requirements, constraints, assumptions, and risks in *Chapter 3, The Design Factors*.

Identifying stakeholders

A stakeholder is anyone who has an interest in or benefits from the design. A virtual datacenter design will have at least some impact on many, if not all, areas of an organization, and not just those associated with technology.

How to do it...

Identify the key stakeholders, including the following:

- ▶ Project sponsors
- ▶ Application owners and providers
- ▶ System, network, and storage administrators
- ▶ Application users

How it works...

Understanding the role of the stakeholders helps an architect identify who can provide the information necessary to design a successful virtual datacenter solution. The details of the stakeholders and their roles are specified in the following table:

Stakeholders	Roles
C-level executives Chief executive officer Chief financial officer Chief technology officer	▶ Strategic planning for the organization ▶ Setting up business policies and goals ▶ Budget approval ▶ Project sponsorship
Business unit managers or directors	▶ Strategic planning for the business unit ▶ Managing day-to-day operations ▶ Influencing business policies and goals ▶ Make and/or influence decisions
Application owners	▶ Consumers of IT infrastructure ▶ Document the application and dependencies ▶ Manage the application functions ▶ Provide day-to-day support for the application

Stakeholders	Roles
IT	▸ Technical **Subject Matter Experts** (**SMEs**)
	▸ Network administrators
	▸ System administrators
	▸ Storage administrators
	▸ Help desk
Application or end users	▸ Consumers of application services
	▸ Rely on the infrastructure and applications to accomplish tasks efficiently

Project sponsors are typically C-level executives, **vice presidents** (**VPs**), or directors. The project sponsor may also be a committee formed by an organization to evaluate the solutions to business problems or to explore new business opportunities. These stakeholders are often the best resource to obtain the business requirements that a design must satisfy. If there is a project or a need to explore opportunities, there is a business goal or need driving it. Project sponsors may make the final decision on whether a design has to be approved and accepted for implementation, or they may provide the recommendations for acceptance.

There's more...

Stakeholders or the project team will ultimately be the ones that sign off on or approve the design factors that will be the basis for the logical and physical design. These design factors are identified by analyzing the data collected from the stakeholder interviews and the current state assessments.

The stakeholder's consensus and acceptance of the design factors must be obtained before proceeding with the design process. If you skip this step, you will end up wasting your time and the time of the stakeholders, having to rework areas of the design when requirements are missed, changed, added, or removed.

Define the design factors and obtain acceptance from the project team or stakeholders before taking the next steps in the design process.

Conducting stakeholder interviews

During the discovery process, the primary source of information will be the stakeholder interviews. These interviews can be face-to-face meetings or can be done over the phone (or the Web). Interviews are not only helpful in collecting information about the business needs and technical requirements, but also keep the stakeholders engaged in the project.

How to do it...

Here are some examples of the questions that should be asked in order to determine the business requirements that will influence the design:

- ▶ What are the business initiatives, challenges, and goals?
- ▶ Are there **Service-Level Agreements** (**SLAs**) in place? What are they?
- ▶ What are the **Recovery Time Objective** (**RTO**) and **Recovery Point Objective** (**RPO**) requirements?
- ▶ Are there any compliance requirements?
- ▶ Who are the SMEs associated with the project?
- ▶ Who are the stakeholders?
- ▶ Who are the decision makers?
- ▶ Are there deadlines that the project must meet?
- ▶ Is there a budget for the project? What is the budget for the project?

Here are some examples of the questions that should be asked in order to determine the technical requirements that will influence the design:

- ▶ Are there any current issues or technical pain points within the environment?
- ▶ What are the technology initiatives, challenges, and goals?
- ▶ How many servers will be virtualized as part of this project?
- ▶ Is there a preferred vendor for the server, network, or storage?
- ▶ Have any servers already been virtualized? What hypervisor is being used to host the servers that are already virtualized?
- ▶ What type of growth is expected over the next 3-5 years?
- ▶ What **Operation-Level Agreements** (**OLAs**) are in place?
- ▶ Is there a current documentation for network, system, storage, and application?

How it works...

Meetings and interviews with stakeholders should maintain some type of structure or formality. Even if it is just a quick call, you should have some type of agenda. I know this may sound like overkill, but it will help you keep the call or meeting on track and, more importantly, help ensure that you collect the information you need.

There are some key items that will help determine the design factors. These key items are explained here:

▶ **Service-Level Agreements**: These are a part of a service contract where a service, its availability (uptime and access), and its performance (application response and transaction processing) are defined

▶ **Service-Level Objective**: This defines specific objectives that must be achieved as part of the SLA

▶ **Recovery Time Objective**: This is the amount of time in which a service must be restored after a disruption or disaster

▶ **Recovery Point Objective**: This is the maximum amount of data loss acceptable due to a disruption or disaster

▶ **Operation-Level Agreements**: This is an internal agreement that defines relationships between support groups

Do not expect to complete the discovery in a single meeting or interview, especially for a large enterprise project. There will be follow-up questions that may need to be asked, and there will likely be questions that require more research to be answered.

In situations where more research is required, make sure that someone has been assigned the responsibility to complete the research. Set an expectation on when the research should be completed and the information should be available. You want to avoid the "I thought so-and-so was getting that" situations and also keep the discovery process moving forward.

VMware Capacity Planner

VMware's Capacity Planner is an inventory and planning tool available to VMware partner organizations. It collects resource utilization information from systems, analyzes the data against industry-standard reference data, and provides the information needed to successfully consolidate the servers into a virtualized environment.

How to do it...

Follow these steps to complete a Capacity Planner engagement:

1. Determine the amount of time for which the Capacity Planner engagement should run based on the business cycle.

2. Choose the type of Capacity Planner assessment to be run: a **Consolidation Estimate** (**CE**) or a **Capacity Assessment** (**CA**).

3. Deploy the Capacity Planner collector in the environment to be assessed.

4. Verify whether the collector is collecting performance metrics for the systems to be analyzed.

5. Collect metrics for the duration of the business cycle.

6. Generate Capacity Planner reports.

How it works...

A Capacity Planner engagement should typically run for at least 30 days to ensure that it covers a complete monthly business cycle. Thirty days is considered typical since this covers a monthly business cycle where the demand for resources increases during the end-of-month or beginning-of-month processing. It is important that the Capacity Planner capture these increases. The time frame for a Capacity Planner engagement can vary depending on the size and nature of the business.

There are two types of Capacity Planner assessments: the CE and the CA. The CE assessment provides the sizing estimates of the current environment, while the CA assessment provides a more detailed analysis of the current environment. The CE assessment helps demonstrate what can be achieved by virtualizing physical workloads, and the CA assessment provides guidance on how systems may be virtualized.

A Capacity Planner collector is installed in the environment that is being assessed. The collector runs as a Windows service and is configured using the VMware Capacity Planner Data Manager. The collector must be installed on a Windows machine, but inventory and performance data can be collected from both Windows and Linux/Unix servers. More than one collector may need to be installed for larger environments. A single collector can collect data from a maximum of 500 systems. The following screenshot depicts the VMware Capacity Planner Data Manager:

The collector or collectors discover systems in the environment and collect inventory and performance data from the systems. The inventory includes information about the installed physical hardware, operating systems, and installed software.

> To run VMware Capacity Planner Data Manager on a Windows 7 workstation, use **Run as administrator**.

Performance data metrics are collected on CPU utilization, RAM utilization, disk capacity, and disk I/O. This data is then sent securely to the VMware Capacity Planner Dashboard at `https://optimize.vmware.com/` to be analyzed. The following screenshot shows the VMware Capacity Planner Data Manager processor utilization report:

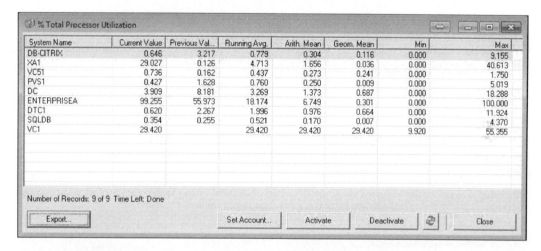

System Name	Current Value	Previous Val...	Running Avg.	Arith. Mean	Geom. Mean	Min	Max
DB-CITRIX	0.646	3.217	0.779	0.304	0.116	0.000	9.155
XA1	29.027	0.126	4.713	1.656	0.036	0.000	40.613
VC51	0.736	0.162	0.437	0.273	0.241	0.000	1.750
PVS1	0.427	1.628	0.760	0.250	0.009	0.000	5.019
DC	3.909	8.181	3.269	1.373	0.687	0.000	18.288
ENTERPRISEA	99.255	55.973	18.174	6.749	0.301	0.000	100.000
DTC1	0.620	2.267	1.996	0.976	0.664	0.000	11.924
SQLDB	0.354	0.255	0.521	0.170	0.007	0.000	4.370
VC1	29.420		29.420	29.420	29.420	9.920	55.355

Number of Records: 9 of 9 Time Left: Done

There can be some challenges to setting up the VMware Capacity Planner. You may encounter issues with setting up the correct credentials required for data collection and configuring Windows Firewall and services to allow the data collection. These issues are common.

The following table includes the services and ports that must be open on target systems to allow the Capacity Planner collector to collect data:

Service	Port
Remote Procedure Call (RPC)	TCP/135
NetBIOS Name Service (NBNS)	TCP/137
NetBIOS Datagram Service (NBDS)	TCP/138
NetBIOS Session Service (NBSS)	TCP/139
Microsoft-DS	TCP/445
Secure Shell (SSH) (Unix/Linux only)	TCP/22

In order to collect data from Windows systems, **Windows Management Instrumentation** (**WMI**), Remote Registry, and PerfMon must be enabled on the target system. For data collection on Linux or Unix systems, port 22 must be open and the **Secure Shell Daemon** (**SSHD**) must be running. Account credentials provided must have at least local administrator rights on the target systems.

There's more...

Once the inventory and performance data have been collected, the results can be analyzed and reports can be generated. Some of this information can be viewed and exported from the VMware Capacity Planner Data Manager, but detailed analysis reports are generated from the VMware Capacity Planner Dashboard at `https://optimize.vmware.com/`.

If server hardware constraints have been identified during the discovery process, report settings can be adjusted. These constraints will then be applied to the Capacity Planner reporting to determine and show the consolidation ratios that can be obtained using the different hardware configurations. The following screenshot shows the report settings:

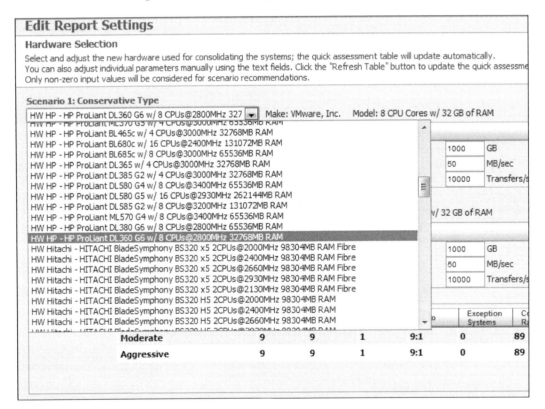

The reports that are available include the Progress Report, which provides an overview of the status of the assessment, the Executive Summary Presentation, which provides a high-level summary of the assessment, and the Assessment Report, which provides information on consolidation ratios and recommendations. Custom reports can also be generated. The following screenshot shows the consolidation recommendations:

System Consolidation Recommendation

Before Virtualization		With VMware Virtualization							
Total Systems	Eligible Systems	Consolidation Scenario and Platform	ESX Hosts	ESX CPU Utilization	ESX Memory Utilization	Average Memory Per VM	Racks Saved	Eligible System Consolidation Ratio	Total System Consolidation Ratio
9	9	Conservative Type	1	23.04%	56.27%	3.25 GB	0	89%	89%
9	9	Aggressive Type	1	23.04%	56.27%	3.25 GB	0	89%	89%

Conservative Type
Make: VMware, Inc.
Model: 8 CPU Cores w/ 32 GB of RAM
CPU: 8
Memory: 32 GB

Aggressive Type
Make: VMware, Inc.
Model: 8 CPU Cores w/ 32 GB of RAM
CPU: 8
Memory: 32 GB

Using Windows Performance Monitor

The Microsoft Windows PerfMon can be used to collect performance information such as CPU utilization, memory utilization, and disk I/O utilization of the Windows servers.

How to do it...

In this example, Microsoft Windows PerfMon is used to collect disk I/O metrics using the following steps:

1. Open **Performance Monitor** and use the **Data Collector Set** wizard to create a user-defined data collector, as displayed in the following screenshot:

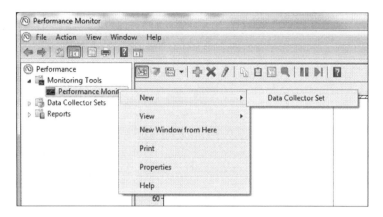

2. Once the **Data Collector Set** application has been created, add new **Data Collector** to the **Data Collector Set**, as shown in the following screenshot:

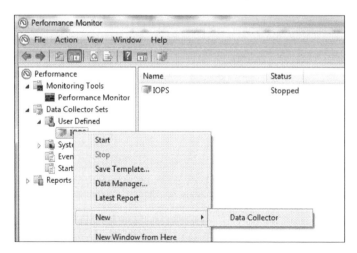

3. Name new **Data Collector** and select the **Performance counter data collector** radio button, as shown in the following screenshot:

4. Add the following counters for the `object _Total` instance to the data collector:

   ❑ `\LogicalDisk\Avg. Disk Sec/Read`

   ❑ `\LogicalDisk\Avg. Disk Sec/Write`

   ❑ `\LogicalDisk\Disk Bytes/Sec`

   ❑ `\LogicalDisk\Disk Reads/Sec`

   ❑ `\LogicalDisk\Disk Writes/Sec`

   ❑ `\LogicalDisk\Split IO/sec`

   ❑ `\LogicalDisk\Disk Transfers/sec`

   The screen should look like the one shown in the following screenshot:

5. Right-click on the new **Data Collector Set**, select the **Stop Condition** tab, and change the stop condition to the period of time for which you want to monitor the **Input/ Output Operations Per Second** (**IOPS**), as shown in the following screenshot:

6. Data collection for the **Data Collector Set** can be configured to start manually or can be scheduled to start at a future date or time. The following screenshot displays the setting of a schedule for **Data Collector Set**:

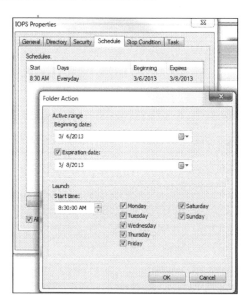

7. Once the collection process has been completed, you can view the report using the **Reports** section of **Performance Monitor**. The following screenshot shows a sample report:

8. A template of the **Data Collector Set** application can be created in order to easily import the **Data Collector Set** on other servers/workstations. This is shown in the following screenshot:

How it works...

The total number of IOPS and the I/O profile of a server are necessary to architect the storage required for a virtualized environment correctly. The IOPS and I/O profile are helpful in determining which **Redundant Array of Independent Disks** (**RAID**) level to use with the number of and the type of disk to be used in order to support the server storage workload.

Windows PerfMon can also be configured to collect metrics associated with CPU and memory usage by simply adding the associated counters to the Data Collector Set.

There's more...

Most organizations will have some form of network- or resource-monitoring system in place, such as Nagios, SolarWinds, Splunk, or vRealize Operations Manager. The information monitored and collected by these systems will be useful for the current state assessments. The SMEs should be asked whether there is monitoring in place and whether there is access to the data collected by these systems.

Many vendors also perform free infrastructure assessments. Often, these free assessments are not thorough enough to provide the details necessary for a complete current state assessment, but they can provide some good information. Again, the project SMEs will be asked whether any type of assessments have been done.

Conducting a VMware Optimization Assessment

The **VMware Optimization Assessment** (**VOA**) is an enhanced evaluation of vRealize Operations Manager. It includes reports providing information about the configuration, capacity, and performance of a vSphere environment. This information is useful for an administrator or architect validating an existing vSphere deployment or planning an expansion to an existing vSphere deployment.

The VOA will provide useful insights into a virtual environment by providing detail analytics. The VOA also does the following:

- ▸ Provides information on misconfigured clusters, hosts, and virtual machines
- ▸ Identifies potential performance problems with root-cause analysis
- ▸ Analyzes virtual machine resource to identify undersized and/or oversized virtual machines providing opportunities to the right-size environment

The information gathered during a VOA will allow an administrator or architect the ability to quickly identify health issues, risks to the environment, and areas where efficiency can be improved.

How to do it...

Follow these steps to obtain, deploy, configure, and conduct an optimization assessment using the VOA appliance:

1. Visit https://www.vmware.com/assessment/voa and download the VOA appliance.
2. Import the VOA appliance OVA into the vCenter inventory.
3. Power on the VOA appliance and access the VOA appliance's IP address with a web browser to launch the **vRealize Operations Manager Initial Setup** wizard and choose **Express Installation**, as shown in the following screenshot:

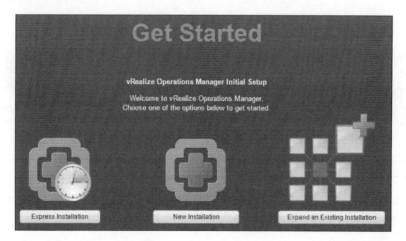

4. Set the administrator password when prompted by the **vRealize Operations Manager Initial Setup** wizard.

5. Configure **vCenter Adapter** by providing **Display name**, the **vCenter Server** IP address, and **Credential**. Use the **Test Connection** button to test connectivity and credentials. Be sure to save the settings using the **Save Settings** button once the test is successful. The **vCenter Adapter** configuration window is shown in the following screenshot:

6. Once **vCenter Adapter** is configured, it will begin collecting performance and configuration information from the configured **vCenter Server**.

7. Access the VOA appliance with a web browser to view information on environment health, risks, and efficiency.

How it works...

Once deployed and configured, the VOA appliance begins collecting information about the virtual environment. The information is analyzed and displayed as part of the VOA dashboard. **Health**, **Risks**, and **Efficiency** of the environment are displayed in the VOA dashboard, as shown in the following screenshot:

The VOA reporting is split up into three phases. The phases correspond with specific metrics that will be available over time as the VOA appliance collects and analyzes information from the environment. The following phases make up the optimization assessment:

▸ **Phase 1–the configuration phase**: This phase provides analysis of the configuration of the environment and corresponds with the **Environment Health** dashboard. The information in this phase is available within 24 hours of deploying the VOA appliance.

▸ **Phase 2–the performance phase**: This phase provides analysis of performance information in the environment and identifies risks associated with exceeding available capacity and performance. This phase requires VOA collection for 5 to 7 days.

▸ **Phase 3–the optimization phase**: In this phase, the areas where capacity and performance can be optimized are identified. This includes details such as virtual machines with resources that have been over allocated. This final phase requires the collection of environment data by the VOA over a period of about 21 days.

Preconfigured reports are included for each phase of the VOA. These reports can be generated for the VOA appliance, as shown in the following screenshot:

These preconfigured reports provide valuable insight to assist an architect in determining what will be necessary to meet requirements around growth or expansion of an existing vSphere environment.

Identifying dependencies

A dependency is a relationship among systems or services. During the discovery process, dependencies should be identified and documented. In *Chapter 1*, *The Virtual Datacenter*, we discussed the importance of taking a holistic view when designing a virtualized environment. Identifying dependencies is the key to the holistic approach of designing.

How to do it...

An architect must identify dependencies in order to understand what effect a design decision or change may have on other services. The architect should identify the following dependencies:

- Physical infrastructure dependencies
- Application and service dependencies

How it works...

Dependencies can be service-to-service; for example, a web application depends on a frontend web server and a backend database. Dependencies can be service-to-infrastructure; for example, the web application requires a static IP address and a minimum of 10 MB of network bandwidth.

Physical and infrastructure dependencies are generally easier to discover and are commonly documented. Applications will have dependencies, which include server resources, network resources, and storage resources. Infrastructure dependencies that are not documented are often readily discovered as part of the current state assessment. The following table is an example of how physical application dependencies can be documented:

Application	OS	CPU cores	Speed (GHz)	RAM (GB)	Network (GBps)	Network (VLAN)	Storage
IIS	Win2k8 R2	4	2.7	16	1	22	50 GB
SQL database	Win2k8 R2	8	2.7	32	1	22	1 TB

Service-to-service or application-to-service dependencies can be a bit more difficult to discover. Application owners, application developers, application documentation, and application vendors will be the best sources to determine these dependencies.

The following diagram is an example of how service dependencies can be mapped and documented:

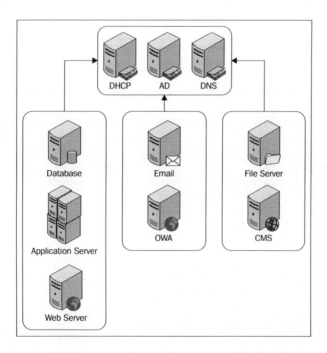

Understanding the dependencies will help an architect understand how a change made to one area of the design may have an effect on another area of the design. Mapping and documenting application dependencies will provide the necessary information to properly design a solution for business continuity and disaster recovery. Understanding the dependencies will also aid in troubleshooting issues with the design implementation.

Beware that there may be undocumented dependencies that are not easily discovered. This can often be a risk to the design, especially in an organization with a legacy of unsupported applications or applications developed in-house that have not been properly documented.

I have seen issues where a specific configuration such as an IP address or a file location has been hardcoded into an application and not documented. A change is made to the environment, and hence, the application becomes unavailable. Dependencies of this type can be extremely difficult to plan for and discover.

3

The Design Factors

In this chapter, we will cover the following topics:

- ▶ Identifying design requirements
- ▶ Identifying design constraints
- ▶ Making design assumptions
- ▶ Identifying design risks
- ▶ Creating the conceptual design

Introduction

During the discovery process, information is collected on the business and technical goals of the virtualization project. This information must be analyzed in order to determine the design factors.

The design factors that must be determined are as follows:

- ▶ Requirements
- ▶ Constraints
- ▶ Assumptions
- ▶ Risks

Determining the requirements, making and proving assumptions, determining constraints, and identifying risks form the conceptual design and provide the foundation to build on for the logical design. Business and technical design factors identified as part of the conceptual design will be mapped to the resources that are necessary to satisfy them during the logical design process. The conceptual design stage is the next phase in the design process as shown in the following diagram:

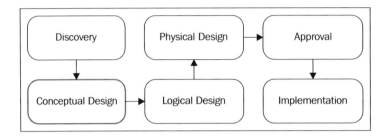

In our example design, after conducting interviews with stakeholders and performing technical assessments of the environment, the following information has been collected about the project's goals, current environment, and business factors that will influence the design:

▶ Currently, there are 100 physical servers, each hosting a single application. Each application services 10 customers.

▶ The business expects to add 50 new customers over the next year.

▶ It expects to support growth over the next 5 years.

▶ Application uptime and accessibility is very important.

▶ Consolidate physical servers to reduce hardware costs associated with the maintenance and deployment of new application servers.

▶ No more than 20 application servers or 200 customers should be affected by a hardware failure.

▶ There should be a one-hour maintenance window each month for application and hardware maintenance. Hardware maintenance is currently a challenge. Since hardware and application maintenance cannot be performed at the same time, the maintenance window does not typically provide the time required to perform both application and hardware maintenance.

▶ Application servers run Microsoft Windows 2008 R2 as the operating system.

▶ Each application server is configured with 8 GB of memory. The peak usage of a single application server is approximately 65 percent or approximately 5.2 GB.

- Each application server is configured with two dual-core 2.7 GHz processors. The peak usage of a single application server is approximately 10 percent of the total or approximately 1 GHz.

- Each application server is configured with 100 GB of disk space. The peak disk capacity usage of a single application server is approximately 65 percent of the total or 65 GB. The peak disk performance of a single application server is 50 IOPS with an IO profile of 90 percent read and 10 percent write.

- Currently, the stakeholders are using HP DL360 servers. The infrastructure team is very familiar with the management and maintenance of these servers and wants to continue using them.

- Currently, there is no shared storage. The current system and infrastructure administrators are unfamiliar with the shared storage concepts and protocols.

- Cisco switches are used for network connectivity. Separate VLANs exist for management connectivity and production application connectivity.

- Currently, each physical server contains a single gigabit network interface card. Peak network usage is 10 Mbps.

- Server logs are auditable and must be retained for 6 months. All logs should also be sent to a central syslog server that is already in place.

- If an application server fails, the current recovery time is around 8 hours. The solution should reduce this time to less than 4 hours.

- The management team expects the implementation to be completed before the third quarter.

- There is an approved project budget of $200,000.

In this chapter, we will use this information to determine the design factors in order to create the conceptual design. Throughout the design process, each design decision is mapped back to these design factors.

Identifying design requirements

The design requirements specify the functions that the design must perform and the objectives that the design must meet.

There are two types of requirements: functional requirements and nonfunctional requirements. Functional requirements specify the objectives or functions that a design must meet. Nonfunctional requirements define how the design accomplishes the functional requirements.

Typical functional requirements include the following:

- Business goals
- Business rules

- ▶ Legal, regulatory, and compliance requirements
- ▶ Application system requirements
- ▶ Technical requirements
- ▶ Administrative functions

Typical nonfunctional requirements include the following:

- ▶ Performance
- ▶ Security
- ▶ Capacity
- ▶ Availability
- ▶ Manageability
- ▶ Recoverability

When identifying and defining the requirements, separate the functional requirements from the nonfunctional requirements. Nonfunctional requirements are design constraints and will be documented separately.

Since functional requirements define what the design must accomplish, once identified and approved, these requirements typically cannot be easily changed during the design process.

How to do it...

1. Analyze the business and technical information collected during the discovery process.
2. Determine the functional and nonfunctional requirements of the design.
3. Document the design requirements.

How it works...

When defining the requirements, each requirement should be clearly stated and specified. Define requirements individually; multiple requirements should not be combined into a single requirement.

During the discovery process, the following information about the current size of the existing environment was identified:

- ▶ Currently, there are 100 physical servers, each hosting a single application. Each application services 10 customers.
- ▶ No more than 20 application servers or 200 customers should be affected by a hardware failure.

- Consolidate physical servers to reduce the hardware costs associated with maintaining and refreshing the hardware of the existing application servers.

One of the goals of the project is to consolidate the physical servers in order to reduce hardware costs. An example design requirement to support this might be as follows:

- Consolidate existing physical servers

This requirement is vague and, with the information available from the discovery, the requirement should be more specific. Based on the number of existing physical servers and the maximum number of customers that should be impacted during a hardware failure, a better requirement example may be as follows:

- Consolidate the existing 100 physical application servers down to five servers

Information about the expected growth of the environment was also discovered:

- The business expects to add 50 new customers each year
- It expects to support growth over the next 5 years

Based on this information, there is a requirement that the environment must be designed to provide the capacity necessary to support future growth. An example requirement to support this might be:

- Provide sufficient capacity to support growth

Again, this requirement is very vague and does not provide any information about how much the growth will be or over what period of time growth is expected. From the discovery, it is known that the business expects to add 50 new customers over the next year. Each server hosts a single application, which will provide service for 10 customers. The solution should support growth over the next 5 years.

Using this information, a requirement that specifies the growth that should be supported and the time period over which this growth is expected is as follows:

- Provide capacity to support growth for 25 additional application servers over the next 5 years

The architect can also determine the availability of requirements for hardware maintenance and application resiliency:

- A 1-hour maintenance window must be there each month for application and hardware maintenance. Hardware maintenance is currently a challenge. Since hardware and application maintenance cannot be performed at the same time, the maintenance window does not typically provide the time required to perform both application and hardware maintenance.
- Application uptime and accessibility is very important.

▶ No more than 20 application servers or 200 customers should be affected by a hardware failure.

From this information, the requirement that might be identified is that the server hardware maintenance should not affect application uptime, and redundancy should be maintained during hardware maintenance operations.

The problem with this requirement is that it includes two separate requirements: one requirement is for application uptime, and another requirement is for redundancy. These requirements should be split into two individual requirements.

Server hardware maintenance should not affect application uptime.

Provide *N+2* redundancy to support a hardware failure during normal and maintenance operations.

There's more...

Once the functional requirements have been identified and defined, the requirements should be recorded in the design documentation as part of the conceptual design. There are a number of formats that can be used, such as bulleted lists and numbered lists, but a simple table works well. Assigning an ID to each requirement makes it easier to reference the requirement later in the design document:

ID	Requirement
R001	Consolidate the existing 100 physical application servers down to five servers
R002	Provide capacity to support growth for 25 additional application servers over the next 5 years
R003	Server hardware maintenance should not affect application uptime
R004	Provide *N+2* redundancy to support a hardware failure during normal and maintenance operations

Identifying design constraints

The design constraints are factors that restrict the options the architect can use to satisfy the design requirements. Once the functional and nonfunctional requirements have been identified, they are separated. The nonfunctional requirements that define how requirements must be satisfied become the constraints on the design.

Design constraints include the following:

▸ Technology constraints such as hardware vendors, software solutions, and protocols

▸ Operational constraints such as performance and accessibility

▸ Financial constraints such as budgets

Unlike functional requirements, the constraints and nonfunctional requirements may change during the design process. This holds true especially if the constraint introduces risks into the design. For example, if an identified constraint that requires a specific model of hardware to be used prevents the design from satisfying a functional requirement, the constraint may need to be changed or adjusted.

How to do it...

1. Analyze the business and technical information collected during the discovery process.

2. Determine the nonfunctional requirements of the design. Nonfunctional requirements are constraints on the design.

3. Identify any other constraints on the design.

4. Document the design constraints.

How it works...

As with functional requirements, when defining nonfunctional requirements or constraints, they should be clearly stated and specified. Define each constraint individually; do not combine multiple nonfunctional requirements into a single constraint. Currently, HP DL360 servers are used. The infrastructure team is very familiar with the management and maintenance of these servers and wants to continue using them.

This statement does not identify something the design must do. It is placing a constraint on the design by providing a specific type of hardware that should be used. Following is an example of the constraint that can be formed from this statement:

▸ HP DL360 servers should be used for compute resources

Budgetary constraints affect nearly all the projects. There will likely be a limit on the amount of money a company will want to spend to accomplish a goal.

 If a budget has not been established for a project, it is likely that the business has not committed to the project. Beware of the infinite budget.

During the design discovery, the following budget was identified for this project:

> ▸ There is an approved project budget of $200,000

This budget constraint can simply be stated as: A project budget of $200,000.

Operational constraints are also common. Often, there will be existing processes or policies in place that will need to be factored into the design. Often, you will need to accommodate the existing monitoring and management applications in the design. An example of an operational requirement is as follows:

> ▸ Server logs are auditable and must be retained for 6 months. All logs should also be sent to a central syslog server that is already in place.

Here, a functional and nonfunctional requirement can be identified. The functional requirement is that the server logs are auditable and must be retained for 6 months. This functional requirement defines something the design must do, but there is also a constraint on how the design must accomplish this, using syslog to send logs to a central server. Based on this information, the constraint is as follows:

> ▸ Syslog should be used to send server logs to an existing central syslog server

There's more...

Constraints should be documented as part of the conceptual design. Just as you used a table to document the design requirements, using a simple table works well when documenting the design constraints. Each constraint is assigned an ID, so it can be easily referenced later in the design document:

ID	Constraint
C001	HP DL360 servers should be used for compute resources
C002	A project budget of $200,000
C003	Syslog should be used to send server logs to an existing central syslog server

Making design assumptions

Assumptions are made by the architect and have not yet been validated. Assumptions are not accepted as a fact until they have been validated. As part of the design process, each assumption needs to be validated as a fact. If an assumption cannot be validated, a risk will be introduced into the design.

How to do it...

Any assumptions that are made will need to be defined and documented as follows:

▶   Identify any assumptions that have been made about the design

▶   Document the design assumptions

How it works...

Common assumptions relate to power, space, and cooling. A common example of an assumption that an architect may make is as follows:

▶   There is sufficient power, cooling, and floor/rack space available in the datacenter to support both the existing and consolidated environment during the migration

When working through the physical design, the power, cooling, and space requirements will need to be identified and the assumption validated. A goal of this project is to consolidate the existing physical servers. The overall need for power, cooling, and space will be reduced once the project is complete, but enough of these resources need to be available to support both the existing physical environment and the new consolidated environment during the consolidation process.

A requirement was identified based on the discovery information to provide *N+2* redundancy. This is documented as a requirement as shown in the following table:

R004	Provide *N+2* redundancy to support a hardware failure during normal and maintenance operations

This requirement was defined based on the following discovery information:

▶   A 1-hour maintenance window each month for application and hardware maintenance. Hardware maintenance is currently a challenge. Since hardware and application maintenance cannot be performed at the same time, the maintenance window does not typically provide the time necessary to perform both application and hardware maintenance.

▶   Application uptime and accessibility is very important.

What assumption may have been made when defining this requirement?

An assumption was made, based on the importance of application uptime and accessibility, that there should be sufficient resources to provide redundancy not only during normal operations but also in the event of a host failure, when a host may be unavailable due to maintenance being performed:

▶   Resources should be provided to support a host failure during both normal and host maintenance operations

A requirement to support growth in the environment was also defined:

▶   The business expects to add 50 new customers over the next year

▶   It expects to support growth over the next 5 years

This requirement is documented as shown in the following table:

R002	Provide capacity to support growth for 25 additional application servers over the next 5 years

An expected growth of 50 customers over the next year was identified, but the design is expected to support growth over the next 5 years. To create this requirement, an assumption was made that growth would be the same over years two through five:

▶   Growth is calculated based on the addition of 50 new customers each year over the next 5 years

The company may have a forecast for growth that exceeds this. If this assumption is incorrect, the design may not meet the defined requirement.

There's more...

Assumptions should be documented in the design document. As with documenting design requirements and constraints, use a table for this. Each assumption is assigned an ID, so that it can be easily referenced later in the design document:

ID	Assumption
A001	Sufficient power, cooling, and floor/rack space is available in the datacenter to support the existing and consolidated environment during the migration
A002	Resources should be provided to support a host failure during both normal and maintenance operations
A003	Growth is calculated based on the addition of 50 new customers each year over the next 5 years

Identifying design risks

Risks include anything that may prevent the design from satisfying the requirements.

Design risks include the following:

▶   Technical risks

▶   Operational risks

▶   Financial risks

Risks are often introduced through constraints or assumptions that have not been proven. Risks resulting from assumptions are mitigated by validating them.

How to do it...

Throughout the design process, design decisions should mitigate or minimize risks by following this process:

1. Identify any risks associated with the design requirements or assumptions.
2. Validate assumptions to reduce the risks associated with them.
3. Determine how design decisions will help mitigate or minimize risks.

How it works...

There are a few risks in the design based on the discovery information, assumption, and constraints.

As part of the discovery process, the following risk was noted:

▸ Currently, there is no shared storage. The current system and infrastructure administrators are unfamiliar with the shared storage concepts and protocols.

These operational risks were identified during discovery. The operational risks can be minimized by providing implementation and operational documentation.

A technical constraint that may also introduce risks is as follows:

C001	HP DL360 servers should be used for compute resources

This constraint may introduce some risks to the environment if the capabilities of the HP DL360 servers are not able to fulfill the requirements. Can the servers be configured with the processing and memory required by the requirements? Are there enough expansion slots to support the number of network ports or HBAs required? It may be necessary to remove or change this constraint if the HP DL360 server is not able to fulfill the technical requirements of the design.

An assumption was also made with regards to the growth of the environment over the next 5 years:

▸ Growth is calculated based on the addition of 50 new customers each year over the next 5 years

If this assumption is not validated and growth is forecasted by the company to be higher in 2 to 5 years, the design will be at risk of not meeting the growth requirements. Validating this assumption will mitigate this risk.

Creating the conceptual design

The conceptual design is created with the documentation of the requirements, constraints, and assumptions. The design documentation should include a list of each of the design factors. The conceptual design guides the design. All logical and physical design elements can be mapped back to the conceptual design in order to provide justifications for design decisions.

How to do it...

To create the conceptual design, follow the given steps:

1. Use the design factors to form the conceptual design.
2. Organize the design factors to be easily referenced during the design process.
3. Create high-level diagrams that document the functional blocks of the design.

How it works...

The conceptual design should include a brief overview that describes the key goals of the project and any factors that may drive the business decisions related to the project. The conceptual design includes all the identified requirements, constraints, and assumptions.

The following paragraphs explain an example of conceptual design.

The primary goal of this project is to lower hardware cost through the consolidation of physical application servers. The design will increase application uptime and resiliency and reduce application recovery time.

The design will attempt to adhere to the standards and best practices when these align with the requirements and constraints of the design.

Design requirements

Requirements are the key demands on the design. The design requirements are as follows:

ID	Requirement
R001	Consolidate the existing 100 physical application servers down to five servers
R002	Provide capacity to support growth for 25 additional application servers over the next 5 years
R003	Server hardware maintenance should not affect application uptime
R004	Provide N+2 redundancy to support hardware failure during normal and maintenance operations

Design constraints

Constraints limit the logical decisions and physical specifications. Constraints may or may not align with the design objectives. The design constraints are as follows:

ID	Constraint
C001	HP DL360 servers should be used for compute resources
C002	A project budget of $200,000
C003	Syslog should be used to send server logs to an existing central Syslog server

Assumptions

Assumptions are the expectations of a system that have not yet been confirmed. If the assumptions are not validated, risks may be introduced. Assumptions are as follows:

ID	Assumption
A001	There is sufficient power, cooling, and floor/rack space available in the datacenter to support the existing and consolidated environments during the migration
A002	Resources should be provided to support a host failure during both normal and maintenance operations
A003	Growth is calculated based on the addition of 50 new customers each year over the next 5 years

There's more...

The conceptual design can also include diagrams that provide high-level overviews of the proposed design. Conceptual diagrams of the functional blocks of the design include the virtualization infrastructure, storage, servers, and networking. A conceptual diagram does not include specifics about resources required or hardware vendors. Here is an example of a conceptual diagram that shows how the virtualization infrastructure will leverage the existing physical network:

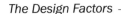

The diagram shows, at a very high level, how servers will be placed in a vSphere **High Availability** (**HA**)/**Distributed Resource Scheduler** (**DRS**) cluster. The existing physical network infrastructure will be leveraged to provide connectivity for IP storage and the virtual machine networks. The diagram does not include any specifics about the type of servers, type of array, or the resources required, but it provides an overview of how the different parts of the design will work together.

4

vSphere Management Design

In this chapter, we will cover the following recipes:

- ▶ Identifying vCenter components and dependencies
- ▶ Selecting a vCenter deployment option
- ▶ Determining vCenter resource requirements
- ▶ Selecting a database for the vCenter deployment
- ▶ Determining database interoperability
- ▶ Choosing a vCenter deployment topology
- ▶ Designing for management availability
- ▶ Designing a separate management cluster
- ▶ Configuring vCenter Mail, SNMP, and Alarms
- ▶ Using Enhanced Linked Mode
- ▶ Using the VMware Product Interoperability Matrix
- ▶ Backing up vCenter Server components
- ▶ Upgrading vCenter Server
- ▶ Designing a vSphere Update Manager Deployment

Introduction

This chapter discusses the design considerations that should be taken into account when designing the management layer of the virtual infrastructure. We will look at the different components that make up vCenter. You will learn how to size them correctly and how to ensure compatibility between VMware products deployed in the environment. This chapter also covers the different deployment options for vCenter and its components as well as the importance of the availability, recoverability, and security of these components.

The following diagram displays how management design is integrated into the design process:

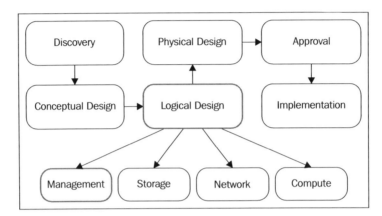

Questions that the architect should ask and answer during the management design process are as follows:

- What components are necessary to manage the virtual environment?
- How will management components be deployed?
- What resources are required to support the management components?
- What impact will the loss of a management component have on the environment?
- How to recover from the loss of a management component?
- How to upgrade and patch management components?

Identifying vCenter components and dependencies

The vCenter Server provides the central configuration and management of the ESXi servers and the services provided by the virtual infrastructure. vCenter 6.x is composed of several components and services such as the **Platform Services Controller** (**PSC**), the vCenter Server Database, and the vCenter Server.

How to do it...

1. Identify the following core components and services of vCenter 6.x:

   - The VMware PSC was introduced in 6.x. The PSC handles security functions in the vSphere infrastructure. The PSC provides the vCenter **Single Sign-On** (**SSO**) service, licensing management, registration services, and the **VMware Certificate Authority** (**VMCA**). The PSC can be deployed as a standalone server or be embedded on the same server with other required vCenter components.

   - The vCenter SSO is deployed as part of the PSC in vSphere 6.x. SSO provides identity management for administrators, users, and applications that interact with the VMware vSphere environment. **Active Directory** (**AD**) domains and **Open Lightweight Directory Access Protocol** (**OpenLDAP**) authentication sources can be added to provide authentication to the vCenter management components.

   - **VMware Certificate Authority** (**VMCA**) issues certificates for users accessing vCenter Services, machines providing vCenter Services, and ESXi hosts. The VMCA service is new to vSphere 6.x and is deployed with the PSC. The VMCA not only issues and manages certificates to vSphere services and components, but it also acts as **Certificate Authority** (**CA**) for these certificates. The VMCA can be used as a subordinate CA in an enterprise CA environment.

   - The VMware vCenter Server provides the configuration, access control, and performance monitoring of ESXi/ESX hosts and virtual machines that have been added to the inventory of the vCenter Server. In vSphere 6.x, the VMware vCenter Inventory Service, the VMware vSphere Web Client, the VMware Content Library Service, and other services not provided by the PSC are all installed with the vCenter Server.

   - The VMware vCenter Inventory Service maintains application and inventory data, so inventory objects including datacenters, clusters, folders, and virtual machines can be searched and accessed. In a vCenter 6.x deployment, the vCenter Inventory Service is installed on the vCenter Server.

❑   The VMware vSphere Web Client allows the connections made to vCenter to manage objects in its inventory using a web browser. Many of the new features and capabilities since vSphere Version 5.1 can only be configured and managed using the VMware vSphere Web Client. To access and configure new features in vSphere 6, the vSphere Web Client is required. The vSphere Web Client Server is installed with the vCenter Server.

❑   The vCenter Server requires a database to store configuration, logs, and performance data. The database can be an external Microsoft SQL, Oracle database server, or the embedded vPostgreSQL database. An external Microsoft SQL Database is only supported with a Windows vCenter Deployment.

2.   Identify the common dependencies required to install vCenter and the PSC:

❑   **DNS**: Forward and reverse name resolution should be working properly for all systems. Ensure that systems can be resolved by the **Fully Qualified Domain Name (FQDN)**, the short name or hostname, and the IP address.

❑   **Time**: Time should be synchronized across the environment.

How it works...

Each vCenter Server component or service has a set of dependencies. The following diagram illustrates the core vCenter Server dependencies:

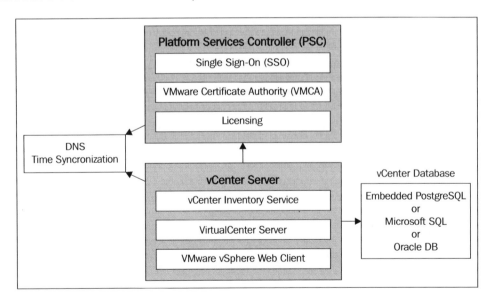

As with earlier vCenter versions, the vCenter 6.x installation media includes several other tools that provide support and automation to deploy, manage, patch, and monitor the vSphere virtual environment. These tools can be installed on the same server as other vCenter Server components or on a separate server. The tools include the following:

- **VMware vSphere Update Manager (VUM)**: This provides a central automated patch and version management for ESXi hosts and virtual appliances. VUM can be installed on the vCenter Server when running on Windows, but it must be installed on a separate Windows Server when using the VCSA.

- **ESXi Dump Collector**: This collects memory dumps over the network in the event of an ESXi host encountering a critical error.

- **VMware vSphere Syslog Collector**: This enables network logging and combines the logs from multiple hosts.

- **VMware vSphere Auto Deploy**: This provides the automated deployment and configuration of ESXi hosts.

Selecting a vCenter deployment option

There are a number of deployment options available to deploy vCenter. The vCenter Server can be deployed on a dedicated physical server running a 64-bit Windows server operating system, on a virtual machine running a 64-bit Windows server guest operating system, or as a Linux-based virtual appliance. vCenter components can be installed on a single server, or the components can be installed on separate virtual or physical machines.

How to do it...

Regardless of the deployment option selected, the vCenter Server components must be installed and configured in a specific order so that the service dependencies are met.

The order of installation of the vCenter Server components is as follows:

1. Deploy VMware Platform Services Controller.
2. Deploy vCenter Server.
3. Other supporting components – VMware Update Manager, VMware Syslog Service, ESXi Dump Collector, and so on.

How it works...

Deploying the vCenter Server components on a virtual machine is a practice recommended by VMware. When vCenter is deployed on a virtual machine, it is possible to take advantage of the portability and availability provided by the virtual infrastructure. One of the primary advantages of deploying vCenter components on virtual machines is that VMware **High Availability** (**HA**) can be leveraged to protect the management environment from a hardware failure or a virtual machine crash.

The **vCenter Server Appliance** (**VCSA**) is a preconfigured Linux-based virtual machine that has been optimized to run the vCenter Server and the associated services. It includes a PostgreSQL-embedded database. A remote database connection can be configured to support larger deployments.

Limitations of the VCSA are as follows:

  ▶ Microsoft SQL is not supported as a remote database

  ▶ VUM must be installed on a separate Windows server

The vCenter Linked Mode creates groups of vCenter Servers that can be managed centrally. Logging in to one member of the vCenter Linked Mode group allows an administrator to view and manage the inventories of all the vCenter Servers in the group. vCenter 6.x provides an Enhanced Linked Mode that allows us to link both VCSA and the Windows vCenter Server deployments.

The PSC, vCenter Server Services, and other supporting components can all be installed on a single Windows server, or each component can be installed on a separate server. Installing all the components on a single server simplifies deployment to support a small environment. Installing each component on a separate server adds some complexity, but allows the resources for each service to be adjusted as necessary and provides flexibility for larger deployments.

Determining vCenter resource requirements

The minimum system requirements for the vCenter Server are dependent on the size of the environment managed by the vCenter Server. Sizing vCenter Server correctly will ensure proper operation. The size of the vCenter inventory, the number of hosts, and the number of virtual machines all have an impact on the amount of resources required. Running multiple vCenter Server components, an embedded PSC, for example, also determines the amount of resources that will need to be allocated to the vCenter Server.

How to do it...

The following steps will help you determine the vCenter system requirements:

1. Estimate the number of host and virtual machines that will be managed by the vCenter Server.

2. Determine whether all the vCenter Server components will be installed on a single server or on separate servers.

3. Size the vCenter Server to support the managed inventory.

How it works...

The vCenter Server 6.x system requirements based on inventory size are given in the following table:

Inventory size	Number of 2 GHz CPU cores	Memory
Tiny 10 hosts/100 virtual machines	2	8 GB
Small 100 hosts/1000 virtual machines	4	16 GB
Medium 400 hosts/4,000 virtual machines	8	24 GB
Large 1,000 hosts/10,000 virtual machines	16	32 GB

The PSC can be installed on separate physical or virtual machines. The following table lists the minimum requirements for the PSC, if installed on separate physical or virtual machines:

Component	2 GHz CPU cores	Memory
PSC	2	2 GB

If the PSC and vCenter Server are all installed on the same machine, the recommended minimum requirements are four CPUs of 2 GHz and 10 GB of RAM. If the databases are installed on the same machine, additional CPU, memory, and disk resources will be necessary.

In vSphere 6.x, the vCenter Server Appliance sizing requirements mirror those of the vCenter on Windows Server based on the size of the managed environment. When deploying the VCSA, the inventory size is selected (tiny, small, medium, or large), and the VCSA appliance is configured with the required resources, as shown in the following screenshot:

There's more...

VMware and third-party plugins and applications may require their own resources. For example, if VUM is installed on the same machine as other vCenter components, the CPU, memory, and disk capacity requirements will need to be adjusted to support the additional resources required.

Selecting a database for the vCenter deployment

The vCenter Server requires a supported database to be deployed to store virtual infrastructure configuration information, logging, and performance statistics. The vCenter Server Appliance and the vCenter Server on Windows both support an embedded or external database.

How to do it...

Perform the following steps to select a database for the vCenter deployment:

1. Estimate the number of host and virtual machines that will be managed by the vCenter Server.
2. Choose a supported database platform that is suitable to support the vCenter inventory.

How it works...

The database stores configuration and performance information. The three database deployment options are as follows:

- Use the embedded vPostgreSQL database on the VCSA or the bundled vPostgreSQL database, if installing the vCenter Server on Windows
- Install a full database server locally on the same server as the vCenter Server components
- Connect to a database hosted on a remote server

The embedded database included with the VCSA can support an inventory of up to 1,000 hosts and 10,000 virtual machines, which makes it a suitable option for even very large deployments. The embedded vPostgreSQL on Windows, which can be deployed as part of the vCenter Server Windows install, is intended for smaller deployments of up to 20 hosts and 20 virtual machines. If a Windows vCenter Server is deployed using the embedded databases where the inventory is expected to grow beyond 20 hosts and 200 virtual machines, a different supported database option should be selected.

The Microsoft SQL Express Database is no longer supported in vCenter 6.x. When upgrading a vCenter 5.x Server, which was deployed using the embedded Microsoft SQL Express Database, the vCenter database will be migrated to the vPostgreSQL database as part of the upgrade process.

Reasons to use the embedded vPostgreSQL database when deploying a Windows vCenter Server are as follows:

- A small environment of less than 20 hosts and 200 virtual machines
- Easy to install and configure
- Free! No need to license a separate database server software

Databases are created as part of the installation process when using the bundled vPostgreSQL and vCenter Server. If a full installation of a database server is used, these databases and the ODBC connections required for them must be manually created prior to the installation.

Installing a full Microsoft SQL or Oracle database locally on the same Windows server as the vCenter components is supported, but this increases the amount of resources necessary for the vCenter Server. Additional resources may be required depending on the size of the vCenter inventory. Hosting the database locally on the same server is fully supported and can provide faster access, since the access to the database does not rely on network resources.

A full installation of Microsoft SQL or Oracle can also be performed on a separate physical or virtual machine. The vCenter components access the databases hosted on the remote database server. The creation of the databases and the configuration of the vCenter components is the same as with a full database installation on the same server as vCenter. Accessing the databases requires network resources. As a result, network congestion or a network outage can affect the accessibility to the databases.

Reasons to choose a remotely installed database are as follows:

▶   Leverage an existing database server already available in the environment

▶   Database administrators are responsible for administering the database servers, while virtual administrators are responsible for administering the virtual environment

▶   High availability to the databases can be provided using Microsoft or Oracle clustering

▶   Reduces the amount of resources that need to be allocated to the vCenter Server

Determining database interoperability

VMware provides an online interoperability matrix in order to make it easy to determine which database versions are compatible and supported with which versions of VMware products.

How to do it...

In order to determine database interoperability with VMware products, perform the following steps:

1. Visit `https://www.vmware.com/resources/compatibility/sim/interop_matrix.php`.

2. Select the **Solution/Database Interoperability** tab.

3. In the **Select a Solution** option, select **VMware vCenter Server** and **Version** from the respective drop-down boxes.

4. Add database versions using the database drop-down box. You can add multiple database versions.

5. The database compatibility with the selected product will be displayed in the table, as shown in the following screenshot:

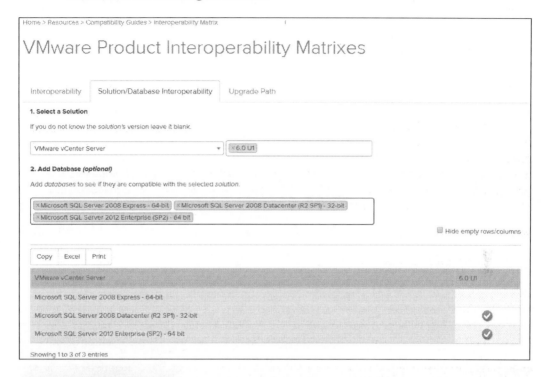

How it works...

Verifying database product interoperability ensures the supportability of the database and the version that has been selected for use with a specific VMware product. The VMware Product Interoperability Matrixes are regularly updated by VMware when new database or VMware product versions are released.

Database and product interoperability should be checked for new installations, and this should be done prior to upgrading VMware products or applying service packs to database servers.

There's more...

The interoperability matrix can be used to determine database operability for all supported VMware products and solutions. It can also be used to determine supported upgrade paths and interoperability between different VMware solutions.

Choosing a vCenter deployment topology

The deployment topology for a vCenter 6.x deployment is dependent on the size of the environment, the number of vCenters that will be deployed, the number of sites, and the availability required.

How to do it...

To determine the vCenter deployment topology for a vCenter 6.x deployment, follow these steps:

1. Identify the use cases for each vCenter deployment topology. Factors to consider include the following:

   ❑ Size of environment

   ❑ Number of vCenter Servers

   ❑ Number of sites

2. Select the vCenter deployment topology based on the environment requirements.

How it works...

vSphere 6 supports up to 10 vCenter Servers linked together in Enhanced Linked Mode and up to 8 PSCs to support the environment. vCenters and PSCs can be deployed on the same site or across multiple sites. In a small environment, with a single vCenter Server, the PSC and the vCenter Server can be combined onto a single appliance.

The embedded deployment is the topology with the least complexity. The embedded deployment topology is suitable for a small, single-site, single vCenter environment. In this topology, the PSC and vCenter Server are installed on the same virtual or physical machine. This is represented in the following image:

Multiple vCenter Servers can be deployed with a single external PSC. This deployment topology is used for a small, single site with multiple vCenter Servers. These vCenter Servers can be VCSA or Windows, or a mix of both. This enables a single-screen management of the environment with Enhanced Linked Mode. This topology is represented in the following diagram:

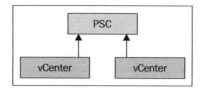

Multiple PSCs can be deployed to provide high availability of the PSC services. A single
vCenter or multiple vCenters access the PSCs within the same site through a load balancer.
There can be up to four PSCs per site behind a load balancer. The following image is a
representation of the topology where multiple PSCs are deployed for high availability:

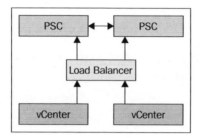

In a multi-site topology, the PSC is deployed at each site. This provides replication of the PSCs
between sites and also enables Enhanced Linked Mode between vCenters at both sites.
The following image represents a multi-site deployment topology:

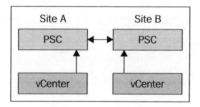

Choose a deployment topology that supports the size and requirements of the environment.
If multiple vCenters are used, the PSCs should not be deployed or embedded with a vCenter.
VMware does not support replication between embedded PSCs or using an embedded PSC to
provide services to external vCenter Servers.

Designing for management availability

The availability of the management functions of an environment becomes more critical, as
with virtual desktop environments and other self-service provisioning environments. In these
environments, if the vCenter Server is unavailable, so is the ability to provide the provisioning
of services.

If the environment does not provide these types of services, the ability to manage the environment, especially during a failure or disaster, is also critical. How can you troubleshoot an issue with a virtual machine or a group of virtual machines if the primary tool that is used to manage the environment is unavailable?

How to do it...

To properly design for management availability, follow these steps:

1. Identify management environment dependencies:

    ❑   Infrastructure dependencies, including storage, networking, and host hardware

    ❑   Service dependencies, including DNS, DHCP, and Active Directory

    ❑   VMware product dependencies, including the PSC, the vCenter Server, and other supporting components

2. Identify the potential single points of failure in the management environment.

3. Create a management design that ensures high availability of the management components.

How it works...

When designing the management network, single points of failure should be minimized. Redundant network connections and multiple network interfaces connected to separate physical switches should be configured to provide connectivity.

The storage that hosts the management components should be configured to support the capacity and performance of the management components. The storage should also be configured to be highly available so that a disk or path failure does not interrupt management operations.

In environments where the vCenter Server provides provisioning, such as virtual desktops or self-service cloud environments, the vCenter uptime is critical.

If the vCenter Server is running on a virtual machine, it can be protected with HA. If the host that vCenter is running on or the operating system crashes, the vCenter Server is restarted on a surviving host. There will be some downtime associated with the failure, but when designed correctly, the vCenter Server services will be quickly restored.

Sufficient resources should be dedicated to the vCenter Server and its components. We discussed correct sizing of the vCenter Server earlier in the chapter. Sizing vCenter correctly and reserving resources ensures not only performance but also availability. If a virtual machine is running on the same host as the vCenter Server or one of its components and it consumes too much of the host's resources, it may impact the performance and availability of the vCenter Server services. Applying resource reservations to the vCenter Server will prevent resource contention.

Another means of preventing resource contention is by designing a separate cluster to host the management components. Management cluster design is discussed in the *Designing a separate management cluster* recipe in this chapter.

Designing a separate management cluster

The management components of a virtual environment can be resource intensive. If you are running vCenter and its dependencies as virtual machines in the same cluster as the cluster managed by the vCenter server, the resources required by the management infrastructure must be factored into the capacity calculations of the logical design. Creating a separate management cluster separates the resources required by the vCenter and other management components from the resources required by the applications hosted in the virtual infrastructure.

How to do it...

Management cluster best practices are as follows:

- CPU and memory resources to support management applications
- Multiple network interfaces and multiple physical network switches to minimize the single points of failure in the management network
- Multiple paths to the storage in order to minimize the single points of failure in the storage network
- Storage designed to support both the capacity and the performance required for management applications

To correctly size the management cluster, the services that will be hosted in the cluster need to be identified. The following questions also need to be answered:

- What is the deployment topology of the vCenter Server environment?
- How many PSCs and vCenter Servers will be deployed to support the environment?
- Will the cluster also provide the resources needed for the vCenter databases?
- What about other management tools such as vCenter Operations Manager and vCenter Log Insight or other third-party management tools?

How it works...

The design of a management cluster follows the same process as designing a cluster hosting the production applications. Requirements need to be identified, and the logical design process for storage, networking, and computing resources must be followed. Functional requirements for the management network will probably include high availability, minimizing single points of failure, and quickly recovering failed components.

There's more...

Affinity rules can be used to keep virtual machines together. For example, keeping the virtual machine running the vCenter Server and the virtual machine running the vCenter Server database on the same host reduces the load on the physical network. This is because all communication between the two servers never leaves the internal host network.

Anti-affinity rules can also be used to separate virtual machines across hosts or groups of hosts. In an environment where multiple PSCs are deployed to provide high availability, separating the PSC using anti-affinity rules will ensure that a single host failure does not impact the services provided by the PSC.

If hosting vCenter in the same cluster as other virtual machine workloads, affinity and anti-affinity rules can be used to keep the vCenter Server running on specific hosts, creating a pseudo management cluster. This will help to easily locate the server in the event of the vCenter Server being unavailable.

Configuring vCenter Mail, SNMP, and Alarms

Alarms can be used to notify an administrator of issues, or potential issues, in a vSphere environment. This notification allows an administrator to take corrective actions. Alarms can be configured to send e-mail notifications and/or SMNP traps when conditions are triggered. Alarm definitions contain a trigger and an action. Triggers include issues such as hardware failures or states such as increased CPU or memory utilization.

Properly designing alarm notifications can ensure successful ongoing operations in a vSphere environment.

How to do it...

The following steps will configure the Mail and SNMP settings for a vCenter Server and to configure a defined alarm to send an e-mail or SNMP notification:

1. Using the vSphere Web Client, go to **Manage | Settings | General**, as shown in the following screenshot:

2. Select **Edit** and **Mail**. Provide the **Mail server** option with an FQDN or an IP address and the **Mail sender** with an address. The vCenter Mail configuration is shown in the following screenshot:

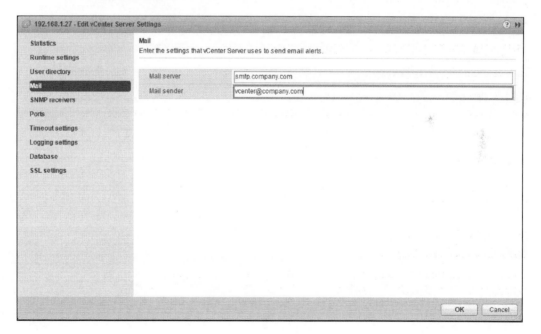

3. To configure SNMP, select **SNMP receivers** and configure **Primary Receiver URL**, **Receiver port**, and **Community string**. Select the **Enabled** checkbox to enable the receiver, as shown in the following screenshot:

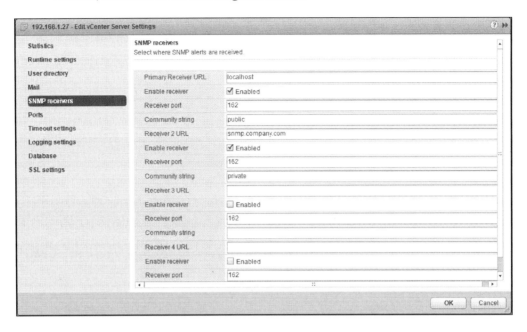

4. To configure an alarm, go to **Manage | Alarm Definitions**. Select the alarm and click on the **Edit...** button:

5. The **Send a notification email** or **Send a notification trap** action can be configured in the alarm **Actions** section. When configuring the **Send a notification email** action, the e-mail address to send the alert to is configured in the **Configuration** field. Multiple actions can be configured for an alarm. Actions can be executed once or they can repeat over a configured period of time, as shown in the following screenshot:

How it works...

In order for the **Send a notification e-mail** alarm action to work, the vCenter Mail settings must be configured with both the Mail server and the Mail sender address. The Mail sender address is the mail from the address included on the vCenter alarm notification. The Mail server is the server through which the SMTP mail will be relayed. The Mail server specified must be configured to accept and relay mail from the vCenter Server.

Configured SNMP receivers will receive notification from alarms configured with the **Send a notification trap** action. The SNMP configuration includes the receiver URL, the receiver port, and the receiver community string. Multiple SNMP receivers can be configured and enabled.

There is an extensive list of pre-configured alarm definitions. Custom alarm definitions can also be created. By default, the **Send a notification e-mail** action is not configured for any of the pre-configured definitions. When an alarm is triggered and the **Send a notification email** action is configured, an e-mail will be sent to the e-mail addresses configured.

Alarm actions can be configured to send a single notification or to send repeat notifications. Repeat notifications can be configured to repeat every set number of minutes while the alarm state is triggered.

Using Enhanced Linked Mode

Enhanced Linked Mode allows multiple vCenter Servers to be connected together to provide a single point of management. Enhanced Linked Mode enables the ability to view, search, and manage multiple vCenter Servers and provides replication of roles, permissions, licenses, and policies between vCenter Servers. This simplifies management of large environments with multiple vCenter Servers deployed in the same site or across multiple sites. vCenter 6.x supports linking vCenter Servers deployed as VCSA and as Windows Servers.

How to do it...

To enable Enhanced Linked Mode, follow these steps:

1. Ensure that Enhanced Linked Mode requirements are met:

   ❏ All PSCs are in the same vSphere SSO domain.

2. Deploy PSC and vCenter Servers in a supported deployment topology.

How it works...

Enhanced Linked Mode enables a single point of management across all vCenter Servers in the same vSphere SSO domain. This allows an administrator to easily manage the different environments, for example, a virtual server environment and a virtual desktop environment, across multiple sites as shown in the following diagram:

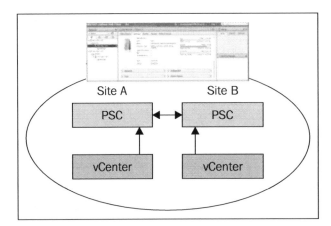

Once enabled, the inventories of all vCenters in the same SSO domain will be linked in Enhanced Linked Mode. Management of these vCenters is then accessible from a single web client interface, as shown in the following screenshot:

As with other new features, Enhanced Linked Mode is not supported when using the Windows thick vSphere Client.

Using the VMware Product Interoperability Matrix

The VMware Product Interoperability Matrix allows you to ensure compatibility between VMware products. It is important to check for compatibility before deploying or upgrading components of a vSphere environment to ensure support operability between product versions.

How to do it...

Perform the following steps to validate interoperability of VMware products in a vSphere deployment:

1. Visit `https://www.vmware.com/resources/compatibility/sim/interop_matrix.php`.

2. Select the **Interoperability** tab button.

3. In the **Select a Solution** option, select the VMware Product and version from the respective drop-down boxes.

4. Add a platform in the **Add Platform/Solution** option using the drop-down box. You can add multiple solutions and versions.

5. Interoperability with the selected products and solutions will be displayed in the table, as shown in the following screenshot:

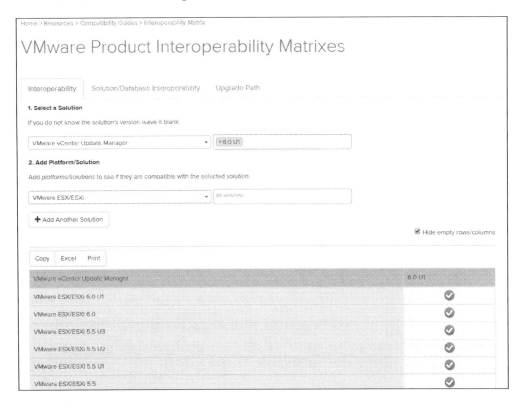

How it works...

Verifying product interoperability ensures supportability and interoperability between different VMware products and versions. The VMware Product Interoperability Matrixes are regularly updated by VMware when new products and versions are released.

Product interoperability should be checked for new installations, and this should be done prior to upgrading VMware products.

There's more...

In many environments, third-party products for monitoring, automation, and protection are used. In a new vSphere design, there will likely be requirements or constraints for integration with these third-party components. It is important to verify interoperability with these products before deploying or upgrading a vSphere environment. The VMware Product Interoperability Matrixes only include VMware products. Third-party product interoperability will need to be verified with the product vendors.

Backing up the vCenter Server components

vCenter and its components have become a critical piece of the virtual infrastructure. The vCenter Server is no longer just the management interface. Provisioning, protection, and the overall availability of the environment rely on the availability of the vCenter Server.

In order to recover the vCenter Server components in the event of an outage that results in data loss or data corruption, it is necessary to perform backups of the databases and the vCenter Server configurations. The PSC and vCenter Server each have specific configuration information that should be backed up.

The frequency of backups depends on the **Recovery Point Objective** (**RPO**) requirement that has been defined for the management environment. The time to recover the vCenter Server or the **Recovery Time Objective** (**RTO**) requirement is also a critical piece of designing a vCenter backup strategy. The RPO defines the maximum period of data loss that can be tolerated as a result of an outage. If the RPO has been determined to be 4 hours, this means backups should occur at least every 4 hours. The RTO determines how quickly the vCenter must be available after an outage.

How to do it...

Follow this process to design a backup and recovery strategy for the vCenter Server environment:

1. Determine the RPO and RTO requirements for the vCenter Server and the supporting components.
2. Develop a backup and recovery strategy that ensures that the RPO and RTO requirements are met.

How it works...

VMware recommends that you use **vSphere Data Protection** (**VDP**) to create full virtual machine backups of the PSC and vCenter Server when these components are running in virtual machines. There are also many other third-party backup software products that can also be used to take full virtual machine backups. This allows the virtual machines to be quickly restored in the event of a failure.

If the PSC or vCenter Server is running as a physical machine, a third-party backup application can be used to take a full bare metal backup. It is important to realize that this type of backup will take longer to restore, impacting the RTO.

Configuration and performance data is stored in the vCenter Server database. How backups are done depends on the database software that is used to host the database. For example, if the database is a Microsoft SQL database, a backup can be performed on demand in the SQL Management Studio or as a scheduled SQL job. Third-party backup tools can also be used to back up the vCenter databases.

If the vCenter is using the embedded vPostgreSQL database on either a Windows vCenter Server or the VCSA, it can be backed up using a scripts from the VMware KB Article 2091961 located at `http://kb.vmware.com/kb/2091961`. There are separate scripts to support a Windows or VCSA vCenter deployment.

The vCenter Server database should be backed up regularly based on the RPO that has been defined for the management components.

Upgrading vCenter Server

Most environments today will already contain at least some virtualization. A vSphere design will likely include upgrading an existing environment in order to enable new features to meet new requirements for availability, security, performance, and manageability.

The management environment for vSphere has become more complex. The vCenter Server and its components have become a critical part of the environment. In the virtualized datacenter, the vCenter Server is no longer just a management interface; it also provides provision, availability, security, and other services. Other vSphere and third-party components require vCenter Server to operate correctly. Because of this, the upgrading of a vCenter Server must be planned correctly.

How to do it...

Follow this high-level process to upgrade a vCenter Server:

1. Identify products and services that depend on the vCenter Server and those that the vCenter Server depends on.

2. Verify product interoperability for all components and the upgraded vCenter version using the VMware Product Interoperability Matrixes. Remember to also validate compatibility with third-party products integrated with vCenter.

3. Verify database support for the upgrade version using the VMware Product Interoperability Matrixes.

4. Determine the proper upgrade path to upgrade VMware products dependent on vCenter using the VMware Product Interoperability Matrixes.

5. Determine the upgrade order necessary to ensure interoperability of all components.

6. Upgrade vCenter and supporting components.

How it works...

It is important to validate support and compatibility of all vCenter Server dependencies before upgrading the vCenter Server. This is the most important process. Secondly, determine the correct upgrade order that will ensure compatibility and interoperability is maintained through the upgrade process.

Once dependencies and interoperability are validated, the upgrade order for components has been determined, and supporting components have been upgraded to ensure interoperability, the process of upgrading of the vCenter Server itself becomes simple. The Windows installer for the vCenter Server on Windows and the VCSA installer both include upgrade installers to upgrade previous versions of vCenter. The following screenshot shows the VCSA installer with the **Upgrade** option:

To upgrade a Windows vCenter Server, simply run the installer from the installation media. The installer will detect the previous version of the vCenter Server and upgrade it in place.

When upgrading an existing vCenter Server environment, consider the following points:

- ▶ Upgrading a Windows vCenter Server that was deployed using Simple Install will upgrade the vCenter Server with an embedded PSC.
- ▶ Upgrading a VCSA deployed with embedded SSO will upgrade the VCSA with the embedded PSC.
- ▶ If Microsoft SQL Express was used for the vCenter deployment, the vCenter database will be migrated to the embedded vPostgreSQL database.
- ▶ A vCenter Server cannot be downgraded after the upgrade. Back up the vCenter Server databases and other supporting components if you ever need to revert to the previous version after the upgrade.

Designing a vSphere Update Manager Deployment

VMware regularly releases patches and updates to provide bug fixes, to address security vulnerabilities, or to add new features. Regularly patching an environment is important to the security and stability of the environment.

VMware vSphere Update Manager (**VUM**) is an optional vCenter component that provides patching and upgrading of ESXi hosts, VMware tools, and VMware Guest Hardware. VUM ensures compliance is maintained through patch and upgrade baselines. VUM also allows the remediation of hosts or virtual machines that are not in compliance with configured baselines.

VUM must be deployed on a Windows Server and requires a supported database, either embedded or external. The VUM architecture is shown in the following diagram:

VUM requires a Windows Server, and there is a one-to-one relationship between VUM and vCenter Servers. VUM 6.x is fully integrated into the vSphere Web Client.

How to do it...

To deploy VUM in a vSphere environment, follow these steps:

1. Verify product and database interoperability using the VMware Product Interoperability Matrixes.
2. Determine the location and type of database to host the VUM database.
3. Allocate the required compute and storage resources to support the VUM server.
4. Run the vSphere Update Manager Server installation on the server selected for VUM, as shown in the following screenshot:

5. Once deployed, use the vSphere Web Client to create baselines and attach hosts and virtual machines to the baselines. The following screenshot provides an example of critical and non-critical host patch baselines associated with a group of hosts:

6. Click on the **Scan for Updates** option to verify compliance with attached baselines. The following screenshot displays a host in compliance with the attached critical and non-critical patch baselines:

7. Remediate hosts or VMs that are not in compliance.

How it works...

VUM supports an embedded or external database. Microsoft SQL Express is included with the VUM installation media. The embedded Microsoft SQL Express database is suitable for small deployments of five hosts and 50 virtual machines. Larger deployments require a Microsoft SQL or Oracle DB that can be installed on the same server or an external one.

VUM cannot be deployed on the same server as the VCSA. If VUM is required in an environment managed by the VCSA, it must be installed on a separate physical or virtual Windows server. VUM can be installed on the same server as a Windows vCenter Server as long as sufficient resources are allocated. The following table lists the minimum requirements for VUM:

Component	2 GHz CPU cores	Memory
VMware Update Manager (VUM)	2	2 GB

The disk space required to support VUM will depend on the size of the environment. VMware provides a VUM Sizing Estimator for vSphere 6, which can be downloaded from `https://pubs.vmware.com/vsphere-60/topic/com.vmware.ICbase/PDF/vsphere-update-manager-60-sizing-estimator.xls`.

Patch and upgrade baselines contain patches or groups of patches. These baselines can be fixed or dynamic. Critical and non-critical patch baselines are included by default. These are dynamic baselines that are regularly updated. Baselines can be attached to a virtual machine, a group of virtual machines, a host, a group of hosts, a cluster, or a datacenter. Hosts, clusters, or datacenters can be scanned against the attached patch baseline and remediated.

There's more...

The default pre-configured dynamic patch baselines poll an external Internet-accessible repository for updates and to download the updates required for remediation. For vSphere environments without access to the Internet, the **Update Manager Download Service** (**UMDS**) can be used to download the patches and updates, and then export the updates and patches information into a repository accessible to the isolated network.

5
vSphere Storage Design

In this chapter, we will cover the following recipes:

- ▸ Identifying RAID levels
- ▸ Calculating storage capacity requirements
- ▸ Determining storage performance requirements
- ▸ Calculating the storage throughput
- ▸ Storage connectivity options
- ▸ Storage path selection plugins
- ▸ Sizing datastores
- ▸ Designing for VMware VSAN
- ▸ Using VMware Virtual Volumes
- ▸ Incorporating storage policies into a design
- ▸ NFS v4.1 capabilities and limits

Introduction

Storage is an essential component of vSphere design and provides the foundation for the vSphere environment. A solid storage design that addresses capacity, performance, availability, and recoverability is the key to a successful vSphere design. The following diagram displays how a storage design is integrated into the design process:

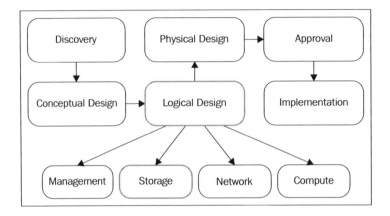

Several storage options and protocols are supported in a vSphere environment. The architecture chosen for a vSphere deployment depends on the capabilities and features required to meet the design requirements.

This chapter will cover the calculation of the storage capacity and performance requirements, sizing datastores, and selecting a storage protocol. The calculations for the recipes in this chapter will be based on the following requirements identified in *Chapter 3, The Design Factors*:

- There are 100 application servers.
- Each application server is configured with 100 GB disk space. The peak disk capacity usage of a single application server is approximately 65% of the total or 65 GB. The average disk performance of a single application server is 65 IOPS with an IO profile of 90% read and 10% write.
- Providing the capacity to support growth for 25 additional application servers over the next 5 years.

Several new storage features have become available with the release of vSphere 6. These new storage features include improvements to **VMware Virtual SAN** (**VSAN**), the introduction of **Virtual Volumes** (**VVOL**), and support for NFS version 4.1. This chapter will also provide an overview of these new storage options so that they can be incorporated into a vSphere 6 design.

Identifying RAID levels

Redundant Array of Independent Disks (**RAID**) combines multiple physical disks into a single unit of storage. The advantages in speed, reliability, and capacity can be realized depending on which RAID level is selected. RAID provides the first level of protection against data loss due to a disk failure.

How to do it...

In order to select the proper RAID level required to support virtual workloads, you need to perform the following steps:

1. Identify the different RAID levels and capabilities.
2. Select an appropriate RAID level to support a virtualized workload based on capacity and performance requirements.

How it works...

RAID0 stripes disks together to appear as a single disk with a capacity equal to the sum of all the disks in the set. It provides excellent performance and capacity efficiency but offers no data protection. If a disk fails in a RAID0 set, the data is lost and must be recovered from a backup or some other source. Since this level offers no redundancy, it is not a good choice for production or mission-critical storage.

The following diagram illustrates the disks in a RAID0 configuration:

RAID1 duplicates or mirrors data from one disk to another. A RAID1 set consists of two disks and data is written on both the disks, which can then be read from either disk. If one of the disks fails, the mirror can be rebuilt by replacing the disk. The following diagram illustrates disks in a RAID1 configuration:

RAID 1+0, RAID1/0, or RAID10 is a stripe of multiple mirrors. RAID10 provides excellent redundancy and performance, making this the best option for mission-critical applications. RAID10 is well suited for applications with small, random, write-intensive IOs, such as high transaction applications, large messaging applications, or large transactional database applications. A RAID10 set can recover from multiple drive failures as long as two drives in the same mirror set do not fail.

Both RAID1 and RAID10 have a capacity efficiency of 50% since half of the disks in a RAID1 or RAID10 set are used to store the mirrored data. The following diagram illustrates disks in a RAID10 configuration:

In RAID5, data is striped across several drives and parity is written equally across all the drives in the set. The parity allows recovery from a failure of a single drive in the set. This level offers a balance of performance and capacity and is suitable for the storage of transactional databases, web servers, application servers, file servers, and mail servers. The following diagram illustrates disks in a RAID5 configuration:

The capacity efficiency of a RAID5 set is calculated using the formula $[(n - 1) / n] * 100$, where *n* is equal to the number of disks in the set. For example, a RAID5 set containing four 100 GB disks would provide 75% of the total capacity or 300 GB:

$$[(4-1)/4]*100 = 75\%$$

$$(100GB * 4) * .75 = 300GB$$

RAID6 is similar to RAID5, except that the two parity blocks are written and distributed equally across all the drives in the set. The second parity increases the write penalty but protects against two drive failures in the set. File archiving and file servers are common workloads hosted on RAID6.

The capacity efficiency of a RAID6 set is calculated using the formula $[(n - 2) / n] * 100$, where *n* is equal to the number of disks in the set. A RAID6 set containing six 100 GB disks would provide approximately 67% of the total capacity or 400 GB:

$$[(6 - 2) / 6] * 100 = \sim 67\%$$

$$(100GB * 6) * .67 = \sim 400GB$$

There's more...

To increase the redundancy of a RAID set, hot spares should be configured in the array. Hot spares are used to automatically replace a failed drive in a RAID set temporarily, until the failed drive can be replaced. A single hot spare can be configured to provide protection against multiple RAID sets.

Calculating the storage capacity requirements

Capacity is typically measured in **Gigabytes (GB)** or **Terabytes (TB)**. It should include the total space required to support the current requirements, the space required to support growth, the space required for virtual machine swapfiles, and the additional slack space for snapshots, logs, and other virtual machine data.

How to do it...

In order to calculate the storage capacity requirements, you need to perform the following steps:

1. Determine the capacity required to support the current workloads.
2. Determine the capacity required to support future growth.

How it works...

Capacity is calculated to support the current and future growth based on the design requirements, as follows:

Current Capacity = 100 Virtual Machines x 100 GB = 10 TB

Growth Capacity = 25 Virtual Machines x 100 GB = 2.5 TB

20% Slack space = 12.5 TB x .20 = 2.5 TB

Capacity = 12.5 TB + 2.5 TB = 15 TB

Each virtual machine will have a swapfile or `.vswp` file that is created when the virtual machine is powered on. The size of the `.vswp` file for each virtual machine is equal to the size of the allocated memory minus the memory reservation:

vSwap Capacity = (100 Virtual Machines + 25 Future Virtual Machines) x 8 GB of Memory = 1 TB

The total capacity required to support the requirements is 16 TB.

There's more...

The application servers are configured with 100 GB disk space, but the maximum space that is actually consumed by a server is only 65 GB. Resizing the virtual machine disk or using thin provisioning can reduce the required amount of storage capacity significantly.

Since only the actual used space is consumed, thin provisioning virtual machine disks allows the disk capacity to be overallocated, which means that more capacity can be allocated to the virtual machine disks than what is actually available in the datastore. This increases the amount of management oversight required to monitor the capacity. vCenter datastore alarms can be configured to monitor overallocation and datastore usage in order to assist capacity management.

Determining the storage performance requirements

Storage performance is an important factor in storage design. The storage must be designed to meet not only the capacity requirements, but also the performance requirements for writes to and reads from the disk. Disk performance is measured in **Input/Output per Second** (**IOPS**). One disk read request or one disk write request is equal to one IO. The storage performance must support the current requirements and growth.

How to do it...

The IOPS required to support an application is calculated based on the percentage of read IO, the percentage of write IO, and the write penalty of the RAID level the workload will be hosted on.

To calculate the IOPS requirements, perform the following steps:

1. Determine the number of IOPS a workload requires.
2. Identify the percentage of read IO to write IO for the workload.
3. Determine the write penalty of the RAID level that will host the workload.
4. Calculate the IOPS the storage must be capable of providing in order to support the workload.

How it works...

To get the total amount of the required IOPS, multiply the number of workloads by the number of functional application IOPS:

Total IOPS = (100 current workloads + 25 future workloads) * 65 IOPS = 8125 IOPS

To calculate the functional IOPS required for a specific workload, use the following formula:

Functional Workload IOPS = (Workload IOPS * %Reads) + ((Workload IOPS * %Writes) * Write Penalty)

The write penalty is based on the number of IO operations a specific RAID configuration requires for a single write request. Writing data to multiple disks in a mirror or parity calculations in a RAID5 or RAID6 configuration adds IO operations to the write request. The write request is not completed until the data and parity are written to the disks.

The following table illustrates the write penalty based on the RAID levels:

RAID	Write penalty
0	1
1	2
5	4
6	6
10	2

Based on the requirements of 65 IOPS per workload with 90% reads and 10% writes on the storage configured in RAID5, the actual workload IOPS will be 85 IOPS:

Functional Application IOPS = (65 * .90) + ((65* .10) * 4) = ~85 IOPS

Each disk in a storage array is capable of providing a number of IOPS. The number of IOPS a single disk can deliver is calculated from the average latency and the average seek time of the disk. The formula to calculate the disk performance is as follows:

IOPS = 1 / (average latency in milliseconds + average seek time in milliseconds)

The following table lists some approximate IOPS provided based on the spindle speed and the drive type:

Drive speed	~ IOPS
SSD	> 2500
15k SAS/FC	175
10k SAS/FC	125
7200 NL-SAS/SATA	75
5400 SATA	50

Based on the number of IOPS required, there will be a need for 47 15k SAS drives to support the workload:

8125 IOPS / 175 IOPS per drive = 46.4 or 47 15k SAS drives

The same workload on drives configured in RAID10 sets would require 52 15k SAS drives to provide the required IOPS:

Functional Workload IOPS = (65 * .90) + ((65* .10) * 2) = 72 IOPS

Total IOPS = (100 current workloads + 25 future workloads) * 72 IOPS = 9000 IOPS

9000 IOPS / 175 IOPS per drive = 51.4 or 52 15k SAS drives

There's more...

Many arrays provide a caching mechanism using memory or SSD disks to increase the number of IOPS the array can deliver. This allows a few slow drives to deliver a higher number of IOPS. This caching can greatly reduce the number of drives required to deliver the same number of IOPS by writing to a faster cache instead of writing to disks directly. FAST Cache of EMC and Flash Cache of NetApp are examples of vendor-specific SSD-caching technologies that can be used to increase the storage IO performance.

Calculating the storage throughput

The data transfer rate, or throughput, is the rate at which data can be read from or written to the storage device, and is typically measured in MB/s. Storage adapters, connectivity, and array controllers will need to support the storage throughput requirements.

How to do it...

Throughput should be calculated in order to ensure that the storage controllers and disk can support the required data transfer rates. Throughput is also used to correctly size the storage connectivity bandwidth.

To calculate the storage throughput requirements, perform the following steps:

1. Determine the IO size of the workload.
2. Determine the number of IOPS required to support the workload.
3. Calculate the throughput required.

How it works...

Throughput is calculated by multiplying the IO size of the workload by the number of IOPS. Transactional databases and application servers typically have an IO size between 4k and 64k, whereas file archiving applications, backup applications, and media streaming applications typically have larger IO sizes from 64k to 1024k.

To calculate the throughput, the following formula is used:

Throughput = Functional Workload IOPS * IO Size

Using the Functional Workload IOPS from the previous recipe and an IO size of 8k, the throughput required can be calculated as follows:

Throughput = 9000 * 8k = 72 MB/s

The Network Interface Card bandwidth is usually expressed in Mbps. To convert MB/s to Mbps, simply multiply by 8:

$$Bandwidth\ Mbps = 72\ MB/s * 8 = 576\ Mbps$$

The array will need to support a throughput of at least 72 MB/s, and the connectivity bandwidth will need to be sufficient enough to support at least 576 Mbps.

Storage connectivity options

vSphere supports multiple storage protocols and connectivity options. Storage can be directly connected to a host, or it can be centralized and shared with multiple hosts. Shared storage is required when implementing many vSphere features, such as VMware **High Availability** (**HA**), VMware **Fault Tolerance** (**FT**), and VMware **Distributed Resource Scheduling** (**DRS**).

How to do it...

In order to determine the storage connectivity requirements, perform the following steps:

1. Identify the supported storage protocols and connectivity options.
2. Select the storage protocol and connectivity that supports the design requirements.

How it works...

Performance, availability, and costs are all factors that should be considered when choosing a storage connectivity option. The following table provides a quick overview of the different storage connectivity options and how they compare with each other in terms of performance, availability, and costs:

Protocol	Performance	Availability	Costs
Local storage	Good	Fair	Low
Fibre channel	Excellent	Excellent	High
iSCSI	Good	Excellent	Medium
NFS	Good	Good	Low
FCoE	Excellent	Excellent	High

Direct attached or local storage is storage directly attached to a host. Since this storage is not shared, many VMware features will not be available for virtual machines hosted on the local storage.

Best practices when using direct attached or local storage are as follows:

- ▸ Configure RAID to provide protection against a hard disk failure
- ▸ Use a hardware RAID controller that is on the VMware HCL

Fibre Channel (**FC**) is a block-level, low latency, high-performance storage network protocol that is well suited for workloads with high I/O requirements. The FC protocol encapsulates the SCSI commands into the FC frames. A Fibre Channel **Host Bus Adapter** (**HBA**) is required to connect the host to the storage network or fabric. FC HBAs can provide a throughput of 2, 4, 8, or 16 Gbps depending on the capabilities of the HBA and the FC network. FC uses zoning and LUN masking to configure which hosts can connect to which targets on the SAN.

The cost of deploying FC-connected storage can be significantly higher than other options, especially if an existing FC infrastructure does not already exist.

The best practices when using FC are as follows:

- ▸ Use multiple HBAs in the host to provide multiple paths from load balancing and redundancy.
- ▸ Ensure all HBAs and switches are configured for the same speed. Mixing the speed of HBAs and switches can produce contention at the FC switch and SAN.
- ▸ Use single-initiator single-target zoning. A single HBA, the initiator, is zoned to a single array target. Separate zones are created for each host HBA.
- ▸ Mask LUNs presented to ESXi hosts from other devices.
- ▸ Ensure firmware levels on FC switches and HBAs are up to date and compatible.

iSCSI provides block-level storage access by encapsulating SCSI commands in TCP/IP. iSCSI storage can be accessed with the iSCSI software initiator, included with ESXi through a standard network adapter or using a dependent or independent iSCSI HBA:

- ▸ A dependent iSCSI adapter depends on VMware networking and iSCSI configuration for connectivity and management.
- ▸ An independent iSCSI HBA provides its own networking and configuration for connectivity and management. Configuration is done directly on the HBA through its own configuration interface.

Throughput is based on the network bandwidth, the speed of the network interface card (1 Gbps or 10 GbE), and the CPU resources required to encapsulate the SCSI commands into TCP/IP packets.

The cost of implementing iSCSI is typically significantly less than implementing FC. Standard network adapters and network switches can be used to provide iSCSI connectivity. Using dedicated iSCSI HBAs not only increases the performance, but also increases the cost. The price of 10 GbE switches and 10 GbE adapters continues to drop as their deployment becomes more widespread.

The best practices when using iSCSI are as follows:

- ▶ Configure multiple vmks bound to multiple vmnics in order to provide load balancing and redundancy for iSCSI connections.

- ▶ Use network cards with **TCP/IP Offload Engine** (**TOE**) enabled in order to reduce the stress on the host CPU.

- ▶ Use a physically separate network for the iSCSI traffic. If a physically separate network is not available, use VLANs to separate the iSCSI traffic from other network traffic.

- ▶ Enable jumbo frames (MTU 9000) on the iSCSI network.

The **Network File System protocol** (**NFS**) can be used to access virtual machine files stored on a **Network Attached Storage** (**NAS**) device. Virtual machine configuration files, disk (VMDK) files, and swap (`.vswp`) files can be stored on the NAS storage. vSphere 5.5 supports NFS Version 3 over TCP, and vSphere 6 added support for NFS v4.1. The capabilities and limitations of NFS v4.1 will be discussed in a separate recipe later in this chapter.

Throughput is based on the network bandwidth, the speed of the network interface card (1 Gbps or 10 GbE), and the processing speed of the NAS. Multiple paths can be configured for high availability, but load balancing across multiple paths is not supported with NFS.

The cost of implementing NFS connectivity is similar to iSCSI. No specialized network hardware is required. Standard network switches and network adapters are used, and there is no need for specialized HBAs.

The best practices when using NFS-connected storage are as follows:

- ▶ Use a physically separate network for the NFS traffic. If a physically separate network is not available, use VLANs to separate the NFS traffic from other network traffic.

- ▶ Hosts must mount NFS version 3 shares and non-Kerberos NFS version 4.1 shares with root access.

- ▶ Enable jumbo frames (MTU 9000) on the NFS network.

Fibre Channel of Ethernet (**FCoE**) encapsulates Fibre Channel in Ethernet frames. A **Converged Network Adapter** (**CNA**) that supports FCoE is required, or a network adapter with FCoE capabilities can be used with the software FCoE initiator included with ESXi.

A common implementation of FCoE is with Cisco UCS blade chassis. The connectivity for TCP/IP network and FCoE storage traffic is converged between the chassis and the Fabric Interconnects. The Fabric Interconnects splits the traffic and provides the connectivity paths to the TCP/IP network and storage network fabrics.

The best practices when using FCoE are as follows:

- ▸ Disable the **Spanning Tree Protocol** (**STP**) on the switch ports connected to FCoE adapters
- ▸ Ensure that the latest microcode is installed on the FCoE network adapter
- ▸ If the FCoE network adapter has multiple ports, configure each port on a separate vSwitch

Storage path selection plugins

Multipathing allows more than one physical path to be used to transfer data between the ESXi hosts and the storage array. In the event of a failure in a storage path, the host or hosts can switch to another available path. Multipathing also provides load balancing by distributing the storage IO across multiple physical paths.

How to do it...

To determine the multipathing policy, we perform the following steps:

1. Identify the different native multipathing policies available and the capabilities of each policy.
2. Select a multipathing policy based on the number of paths and the array type used.
3. Change the default multipathing policy using the `esxcli` command.
4. Configure the multipathing policy on the storage devices presented to the ESXi host.

How it works...

The VMware **Native Multipathing Plugin** (**NMP**) supports storage arrays listed on the VMware **Hardware Compatibility List** (**HCL**). NMP provides path selection based on the array type by associating a set of physical paths with a storage device or LUN.

The **Storage Array Type Plugin** (**SATP**) monitors the available storage paths, reports changes in the path status, and initiates failover between the paths when required. The **Path Selection Plugins** (**PSP**) determine which available path to use for IO. There are the following three Native Multipathing PSPs available:

- ▸ **Fixed**: The host always uses a preferred path if it is available. If the preferred path fails, another available path is selected and used until the preferred path becomes available. This is the default policy for active/active storage devices.
- ▸ **Most Recently Used** (**MRU**): The host uses the most recently used path. If the current path fails, another path is selected. IO does not revert to the previous path when it becomes available. This is the default policy for active/passive storage devices.

▶ **Round Robin** (**RR**): IO is rotated through all active paths. This provides load balancing across all physical paths available to the hosts. This PSP can be used on active/passive or active/active arrays.

Array vendors may provide their own path selection plugins in order to provide storage multipathing. The use of third-party MPPs will depend on array-and-vendor best practices. The NMP can be used for any supported array.

The optimal PSP to choose is dependent on the recommendations of the array vendor.

By default, a PSP is set based on the SATP used for the array. The SATP to use is identified by the **Pluggable Storage Architecture** (**PSA**) using a set of claim rules that base the selection on the vendor and the model of the array. The SATP then determines the default PSP to be used.

The NMP PSP policies are as follows:

▶ VMW_PSP_MRU for MRU

▶ VMW_PSP_FIXED for Fixed

▶ VMW_PSP_RR for RR

The default PSP for an SATP can be changed using the following `esxcli` command:

```
esxcli storage nmp satp set –default-psp=<psp policy to set>
--satp=<SATP_name>
```

Using the command line changes the default PSP for all new devices identified by the SATP. The PSP for an individual device or LUN can also be changed. This can be done in the vSphere Client or vSphere Web Client by managing the paths for a single storage device on a host.

To change the PSP of a device using the vSphere Client, navigate to **Host and Clusters | Hosts | Configuration | Storage Adapters** and select the storage adapter that services the paths you want to modify. In the **Details** section of the **Storage Adapters** window, right-click on the device you want to modify the PSP on and select **Manage Paths**.

From the **Manage Paths** window, select the **Path Selection** option with the drop-down menu and click on **Change**.

The following screenshot displays how to select and change the path selection policy for a device using the vSphere Client:

Changing the default PSP for an SATP or the PSP for a device can be done without impacting normal operations. A change made to the PSP for a single device takes effect immediately. Changing the default PSP for the SATP changes only the settings of newly discovered devices and not the PSP settings of the current devices.

Sizing datastores

A datastore is a logical representation of storage presented to an ESXi host where virtual machine files are stored. A datastore can be a VMFS-formatted volume, an NFS export, a Virtual Volume datastore, a Virtual SAN datastore, or a path on the local ESXi filesystem.

How to do it...

Design requirements, the virtual machine disk size, IOPS, and recovery are all factors that can determine the number of virtual machines to store on a single datastore. The size of the datastore is calculated based on the number of virtual machines per datastore and the size of the virtual machines:

1. Determine the number of virtual machines per datastore based on the capacity, performance, and recovery requirements.
2. Understand the impact the SCSI reservations may have on the datastore sizing.
3. Understand how the recovery time impacts the datastore sizing.

How it works...

A design factor that was identified in *Chapter 3, The Design Factors*, specified that no more than 20 application servers should be affected by a hardware failure. Applying the same requirement to datastore sizing would mean that no more than 20 application servers should be hosted on a single datastore:

*Number of VMs per datastore * (VM disk size + .vswp size) + 20% = Minimum datastore size*

The datastore size for 20 application server workloads, each with 100 GB of disk storage and 8 GB of RAM with no reservations plus 20% for slack would be approximately 2.5 TB:

$$20 * (100GB + 8GB) + 20\% = 2{,}592 \; GB \; or \sim 2.5TB$$

The storage backing the datastore has to provide enough IOPS to support the virtual machines running on it. If a virtual machine generates 50 IOPS and there are 20 virtual machines on the datastore, the storage must be able to support 1000 IOPS.

 The maximum size of a VMFS5 datastore is 64 TB.

Block storage formatted as a VMFS volume is susceptible to SCSI reservations or the locking of the entire LUN for a very short period of time by a single host. A few operations that cause SCSI reservations to occur are as follows:

- ▶ Creating a VMFS datastore
- ▶ Expanding a VMFS datastore
- ▶ Powering on a virtual machine
- ▶ Creating a template
- ▶ Deploying a virtual machine from a template

- ▸ Creating a virtual machine
- ▸ Migrating a virtual machine with vMotion
- ▸ Developing a virtual machine disk
- ▸ Creating or deleting a file

With the introduction of VMFS5 along with the **vStorage APIs for Array Integration** (**VAAI**) hardware-assisted locking feature, the impact of SCSI reservations has become minimized. If an array does not support the VAAI hardware-assisted locking feature, then the number of virtual machines per datastore may need to be decreased in order to reduce the impact of LUN locking for SCSI reservations.

The **Recovery Time Objective** (**RTO**) must also be taken into account when determining the size of a datastore. If the datastore is lost or becomes inaccessible, how long will it take to restore the virtual machines that were running on it?

Size of Datastore / GBs recovered per hour <= RTO

If 500 GB is to be recovered per hour, the time to recover a failed datastore can be calculated as follows:

2.5 TB / 500GB = 5 hours to recover

If the RTO for the applications or workloads running on the datastore is less than 5 hours, the datastore would need to be resized in order to ensure that recovery would take place within the defined RTO.

There's more...

Multiple datastores can be aggregated to create a datastore cluster. A datastore cluster is a collection of the member datastore resources with a shared management interface. vSphere Storage DRS manages the datastore cluster resources to determine the initial placement and the ongoing balancing of virtual machine VMDKs across the datastores in the cluster. Datastore clusters are supported for both VMFS and NFS datastores.

A few recommended practices when using datastore clusters and Storage DRS are as follows:

- ▸ Cluster datastores with similar IOs and capacity characteristics
- ▸ Use separate datastore clusters for replicated and non-replicated datastores
- ▸ Do not mix NFS and VMFS datastores in the same datastore cluster
- ▸ Do not place datastores shared across multiple datacenters in a datastore cluster

When a virtual machine is placed in a datastore cluster, Storage DRS determines which datastore in the cluster the files will be stored in based on the space utilization and/or the performance. The following diagram is a logical representation of the virtual machines placed in a datastore cluster:

The best practices when using datastore clusters are as follows:

 ▸ Datastores in a cluster should have similar performance capabilities

 ▸ Keep similar virtual machine IO workloads together on the same cluster

 ▸ Do not mix replicated and non-replicated datastores in the same cluster

 ▸ Do not mix NFS and VMFS datastores in the same datastore cluster

 ▸ Use VMDK affinity rules to keep virtual machine disk files together on the same datastore within the datastore cluster

 ▸ Use VM anti-affinity rules to ensure that virtual machines run on different datastores within the datastore cluster

The VMware vSphere Storage DRS Interoperability whitepaper can be found at http://www.vmware.com/files/pdf/techpaper/vsphere-storage-drs-interoperability.pdf. This whitepaper provides an overview of the datastore cluster's best practices and the interoperability of datastore clusters along with other VMware products.

Designing for VMware VSAN

VMware **Virtual SAN** (**VSAN**) is integrated into the ESXi hypervisor. VSAN virtualizes and aggregates the local direct-attached disks in ESXi hosts. This creates a single pool of storage resources from the local disks with each host, which is shared across all hosts in the VSAN cluster, as shown in the following illustration:

How to do it...

To use VSAN for storage in a vSphere virtual infrastructure design, follow these steps:

1. Identify the hardware requirements to support VSAN.
2. Verify that disks and controllers are on the VSAN **Hardware Compatibility List** (**HCL**).
3. Size VSAN to support performance and availability.
4. Enable VSAN on the vSphere Cluster.

How it works...

VSAN presents shared storage to ESXi hosts across a vSphere Cluster. Each host providing storage to the VSAN cluster requires the following:

- ▶ **Solid-state disks** (**SSD**) to provide performance
- ▶ **Hard disk drives** (**HDD**) or SSDs to provide capacity
- ▶ Disk controller
- ▶ Network connectivity between hosts

As with all hardware in a vSphere environment, the hardware supporting VSAN must be verified on the HCL located at `http://www.vmware.com/resources/compatibility/search.php?deviceCategory=vsan`. The compatibility of the SSD, HDD, and disk controller, including the firmware, should all be validated on the HCL. Many server hardware vendors offer VSAN-ready nodes that have been preconfigured with supported hardware/firmware.

VSAN can be deployed as a hybrid, SSD and HDD disks, or as All-Flash. VSAN requires network connectivity between hosts. A 10 GbE network should be used for VSAN to provide the best performance, but 1 GbE is supported in a hybrid VSAN. 10 GbE is required for All-Flash VSAN. A VMkernel is configured and enabled for VSAN traffic, as shown in the following screenshot:

VSAN is enabled on a vSphere Cluster. ESXi hosts participating in the VSAN, whether the host is providing storage or consuming storage, must be in the same cluster. The VSAN storage cannot be directly consumed by hosts outside the cluster. VSAN is enabled by simply turning on VSAN for a vSphere Cluster, as shown in the following screenshot:

When enabling VSAN, disks can be automatically or manually claimed. Disks are claimed to be used by VSAN and placed into disk groups. A disk group must contain at least one flash (SSD) disk and one or more HDDs. A single host can be configured with up to five disk groups, and each disk group can contain up to 8 disks, 1 SSD, and 7 HDDs. All flash disk groups are supported as well. In a VSAN disk group, the flash disk provides performance and the HDD disk provides capacity. Claiming disks for VSAN is shown in the following screenshot:

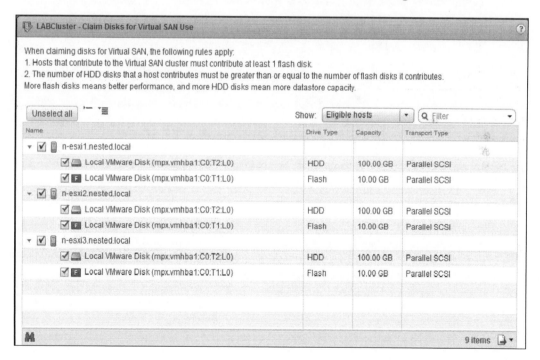

When sizing VSAN, VMware recommends that the SSDs be sized to 10% of the HDD capacity in a disk group. For example, if there is 1 TB of HDD capacity, the SSD should be at least 100 GB. The capacity of the disk group is the sum of the HDD capacity. If there are three 1 TB HDDs in the disk group, the group will provide 3 TB of capacity storage. The size of the VSAN in a datastore is the aggregate of all disk groups claimed by VSAN across all hosts.

Three hosts participating in a VSAN cluster, each with a disk group of three 1 TB HDD to provide capacity, will present a VSAN datastore with approximately 9 TB of usable capacity.

When sizing VSAN, it is important to take into account **failures to tolerate** (**FTT**) and Fault Domain policies for virtual machines. A virtual machine consuming 100 GB of storage on a VSAN datastore with the FTT policy configured to 1 will consume twice the capacity, or 200 GB. This is due to the virtual machine storage being duplicated across two hosts, so the virtual machine disks will be available in the event that a single host fails. If the FTT is set to 2, then a virtual machine will consume thrice the capacity. We will take a deeper look at storage policies later in this chapter.

There's more...

At the time of writing, VMware has just released the latest version of VSAN. This new version, VSAN 6.2, includes a number of significant features and improvements, including the following:

▶ Deduplication and compression in order to improve the capacity efficiency

▶ Erasure coding to provide better resiliency

▶ Quality of service to control IOPS on a per-virtual machine basis

VMware continues to develop and improve the capabilities, efficiencies, and the performance of VSAN storage, making it a suitable alternative to traditional storage for virtual machine workloads. More details on VSAN design and sizing can be found in the *VMware Virtual SAN 6.0 Design and Sizing Guide* found at `http://www.vmware.com/files/pdf/products/vsan/VSAN_Design_and_Sizing_Guide.pdf`.

Using VMware Virtual Volumes

Virtual Volumes (**VVOL**) is a virtual disk management and array integration framework introduced with vSphere 6. VVOLs enables policy-based storage for virtual machines. A datastore is presented backed by raw storage supporting multiple different capabilities, such as snapshotting, replication, deduplication, raid level, performance, and so on. These capabilities are exposed to the vSphere environment. Policies are created and assigned to virtual machines. When a virtual machine is placed on a VVOL datastore, the placement on the array is based on the requirements defined in the policies.

How to do it...

To successfully incorporate VVOLs as part of a vSphere infrastructure design, perform these steps:

1. Identify the components and characteristics of VVOL.
2. Identify the limitations and interoperability of VVOLs with other vSphere components.
3. Create a new storage provider in vCenter.
4. Add a VVOL datastore.

How it works...

The following table outlines the different components that are required to make up a VVOL environment:

Component	Description
vSphere APIs for Storage Awareness (VASA)	The VASA provider is a software component developed by the storage array vendor. It provides storage capability awareness to vCenter and ESXi hosts.
Storage Containers (SC)	A pool of storage capacity and storage capabilities in the array. A storage container represents a virtual datastore.
Protocol Endpoint (PE)	A logical IO proxy that provides a data path from virtual machines to virtual volumes.
VVOL Objects	Encapsulation of virtual machine files and disks. Objects are stored natively on the array storage containers.

VVOLs differ from other vSphere storage in that there is no filesystem. The storage container is comprised of raw storage capacity grouped by capabilities. This storage container is presented as a datastore to the vSphere environment through the protocol endpoint. The protocol endpoint can provide a data path and supports IP-based (iSCSI, NFS, and FCoE) and FC connectivity. The VASA provider communicates with vCenter and ESXi hosts to expose the storage capabilities of the VVOLs.

The following figure provide a logical overview of VVOLs and the connectivity between the components:

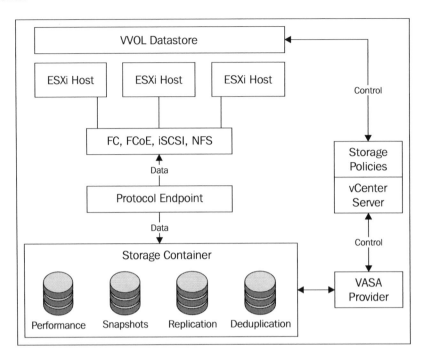

VVOLs is a new feature that has only just been introduced with vSphere 6. There are still a number of limitations to the features and the products supported. For example, features such as **Storage IO Control** (**SIOC**), IPv6, **Fault Tolerance** (**FT**), and **Raw Device Mapping** (**RDM**) are not supported on VVOL. Products such as **vSphere Data Protection** (**VDP**) and VMware **Site Recovery Manager** (**SRM**) do not currently support the use of VVOLs. If a vSphere design requires these features or products, VVOLs will most likely not be a viable choice to provide storage to the environment. For a complete list of supported/unsupported features and products, refer to the VMware *Knowledge Base* article at `https://kb.vmware.com/kb/2112039`.

To create a new storage provider, the name of the provider, the URL for the VASA 2.0 provider, and a username and password or a certificate for authentication are required. Storage providers are configured per vCenter Server, as shown in the following screenshot:

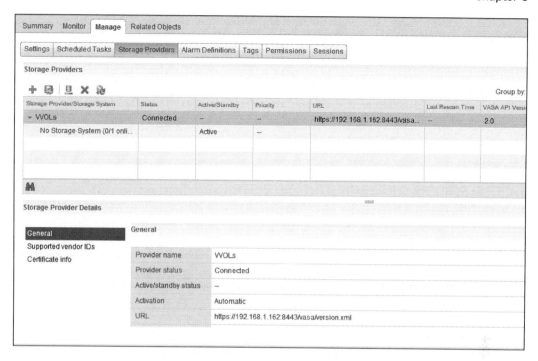

Once the storage provider has been configured the VVOL, the datastore is added using the **New Datastore** wizard and by selecting the **VVOL** datastore type, as shown in the following screenshot:

When VVOL is selected as the type in the **New Datastore** wizard, the available storage containers will be displayed. Enter a name in the **Datastore name** field and select the **Backing Storage Container** option, as shown in the following screenshot:

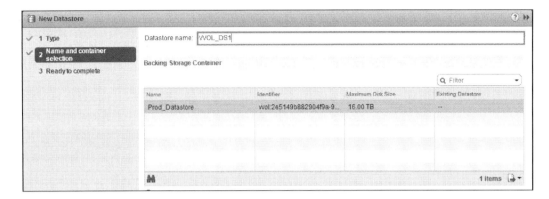

Once complete, the datastore will be created, presented to the hosts in the environment, and available for virtual machine storage.

Incorporating storage policies into a design

Storage policies are configured to simplify the provisioning of a virtual machine in the storage. Storage policies ensure that service levels are met for the storage performance, protection, and availability. For **Software Defined Storage** (**SDS**), including VSAN and VVOL, these policies are a key component required to determine the virtual machine placement during provisioning and throughout a virtual machine's life cycle.

How to do it...

When incorporating storage policies into a vSphere design, perform the following steps:

1. Determine the storage services and capabilities required by virtual machine workloads:

   ❑ What data protection service will be required for virtual machines?

   ❑ Are capabilities such as encryption at rest, deduplication, or compression required?

   ❑ Are different tiers of storage required?

2. Identify how storage array capabilities will be discovered:

    ❑ Is a VASA provider available for providing awareness about storage capabilities?

    ❑ Will tags be used to manually tag datastores based on capabilities?

3. Create the policies' mapping storage capabilities to virtual machine requirements.

4. Assign storage policies to virtual machines and virtual machine disks.

How it works...

VM Storage Policies are created and managed through the vSphere Web Client, as shown in the following screenshot:

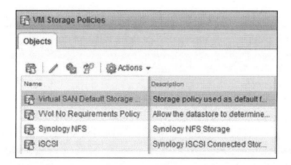

VM Storage Policies contain a rule or a set of rules. These can be based on tags or data services. Tag-based rules are created from tags the administrator creates for storage capabilities and then manually assigns to datastores. Data services-based rules are created from capabilities discovered from a data service provider, for example, for a VASA provider on a VVOL-enabled array. A rule set based on data services is shown in the following screenshot:

VM Storage Policies can be assigned to a virtual machine or to individual virtual machine disks. The **Manage VM Storage Policies** dialog box for a virtual machine is displayed in the following screenshot:

This is based on the requirements for the virtual machine; for example, a virtual machine running SQL may require different storage capabilities for the disks containing the OS, the logs, the tempDB, and the databases. Policies can be assigned to each virtual disk in order to ensure the correct placement of the disks and also to ensure compliance through the virtual machines' life cycle.

NFS version 4.1 capabilities and limits

vSphere 6 has added support for NFS version 4.1. NFS clients for both NFS version 3 and NFS version 4.1 are included as part of ESXi. Using NFS version 4.1 provides additional features and functionalities over NFS version 3, but there are some significant caveats and limitations that must be accounted for when using NFS version 4.1 in a vSphere design.

How to do it...

To determine how NFS version 4.1 can be incorporated into a vSphere 6 design, follow these steps:

1. Identify the capabilities of NFS version 4.1:

   ❑ What design requirements will NFS version 4.1 satisfy?

2. Determine the limitations of NFS version 4.1.

3. Identify the requirements for configuring a NFS version 4.1 datastore.

How it works...

NFS version 4.1 in vSphere 6 provides the following capabilities:

▸ Multipathing support for NFS datastores

▸ Non-root user access when using Kerberos

▸ Stateful server-side locking

▸ Better error recovery

These features provide enhancement to performance, security, and availability. There are still a number of limitations that will have an impact on using NFS version 4.1 in a vSphere design. These limitation include the following:

▸ No support for vSphere **Fault Tolerance** (**FT**), VMware **Site Recovery Manager** (**SRM**), **Virtual Volumes** (**VVOL**), or **Storage IO Control** (**SIOC**)

▸ IPv6 is only supported for non-Kerberos datastores

▸ NFS version 3 datastores cannot be upgraded to NFS version 4.1

▸ No VAAI-NAS hardware acceleration

Features including vSphere High Availability, vSphere vMotion, and vSphere **Distributed Resource Scheduler** (**DRS**) are all supported when using NFS version 4.1 datastores.

Presenting both NFS version 3 and NFS version 4.1 datastores is supported. ESXi includes separate NFS clients to support each version. However, a single NFS share should not be accessible by both protocol versions; this will most likely result in data corruption.

The NFS server providing storage must support NFS version 4.1, and as with all IP connected storage, VMkernel interfaces are required on each ESXi host to support the storage connectivity.

NFS Kerberos Credentials provides significant security improvements, and this allows non-root access to the NFS export. NFS Kerberos credentials are configured for each hosts. Only a single credential can be created.

The NFS Kerberos credentials are created and managed from the **Authentication Services** settings on a host, as displayed in the following screenshot:

NFS version 4.1 datastores are mounted to ESXi hosts using the **New Datastore** wizard. A datastore name and the folder location of the NFS share are required just as with NFS version 3. Multiple NFS servers can be added to provide multiple paths to the NFS version 4 share, as shown in the following screenshot:

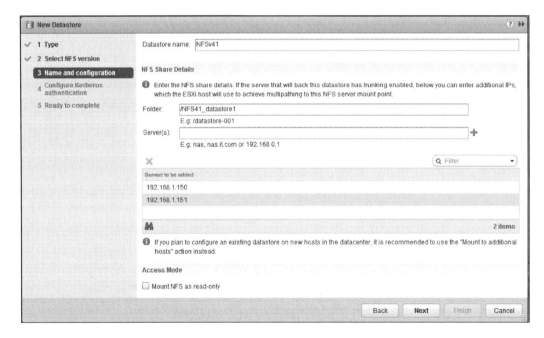

6
vSphere Network Design

In this chapter, we will cover the following topics:

- ▶ Determining network bandwidth requirements
- ▶ Standard or distributed virtual switches
- ▶ Providing network availability
- ▶ Network resource management
- ▶ Using private VLANs
- ▶ IP storage network design considerations
- ▶ Enabling jumbo frames
- ▶ Designing for VMkernel services
- ▶ Creating custom TCP/IP stacks
- ▶ vMotion network design considerations
- ▶ IPv6 in a vSphere design

Introduction

In order to effectively design a virtual network infrastructure, a design architect must understand the virtual network architecture, including which features are available and how they are configured. This chapter contains recipes that a design architect can use to design a virtual network architecture that provides the capacity and availability required to support the virtual infrastructure.

The logical network design includes the calculation of the network capacity or the bandwidth required to support the virtual machines and the determination of the capacity required to support VMware technologies, such as vMotion and fault tolerance. If IP-based storage connectivity is required, the design must account for the networking required to support the storage traffic as well. The following diagram displays how a network design is integrated into the design process:

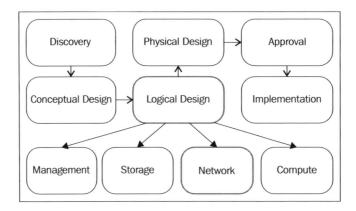

This chapter discusses the different virtual network switch technologies available in vSphere and the different features available in each. It also covers how load balancing and teaming are used to improve network utilization efficiency and increase availability. Network capacity resource management using traffic shaping, jumbo frames, and network I/O control is also covered.

Determining network bandwidth requirements

Bandwidth refers to the capacity of the network and is measured in either **gigabits per second** (**Gbps**) or **megabits per second** (**Mbps**). The bandwidth required is based on the amount of data transferred or the throughput required by the virtual machines. Most modern networks are capable of transferring data at 1 Gbps or 10 Gbps. Network adapters that support 40 Gbps have recently become available.

The number of physical network adapters in each host required to support a solution is dependent on the amount of bandwidth required to support virtual machine network traffic, the number of virtual switches required, and the network redundancy requirements.

From the case example in *Chapter 3, The Design Factors*, the following information is used to help calculate the network bandwidth requirements:

- Cisco switches are used for network connectivity. Separate VLANs exist for management connectivity and production application connectivity.

- No more than 20 application servers, or 200 customers, should be affected by hardware failure.
- Currently, each physical server contains a single gigabit network interface card. Peak network usage is 10 Mbps.

How to do it...

1. Calculate the total amount of bandwidth required to support virtual machine network traffic using the following formula:

   Total Number or Virtual Machines x Bandwidth per Virtual Machine (Mbps) = Total Bandwidth Requirement (Mbps)

2. Calculate the amount of bandwidth required per host. This is dependent on the maximum number of virtual machines that can be run on a single host.

3. Determine the network requirements for other vSphere services and features, such as vMotion, iSCSI, NFS, and fault tolerance.

4. Select the type and number of network adapters in order to provide the network connectivity required to support the design requirements.

How it works...

The physical network infrastructure must be capable of supporting the total throughput requirement of the environment. The total throughput requirement is calculated by multiplying the number of virtual machines by the throughput required by a single virtual machine:

100 Virtual Machines x 10Mbps = 1000 Mbps Total

The throughput required for a single host is calculated by multiplying the number of virtual machines that will run on a host by the throughput required by a single virtual machine:

20 Virtual Machines x 10 Mbps = 200 Mbps per Host

Network adapters are generally capable of delivering throughput equal to approximately 80% of the adapter speed, for example, 800 Mbps for a 1 Gbps network adapter. A single gigabit Ethernet connection would provide sufficient bandwidth to support the virtual machine throughput requirements calculated previously. An additional network adapter would be required to support failovers.

There are also network bandwidth requirements to support VMkernel interface network connectivity for management, vMotion, IP storage, and fault tolerance. The minimum bandwidth requirements for VMkernel network connectivity are as follows:

- **Management**: 100 MB
- **vMotion**: 1 GB

> ▸ **IP storage**: This is dependent on the amount of storage throughput required but is limited to the bandwidth of a single path

> ▸ **Fault tolerance**: 1 GB (10 GB required for multi-vCPU fault tolerance)

Sufficient physical network connectivity and bandwidth must be included in the design to support these services.

Network connectivity can be provided using multiple 1 GB network adapters, or 10GbE **Converged Network Adapters** (**CNA**) can be used to carry multiple network traffic types, including virtual machine network traffic and VMkernel (management, vMotion, fault tolerance, and IP storage) network traffic on a single 10GbE network adapter, as shown in the following figure:

When CNAs are used to provide physical uplink connectivity to virtual switches, traffic shaping or **Network I/O Control** (**NIOC**) can be configured in order to ensure that sufficient network bandwidth is available to each traffic type serviced by the CNAs.

There's more...

For a virtual machine with very high network I/O requirements, DirectPath I/O allows a physical network adapter to be passed through directly to the virtual machine.

The following figure shows how a virtual machine is provided direct access to a physical network card using **DirectPath I/O**:

When DirectPath I/O is used, the network adapter is made available only to the virtual machine, it is passed to and cannot be shared with other virtual machines. The full bandwidth capacity of the network adapter is available to the virtual machine. Because a virtual machine with DirectPath I/O configured is dependent on the physical network card in the host, neither can it be moved to other hosts using vMotion, nor be protected using VMware HA.

Standard or distributed virtual switches

The connectivity of the virtual network to the physical network in a vSphere environment is accomplished using one of two virtual switch technologies: the standard **virtual switch** (**vSwitch**) or the **virtual distributed switch** (**vDSwitch**). VMware technologies such as VMware HA, VMware DRS, and fault tolerance require that virtual switch configurations be consistent across all ESXi hosts in a cluster.

How to do it...

1. Identify the features and capabilities of virtual standard switches and distributed virtual switches.

2. Based on the design requirements, determine which virtual switch technology should be selected to support them.

How it works...

The virtual switch technology chosen is dependent on the connectivity, availability, manageability requirements, and the features available in the virtual switch.

A standard virtual switch is configured and managed independently on each ESXi host and supports up to 1024 virtual switch ports per vSwitch. Because vSwitches are configured on each individual host, it increases the administrative overhead required to support large environments. Advanced network features such as port mirroring, NetFlow integration, and private VLANs are not available when using standard virtual switches. vSwitches are available on all vSphere license levels.

Several networks can use the same vSwitch, or networks can be separated across multiple vSwitches. Multiple physical uplinks can be associated with a vSwitch to provide redundancy and load balancing. vSwitches can be created with no physical uplinks to keep the virtual machine network traffic isolated on a single host.

The following figure depicts a common logical network design using standard virtual switches to provide virtual machine network connectivity:

vDSwitches are configured and managed by vCenter. A vDSwitch guarantees consistent network policy configurations and PortGroup configurations across all hosts with uplinks that are connected to it. vSphere Enterprise Plus Licensing is required to use vDSwitches.

Multiple physical uplinks from each host can be associated with a vDSwitch in order to provide redundancy and load balancing. A vDSwitch will not be available for use by a host without any physical uplinks associated with it. The following figure depicts a logical virtual network design using a virtual distributed switch:

vCenter is required to manage vDSwitches. vCenter controls the configuration state and keeps track of virtual machine connection information for the vDSwitch. If the vCenter Server managing the vDSwitch is unavailable, new connections to the vDSwitch will not be possible.

The features available when using a vDSwitch are as follows:

▸ The central management of the virtual switch and virtual machine port groups

▸ Link Aggregation Control Protocol

▸ Ingress and egress traffic shaping

▸ Load balancing based on physical NIC load

▸ NetFlow integration

▸ Port mirroring

▸ Third-party virtual switches (Cisco Nexus 1000v)

▸ Private VLANs

▸ Network I/O Control

There's more...

Third-party virtual switches, such as the Cisco Nexus 1000v, can be used to extend the functionality of a vDSwitch. They provide an interface for the provisioning, monitoring, securing, and configuring of the virtual network using standard vendor network management tools.

Providing network availability

Network availability is obtained by minimizing **Single Points of Failure** (**SPOF**) and providing sufficient capacity. Multiple network ports, network adapters, and physical switches can be used to minimize single points of failure, and link aggregation can be used to provide load balancing across multiple network adapters.

vSphere virtual network configurations offer multiple NIC teaming and load balancing options. The options used are dependent on the number of network adapters available, the number of virtual machines connected, the physical network's topology, and the amount of bandwidth required.

How to do it...

1. Identify the availability options on virtual switches and virtual switch port groups.

2. Determine the load balancing policies to provide availability based on the design requirements.

3. Determine the network adapter teaming policies to provide availability based on the design requirements.

How it works...

Load balancing distributes the network load across multiple available adapters. Load balancing policies are configured as part of the NIC **Teaming and failover** options on virtual switches, virtual machine port groups, and VMkernel interfaces.

The following screenshot illustrates the **Edit Settings** dialog to configure **Teaming and failover** options on a virtual machine port group on a standard virtual switch:

The following load balancing policies can be applied to virtual switches or virtual port groups:

► **Route based on originating virtual port**: This is the default load balancing policy. When it is used, the load is balanced based on the number of physical NICs and the number of virtual switch ports in use. Virtual port connections are distributed across the physical NICs available to the virtual switch. A virtual machine connected to the virtual port will always use the same physical NIC, unless the NIC becomes unavailable.

► **Route based on IP hash**: This load balancing policy uses a hashing algorithm that determines the physical path based on the source and destination IP addresses of the virtual machine traffic. A virtual machine's network traffic can use multiple available NICs. This policy is used when using either EtherChannel or the LACP link aggregation.

► **Route based on source MAC hash**: This load balancing policy is similar to the Route based on originating virtual port policy, except that the physical NIC used for the virtual machine traffic is based on the virtual network adapter's MAC address and not the virtual port connection.

- ▸ **Use explicit failover order**: This policy is not really a load balancing policy because network traffic always uses the physical NIC uplink that is configured as the highest order active physical uplink available.

- ▸ **Route based on physical NIC load**: This is an additional load balancing option offered by vDSwitches that is not available to vSwitches. It is the most efficient because it distributes the load across active uplinks based on the actual workload of the physical NICs.

Redundancy in the virtual network is provided by configuring **Failover order**. These configurations define the physical uplinks that are actively used to pass the network traffic, and those that are available stand in the event of an active uplink failing.

The available adapters are as follows:

- ▸ **Active adapters**: These are adapters that are available for use by the virtual switch, a virtual machine network port group, or a VMkernel interface.

- ▸ **Standby adapters**: These are adapters that become active only in the event that an active adapter becomes unavailable.

- ▸ **Unused adapters**: These adapters are unused. They will never be used by the virtual switch, a virtual machine port group, or a VMkernel interface.

The following screenshot shows adapters configured in **Active** and **Standby**. If **Active adapters** (**vmnic0**) fails, **Standby adapters** (**vmnic1**) will become active:

The following figure shows an example of an active/standby network configuration commonly used in small environments to provide connectivity and redundancy for the host management and vMotion networks:

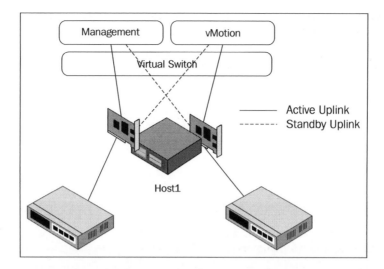

Network Failover Detection and **Failback** are settings that control how a network failure is detected and what happens when an Active adapter is returned to service after a failure.

How a network failure is detected is configured using the **Network Failover Detection** option. Two failure detection options are available: **Link Status Only** and **Beacon Probing**. The **Link Status Only** option uses the link state, up or down, of the physical NIC to determine whether the uplink is available. The **Beacon Probing** option detects network failures by sending and receiving beacon probes to all physical uplinks on the virtual switch and can detect the link state and switch failures. At least three active uplinks are required for beacon probing to work effectively. The VMware *Knowledge Base* article located at `http://kb.vmware.com/kb/1005577` provides more information on how beacon probing works with virtual switches.

The **Failback** setting defines whether or not an Active adapter is returned to the service if the adapter becomes available after a failure based on the value set for **Network Failover Detection**. If a physical switch fails and **Failback** is enabled with **Link Status Only** being used for **Failover Detection**, the adapter may become active and will be returned to the service before the physical switch is available to pass the traffic.

Network resource management

In a vSphere environment, physical network resources are shared across multiple virtual machines and services. The ability to ensure that sufficient capacity is available across shared resources, therefore, becomes important. If a single virtual machine or a VMkernel network service, such as vMotion or fault tolerance, saturates the available network capacity, other virtual machines and services, including host management services, may be adversely impacted.

How to do it...

1. Identify the traffic shaping and network resource controls available in the virtual network switches.

2. Determine the network resources required for different traffic types: management, IP storage, vMotion, and virtual machine traffic.

3. Design traffic shaping, **Network I/O Control** (**NIOC**) policies, and Network Resource Pools to guarantee or limit network resources for the network traffic types based on the design requirements.

How it works...

Traffic shaping is used to limit the amount of bandwidth available to virtual switch ports. NIOC is used to apply limits and guarantee traffic to different virtual network service types.

Traffic shaping can be configured on vSwitches, vDSwitch uplinks, VMkernel interfaces, and port groups to restrict the network bandwidth available to the network ports on the virtual switch. Traffic shaping is applied at all times regardless of the amount of network capacity available. This means that if traffic shaping is enabled and configured on a virtual switch or port group to limit the peak bandwidth to 1,048,576 Kbps (1 Gbps), only 1,048,576 Kbps of bandwidth will be used even if more bandwidth is available.

The following bandwidth characteristics can be applied to the traffic shaping policy:

▶ **Average bandwidth**: This is the allowed average load measured in Kbps

▶ **Peak bandwidth**: This is the maximum allowed load measured in Kbps

▶ **Burst size**: This is the maximum number of bytes, measured in Kbytes, that can be burst over the specified average bandwidth

Traffic shaping policies on a vSwitch apply only to egress or outbound traffic. vDSwitch traffic shaping policies can be configured for both ingress (inbound) and egress (outbound) traffic.

The following is a screenshot of the configuration screen in order to apply **Traffic shaping** to a virtual machine port group on a standard virtual switch:

The following screenshot shows the **Ingress traffic shaping** and **Egress traffic shaping** settings that can be applied to a virtual machine port group on a vDSwitch:

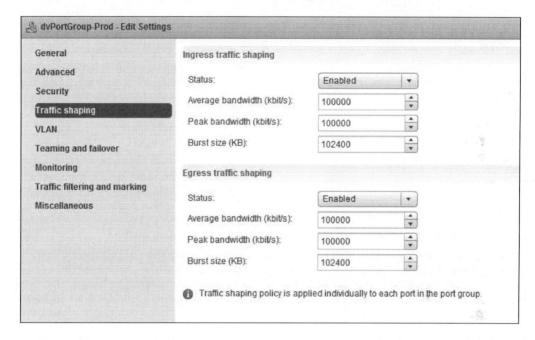

Unlike traffic shaping, NIOC provides control over network bandwidth for specific network protocols only during times of network contention. NIOC can only be enabled on vDSwitches.

Shares, limits, and reservations can be applied to network traffic types in order to limit and guarantee bandwidth to the different network traffic types, including the following:

- ▸ Management traffic
- ▸ vMotion traffic
- ▸ IP storage traffic (NFS/iSCSI)
- ▸ Virtual SAN traffic

- ▶ Fault tolerance traffic
- ▶ vSphere replication traffic
- ▶ vSphere Data Protection backup traffic
- ▶ Virtual machine traffic

The **System traffic** screen in the vSphere Web Client provides information about the bandwidth capacity and the allocation of network resources across the different traffic types. The following screenshot illustrates the NIOC configurations of a vDSwitch:

Shares define the share a specific traffic type will receive from the available bandwidth on a physical NIC attached to the vDSwitch at the time of network bandwidth contention. **Reservation** is the Mbps guaranteed to a specific traffic type. **Limit** is the Mbps limit applied to all hosts connected to the vDSwitch.

The percentage of bandwidth a traffic type receives is based on the total number of shares available; for example, in the default configuration, the virtual machine traffic receives 100 shares of the 400 (50 + 50 + 50 + 50 + 100 + 50 + 50) shares available. The formula for this is as follows:

Shares Value / Total Available Shares = Percentage of Physical Network Bandwidth

Therefore, *100 / 400 = 25%*.

The amount of bandwidth available to vMotion would be calculated based on the 50 shares allocated to the vMotion traffic, as follows:

50 / 400 = 12.5%

Network resource pools can be created in order to allocate virtual machine traffic reservations across distributed port groups. For example, if 100 Mbps is reserved for virtual machine traffic, this reservation can be applied across different port groups. In the following screenshot, **New Network Resource Pool** is created, allocating 90 Mbps of the 100 Mbps reservation to a pool named CriticalVMs:

Note that **Reservation quota** is the bandwidth network resource pool will be guaranteed out of the overall reservation. **Reservation quota** cannot be set to a value higher than the total reservation allocated to the virtual machine traffic.

Network resource pool is then assigned to a portgroup on the virtual distributed switch, as shown in this screenshot:

This allocates the reservation from the CriticalVMs network resource pool to the **DPortGroup** port group.

Using private VLANs

Private VLANs (**PVLANs**) are an extension of the VLAN standard. PVLANs can be configured on virtual distributed switches in order to isolate traffic between virtual machines in the same VLAN.

How to do it...

1. Identify the types of PVLANs available and the functionalities of each.
2. Determine the use cases for the PVLANs and identify whether the PVLANs can be used to satisfy the design requirements.
3. Design the PVLANs to meet the design requirements.

How it works...

A primary PVLAN is created on a vDSwitch, and secondary PVLANs are associated with the primary PVLAN. There are three types of secondary PVLAN: **Promiscuous**, **Community**, and **Isolated**. They are depicted in the following diagram:

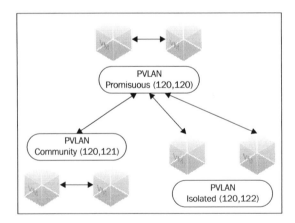

The virtual machine connections in a **Promiscuous PVLAN** can communicate with all the virtual machine connections in the same primary PVLAN. When a primary PVLAN is created, a Promiscuous PVLAN is created with the same PVLAN ID as the primary PVLAN.

Virtual machine connections in a **Community PVLAN** can communicate with other virtual machine connections in the same Community PVLAN and virtual machine connections in the Promiscuous PVLAN. Multiple Community PVLANs can be associated with a single primary PVLAN.

Virtual machine connections in an **Isolated PVLAN** can only communicate with virtual machine connections in the Promiscuous PVLAN. Only one Isolated PVLAN can exist per primary PVLAN.

PVLANs are created by editing the settings of a vDSwitch, as follows:

Once the PVLAN has been configured on the vDSwitch, a virtual machine network portgroup is created with the PVLAN type and ID assigned, as follows:

There's more...

In order for PVLAN traffic to be passed between ESXi hosts connected to a vDSwitch, the physical switch must be PVLAN-aware and properly configured to support PVLANs. The process to configure PVLANs on a physical switch will vary from vendor to vendor. The following process shows the steps required to configure PVLANs on a Cisco IOS switch:

1. Enter the Cisco switch configuration mode:

    ```
    switch# configure terminal
    ```

2. Enable the PVLAN feature on the switch:

    ```
    switch(config)# feature private-vlan
    ```

3. Create the PVLAN on the switch and set the PVLAN type:

    ```
    switch(config)# vlan <vlan-id>
    switch(config-vlan)# private-vlan primary
    ```

4. Associate the secondary PVLANs with a primary VLAN:

    ```
    switch(config-vlan)# private-vlan association <secondary
    pvlan>
    ```

5. The switch ports that are connected to the vDSwitch uplinks need to be configured to allow the PVLAN traffic:

    ```
    switch(config)# interface GigabitEthernet1/1
    switch(config-if)# switchport mode trunk
    switch(config-if)# switchport trunk allowed vlan
    <vlan/pvlan ids>
    ```

IP storage network design considerations

iSCSI, NFS, and **Fiber Channel over Ethernet** (**FCoE**) are IP-based storage protocols supported in a vSphere environment. This recipe covers the design considerations when designing the IP networks that will be used for storage traffic.

How to do it...

1. Identify the network connectivity and virtual switch configurations required for IP-connected storage.
2. Determine the best practices to be used to provide connectivity for IP-connected storage.
3. Design the IP storage connectivity to meet the design requirements.

How it works...

IP storage traffic should be separated from other IP traffic. This separation can be provided by either using physically separate hardware (network adapters and physical switches), or separate VLANs for IP storage traffic. The networks associated with IP storage should be directly connected and non-routable.

Multiple network paths to storage should be configured to provide redundancy and load balancing. Single points of failure should be minimized so that the loss of a single network path does not result in the loss of storage connectivity.

Software iSCSI, NFS, and software FCoE each require a VMkernel interface to be created on a virtual switch. VMkernel interfaces used for iSCSI and FCoE must be bound to a single physical active adapter. Having more than one Active adapter or a Standby adapter is not supported with software iSCSI or software FCoE.

NFS v3 over TCP does not provide support for multipathing. Using link aggregation will only provide failover and not load balancing. NFS will always use a single physical network path even if multiple VMkernels are configured. To manually load-balance NFS traffic, create separate VMkernel ports connected to separate networks and mount separate NFS v3 datastores.

NFS v4.1 supports multipathing for NFS servers that support session trunking. Multiple VMkernel ports can be configured to provide access to a single NFS volume configured with multiple IP addresses. This provides load balancing and resiliency for NFS v4.1.

The VMkernel port binding for software iSCSI is configured in the properties of the software iSCSI adapter. Only VMkernel ports that are compliant will be available for binding, as shown in the following screenshot:

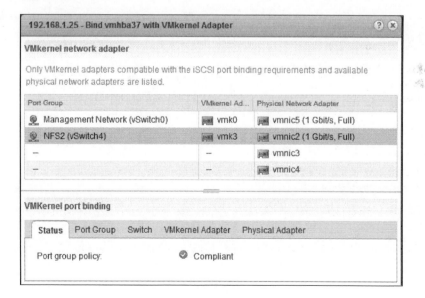

To enable the software FCoE adapter, an NIC that supports FCoE offloads must be installed on the host. If a supported NIC is not installed, the ability to add the software FCoE adapter will not be available.

Physical network binding for FCoE is done when enabling a software FCoE adapter. Compliant and supported physical adapters are available when adding the software FCoE adapter. Separate FCoE adapters should be enabled and connected to each storage network fabric. A single ESXi host can support up to four software FCoE adapters. Each software FCoE adapter requires a dedicated VMkernel port bound to a dedicated physical adapter.

Using jumbo frames

Enabling jumbo frames on the networks used for vMotion or IP Storage can increase performance and throughput. When jumbo frames are configured, iSCSI or NFS packets can be transferred over the network in a single frame; there is no fragmentation. This decreases the amount of CPU overhead required to encapsulate and de-encapsulate IP storage packets.

How to do it...

1. Determine use cases to enable jumbo frames.
2. Configure jumbo frames on virtual switches.
3. Configure jumbo frames on VMkernel ports.
4. Ensure jumbo frames are configured end to end on the physical network: physical switches and array network interfaces.
5. Test the network for proper end-to-end jumbo frames configuration.

How it works...

Jumbo frames must be supported and enabled on the network from end to end; this includes the physical network infrastructure as well. In vSphere, jumbo frames are enabled either in the vSwitch configuration or on the vDSwitch uplinks by setting the **Maximum Transmission Unit (MTU)** value to 9000. Jumbo frames must also be enabled on VMkernel interfaces by setting the value of **MTU (Bytes)** for the PortGroup to 9000.

To enable jumbo frames, set the value of **MTU (Bytes)** on the vSwitch to 9000, as shown in the following screenshot:

If using a vDSwitch, **MTU (Bytes)** is set to 9000 in the **Advanced** settings in order to enable jumbo frames:

The **MTU** setting must also be changed to `9000` on a VMkernel interface on the vSwitch or vDSwitch in order to enable jumbo frames, as shown in the following screenshot:

When using jumbo frames, the physical switch must also be configured to support the MTU. This will vary depending on the switch vendor and version. To enable jumbo frames on a Cisco Catalyst Series switch, use the following command:

```
Switch(config)# system mtu jumbo 9000
```

In this case, the switch must be reloaded for the setting to take effect. Other switches may allow, or require, per-port MTU configuration.

If using jumbo frames for the storage network, jumbo frames will need to be enabled on the network interfaces of the array. The process for this will vary greatly between array vendors. If the array interfaces are not configured correctly, traffic may not pass or performance may be significantly impacted.

The jumbo frame configuration can be tested from the ESXi shell using the `vmkping` command with the **data fragment** (**DF**) bit (`-d`) and the size (`-s`) options set, as shown here:

```
ESX1 # vmkping -d -s 8972 <IP_Address_of_IP_Storage_Array>
```

If jumbo frames are not configured correctly, `vmkping` will fail.

Creating custom TCP/IP stacks

TCP/IP stacks provide flexibility in the VMkernel interface design by allowing you to apply specific DNS and default gateway configurations to a VMkernel interface on a host.

There are three preconfigured TCP/IP stacks:

- **Default TCP/IP stack**: Supports management traffic
- **vMotion TCP/IP stack**: Supports live migration, vMotion, of virtual machines
- **Provisioning TCP/IP stack**: Supports cold migration, cloning, and snapshot creation of virtual machines

Custom TCP/IP stacks can be used to handle the network traffic of other applications and services, which may require separate DNS and default gateway configurations.

How to do it...

1. Create a custom TCP/IP stack on an ESXi host.
2. Configure **DNS**, **Default Gateway**, and **Advanced** settings on TCP/IP stack.
3. Assign TCP/IP stack to a VMkernel adapter.

How it works...

Using TCP/IP stacks for VMkernel network traffic provides the following benefits:

- ▶ It separates VMkernel routing tables
- ▶ It provides a separate set of buffers and sockets
- ▶ It isolates traffic types to improve performance and security

Currently, a custom TCP/IP stack cannot be created in the Web Client interface. A custom TCP/IP stack is created using `esxcli` on the ESX host, as shown here:

```
ESX1 # esxcli network ip netstack add -N "Name_of_Stack"
```

DNS configuration associated with the TCP/IP stack can then be configured. This can be automatically obtained from a VMkernel adapter using DHCP or set manually, as shown in the following screenshot:

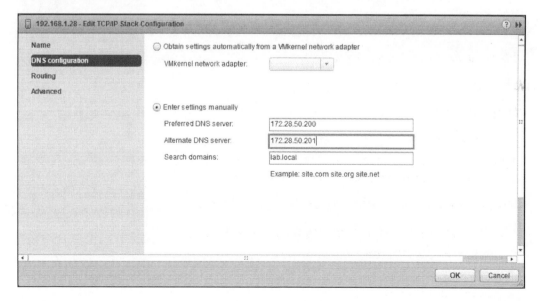

VMkernel gateway can be assigned to the TCP/IP stack, as shown in the following screenshot:

Advanced TCP/IP stack settings include the maximum number of connections and the congestion control algorithm to be used for the stack.

The **TCP/IP stack** option is then assigned to a VMkernel adapter when it is created, as shown in this screenshot:

Designing for VMkernel services

VMkernel interfaces are configured to provide network connectivity for services in the vSphere environment. VMkernels provide network paths for service connectivity. Multiple VMkernel interfaces can be created to provide physical or logical separation for these services.

How to do it...

1. Identify services that require a VMkernel interface.
2. Create a VMkernel interface to support the service.
3. Enable services on the VMkernel interface.

How it works...

Most vSphere services require a VMkernel interface to provide network connectivity. These services include the following:

- ESXi management
- vMotion
- Fault tolerance
- Virtual SAN
- vSphere replication
- IP storage (NFS, iSCSI, FCoE)

Multiple services can share a single VMkernel port, or the services can be separated across multiple VMkernel ports for performance, management, and security. Services can be enabled on VMkernel interfaces at the time of creation or by editing **Port properties**, as shown in the following screenshot:

Once services have been enabled, the VMkernel interface will provide connectivity for the services selected. As discussed in the previous recipe, TCP/IP stacks can be used to configure specific DNS settings and a default gateway for a service.

vMotion network design considerations

vMotion allows the running state of a virtual machine to be transferred from one ESXi host to another. The network traffic required for the migration uses the VMkernel interfaces that have been enabled for vMotion. vMotion connectivity between ESXi hosts is required when using **Distributed Resource Scheduler** (**DRS**) in order to balance the virtual machine load across hosts in a DRS-enabled cluster.

How to do it...

1. Identify vMotion network requirements.

2. Determine the best practices to configure the network connectivity required to support vMotion.

3. Identify the benefits of keeping virtual machines together on the same host in order to minimize the network traffic that must transverse the physical uplinks.

4. Design the vMotion network connectivity to support the design requirements.

5. Design DRS rules to support the design requirements.

How it works...

vMotion requires, at a minimum, a single, active 1 Gb network adapter. A second standby adapter should be configured to provide redundancy for the vMotion network.

A vMotion migration can consume all available network bandwidth. If the vMotion network is shared with other network traffic, traffic shaping or NIOC should be enabled in order to prevent vMotion from impacting other virtual network traffic. If possible, vMotion should be configured on a separate physical network or a separate VLAN.

vSphere 5 introduced the ability to configure multiple adapters for use with vMotion. Multiple-NIC vMotion allows the bandwidth of multiple physical NICs to be leveraged by vMotion in order to speed up the migration of virtual machines between hosts.

To configure Multiple-NIC vMotion, create multiple VMkernel interfaces with vMotion enabled. Configure each VMkernel interface to use a single Active adapter, and configure other available adapters as standby adapters. When a virtual machine is vMotioned, either manually or by DRS, all available links will be used for the vMotion traffic. More information on Multiple-NIC vMotion can be found in the VMware *Knowledge Base* article at `http://kb.vmware.com/kb/2007467`.

There's more...

Network communications between virtual machines that are connected to the same virtual switch on the same ESXi host will not use the physical network. All the network traffic between the virtual machines will remain on the host.

Keeping virtual machines that communicate with each other together on the same host will reduce the load on the physical network; for example, keeping a web frontend server, application server, and database server together on the same host will keep network traffic between the virtual servers from leaving the host.

If the VMware DRS is configured on a vSphere Cluster, DRS rules can be configured on the cluster to keep virtual machines together on the same host.

In the following screenshot, a virtual machine affinity rule has been created to keep two virtual machines together on the same host:

With DRS enabled, the virtual machines assigned to the DRS rule will use vMotion to run on the same host.

Virtual machine anti-affinity rules (**Separate Virtual Machines**) can also be configured to ensure that virtual machines run on separate hosts. This can be used when service redundancy is provided by multiple virtual machines, such as with multiple virtual domain controllers. Keeping virtual machines separate will ensure that a host failure does not impact the service redundancy.

IPv6 in a vSphere Design

Internet Protocol version 6 (**IPv6**) was developed to replace **IP version 4** (**IPv4**). IPv6 addresses are 128-bit IP addresses compared to the 32-bit addresses in IPv4. IPv6 is becoming more common in datacenter network environments, and vSphere has included support for IPv6 since vSphere 5.x.

How to do it...

1. Enable IPv6 on the ESXi host.
2. Determine the vSphere features and services with IPv6 support.
3. Configure VMkernel interfaces to use IPv6.

How it works...

By default, IPv6 support is enabled on ESXi hosts. If the IPv6 support is changed, disabled, or enabled, a host reboot is required. Enabling or disabling IPv6 is done on each ESXi host by editing **Advanced Network Settings** from the **Networking** management tab for the host, as shown in the following screenshot:

Once enabled, IPv6 can be configured for supported vSphere features and services. The following vSphere features and services support IPv6:

- ESXi and vCenter Management
- vMotion and vSphere DRS
- Fault tolerance
- vSphere HA
- NFS v3 storage
- iSCSI (software or hardware)

Currently, IPv6 is not supported with the following vSphere features:

- Auto deploy
- DPM with IPMI/iLO
- Virtual Volumes
- Virtual SAN
- Authentication proxy
- NFS v4.1

When **IPv6** is enabled on an ESXi host, VMkernel interfaces can be created with **IPv4**, **IPv6**, or both **IPv4 and IPv6** settings, as shown in the following screenshot:

IPv6 addresses can be configured automatically using DHCP or router advertisement, or the IPv6 address can be a static address that is manually assigned.

7
vSphere Compute Design

In this chapter, we will cover the following topics:

- ▶ Calculating CPU resource requirements
- ▶ Calculating memory resource requirements
- ▶ Transparent Page Sharing
- ▶ Scaling up or scaling out
- ▶ Determining the vCPU-to-core ratio
- ▶ Clustering compute resources
- ▶ Reserving HA resources to support failover
- ▶ Using Distributed Resource Scheduling to balance cluster resources
- ▶ Ensuring cluster vMotion compatibility
- ▶ Using resource pools
- ▶ Providing fault tolerance protection
- ▶ Leveraging host flash

Introduction

This chapter covers logical compute design. Compute refers to the processor and memory resources required to support the virtual machines running in the vSphere environment. Calculating the required CPU and memory resources is an important part of the design process and ensures that the environment will be able to support the virtual machine workloads. Design decisions, such as scaling up, scaling out, and clustering hosts, are covered as well. The following diagram displays how the compute design is integrated into the design process:

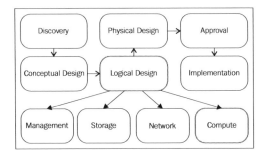

In a physical environment where a single operating system or a single application is installed on a dedicated physical hardware, compute utilization usually averages 10-20 percent of the available resources. A majority of the memory and CPU resources are idle and wasted. In a virtual environment, the resources available are utilized by multiple operating systems and applications. It is not uncommon to see a usage of 65-80% of the available resources.

This chapter takes a look at the clustering hosts' resources in order to take advantage of the advanced VMware features: vSphere **High Availability** (**HA**), vSphere **Distributed Resource Scheduler** (**DRS**), and vSphere **Fault Tolerance** (**FT**). Ensuring that significant resources are available for failover and providing vMotion compatibility are key factors of cluster design. Methods to reserve or limit resources and provide flash-based caching are also covered.

Calculating CPU resource requirements

There are several factors that must be considered when calculating CPU resources' requirements, such as the amount of CPU resources required to support the current workloads, the amount of CPU resources required to support future growth, and the maximum CPU utilization threshold.

The following discovery information from *Chapter 3, The Design Factors*, will be used to calculate the CPU requirements:

> ▶ Currently, there are 100 physical servers, each hosting a single application. Each application services 10 customers.

- ▸ The business expects to add 50 new customers over the next year.
- ▸ Support growth over the next 5 years.
- ▸ Each application server is configured with two dual core 2.7 GHz processors. The peak usage of a single application server is approximately 10% of the total or approximately 1 GHz.

How to do it...

1. Determine the amount of CPU resources required to support the current workloads:

   Number of Workloads x CPU Speed in MHz or GHz = Current CPU Resources Required

2. Determine the maximum utilization threshold. This is the maximum percentage of available resources that should be consumed.

3. Determine the amount of growth in CPU resources that the environment should support.

4. Calculate the amount of CPU resources required:

   Current Workload CPU Resources + Future Growth + Maximum Utilization Threshold = Total CPU Resources Required

How it works...

Calculating the required CPU resources required to support the current workloads is straightforward using the following formula:

Number of Workloads x CPU Speed in MHz or GHz = Current CPU Resources Required

100 x 1 GHz = 100 GHz

In order to determine the total CPU resources required, the amount required to support future growth should also be calculated. The amount of CPU resources required for future growth will be determined by the design requirements. Based on the requirements identified in *Chapter 3*, *The Design Factors*, the environment should be designed to support a growth of 25 additional virtual machines over the next 5 years.

A maximum utilization threshold must also be determined and accounted for in CPU resource requirements. This threshold determines the maximum percentage of total CPU resources that will be consumed. It is unlikely that the environment would be configured to consume 100% of the CPU resources available. If the maximum utilization threshold is 75%, an additional 25% of CPU resources will be added to calculate the total CPU resources required:

Current CPU Resources Required + Future Growth = Total CPU Resources Required

100 GHz + (25 x 1 GHz) = 125 GHz

When the maximum utilization threshold is 75%, the calculation will be as follows:

$$125\ GHz * (100/75) = \sim 167\ GHz$$

The environment must be designed to support the 167 GHz of CPU resources that are in turn required to support the current workloads, future workloads, and provide for a maximum utilization threshold of 75%.

Calculating memory resource requirements

There are several factors that must be considered when calculating memory requirements; these factors include the amount of memory required to support the current workloads, the amount of memory required to support the future growth, the amount of memory required for the virtual machine memory overhead, and the maximum memory utilization threshold.

As with CPU requirements, the discovery information from *Chapter 3, The Design Factors*, will also be used to calculate the memory requirements:

► Currently, there are 100 physical servers, each hosting a single application. Each application services 10 customers.

► The business expects to add 50 new customers over the next year.

► Support growth over the next 5 years.

► Each application server is configured with 8 GB of memory. The peak usage of a single application server is approximately 65% or around 5.2 GB.

How to do it...

1. Determine the amount of memory resources required to support the current workloads:

   Number of Workloads X Memory Usage = Current Memory Required

2. Determine the memory overhead required.

3. Determine the maximum utilization threshold. This is the maximum percentage of available resources that should be consumed.

4. Determine the amount of growth in the memory resources that the environment should support.

5. Calculate the amount of memory resources required:

   Current Workload Memory Usage + Memory Overhead + Future Growth + Maximum Utilization Threshold - TPS Savings = Total Memory Resources Required

How it works...

To calculate the amount of memory required to support the current workloads, the following formula is used:

Number of Workloads x Memory Usage = Current Memory Required

100 x 5.2 GB = 520 GB

The memory overhead of a virtual machine must also be accounted for when calculating memory requirements. The amount of memory required for an overhead depends on the configuration of the virtual machine.

The number of vCPUs allocated to the virtual machine, the amount of memory allocated to the virtual machine, and the virtual hardware configured for the virtual machine will have an impact on the amount of memory required for the overhead:

▼ Virtual Machine Memory	□
0 GB	2.00 GB
▓ VM Consumed	540.00 MB
▓ VM Overhead Consumed	30.00 MB
▸ Reservation	1.00 GB
◂ Limit	Unlimited
Configured	2.00 GB
Shares	Normal (20480)
▾ Worst Case Allocation	2.06 GB
Overhead Reservation	40.49 MB

Typically, the memory overhead required for a virtual machine is between 20 MB and 150 MB. Memory overhead estimations based on the amount of RAM and the number of vCPUs can be found in the vSphere documentation:

  ▸ **vSphere 5.5**: `https://pubs.vmware.com/vsphere-55/topic/com.vmware.vsphere.resmgmt.doc/GUID-B42C72C1-F8D5-40DC-93D1-FB31849B1114.html`

  ▸ **vSphere 6.0**: `https://pubs.vmware.com/vsphere-60/topic/com.vmware.vsphere.resmgmt.doc/GUID-B42C72C1-F8D5-40DC-93D1-FB31849B1114.html`

This may seem like a small amount of memory, but over dozens or even hundreds of virtual machines, it can have a significant impact on the amount of total memory required:

(Number of Workloads x Memory Usage) + (Number of Workloads x Memory Overhead) = Current Memory Required

(100 x 5.2 GB) + (100 x 50 MB) = 525 GB

To calculate the total memory required, future growth must be considered. When memory is calculated for growth, the memory overhead required to support the additional virtual machines must also considered.

The maximum utilization threshold must also be determined for memory resources. This threshold defines what the maximum percentage of the total memory resources that will be consumed is. If the maximum utilization threshold is 75%, an additional 25% of memory resources will need to be added in order to calculate the total memory resources required:

*Current Memory Required + Future Growth * (100/Maximum Threshold%) = Total Memory Resources Required*

*525 GB + [(25 x 5.2 GB) + (25 x 50 MB)] * (100/75) = ~875 GB*

875 GB of memory is required to support the current workloads, future growth, and a maximum utilization threshold of 75%.

Transparent Page Sharing

Transparent Page Sharing (**TPS**) is a memory saving technology used by vSphere, which allows duplicate memory pages to be shared between virtual machines. To address security concerns with sharing memory between virtual machines across security domains, TPS can be disabled, enabled across groups of virtual machines with the same salt setting, or enabled across all virtual machines in the environment.

How to do it...

1. Identify the different options to share duplicate memory pages within a virtual machine and across groups of virtual machines.

2. Configure TPS to meet the requirements for security and the performance of the environment.

3. Configure salt values on virtual machines to enable or disable page sharing between virtual machines.

How it works...

TPS deduplicates pages of memory, both within a virtual machine, Intra-VM, and across virtual machines, Inter-VM. By default, Inter-VM TPS is disabled due to security concerns on sharing memory pages between virtual machines that cross security boundaries, for example, virtual machine guests within the DMZ and virtual machine guests in the production environment. TPS can be configured to allow Inter-VM sharing between all virtual machines or only across certain groups of virtual machines by adding a salt value to the virtual machines. The VMware *Knowledge Base* article, `http://kb.vmware.com/kb/2097593`, provides more information on changes and enhancements to TPS.

The host advanced configuration option, **Mem.ShareForceSalting**, can be set to configure how TPS will be used. This setting is configured per ESXi host, as shown in the following screenshot:

Mem.ShareForceSalting can be set to a value of 0, 1, or 2, adding the **sched.mem.pshare. salt** setting to a virtual machine to set the salt value. Page sharing can be configured to share pages only between virtual machines with the same salt value. The following table outlines how Intra-VM and Inter-VM page sharing is impacted based on the **Mem.ShareForceSalting** setting:

The following screenshot displays the memory utilization for a specific virtual machine, showing the amount of the shared memory:

Mem.ShareForceSalting settings	Inter-VM sharing	Intra-VM sharing
0	Yes, between all virtual machines on the host. Virtual machine salt value is ignored.	Yes
1	Sharing between virtual machines with the same **sched.mem.pshare.salt** setting. Sharing between virtual machines where **sched.mem.pshare.salt** is not present.	Yes
2 (default)	Only among virtual machines with the same **sched. mem.pshare.salt** setting. The virtual machine vc.uuid is used as the salt value by default.	Yes

The following screenshot displays the memory utilization for a specific virtual machine, showing the amount of the shared memory:

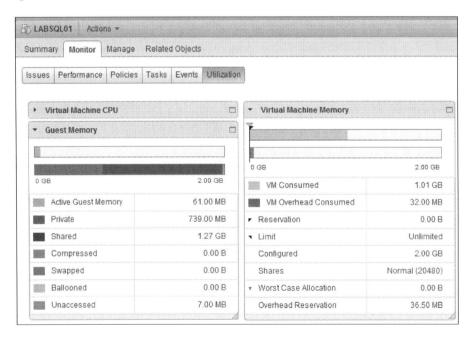

Note the savings the **Shared** memory provides when compared to the **VM Consumed** memory, which is the amount of physical memory consumed on the host. The following screenshot shows the TPS savings across a vSphere cluster:

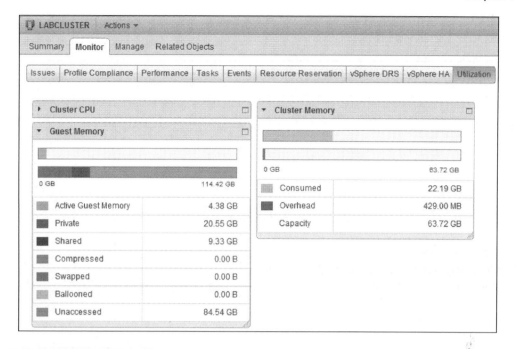

There's more...

When large memory pages are used, TPS only provides a benefit when there is memory pressure on the host. When memory utilization on a host reaches 95%, large pages are broken down into small pages in order to enable TPS. Large memory pages can be disabled on the ESXi hosts. This is done by setting **Mem.AllocGuestLargePage** to **0**. This configuration must be done on each host. Disabling large pages will increase sharing and decrease the amount of physical memory required, but it can have a performance impact, especially with memory-intensive workloads.

Scaling up or scaling out

Once the total CPU and memory resource requirements have been calculated, the amount of resources per host must be determined. Host resources can be designed based on two resource-scaling methodologies, scaling up or scaling out.

When scaling up, fewer, larger hosts are used to satisfy the resource requirements. More virtual machines run on a single host; because of this, more virtual machines are affected by a host failure.

When scaling out, many smaller hosts are used to satisfy the resource requirements. Fewer virtual machines run on a single host, and fewer virtual machines will be affected by a host failure.

How to do it...

1. Determine whether the host in the environment should scale up or scale out.

2. Determine the number of virtual machine workloads per host.

3. Based on the number of virtual machines per host, calculate the number of hosts required. This should also include the number of hosts required to support growth and failover:

   (Number of Workloads / Number of Workloads per Host) + (Number of Future Workloads / Number of Workloads per Host) + Number of Failover Hosts = Number of Physical Hosts Required

4. Using the identified CPU requirements, calculate the CPU resources required per host:

   Total CPU Resources Required / (Number of Physical Hosts Required - Failover Hosts) = CPU Resources per Host

5. Using the identified memory requirements, calculate the memory resources required per host:

   Total Memory Resources Required / (Number of Physical Hosts Required - Failover Hosts) = Memory Resources per Host

How it works...

Many CPU and memory resources were calculated in the earlier recipes in this chapter and are stated as follows:

▸ The total number of CPU resources required is 167 GHz

▸ The total number of memory resources required, taking into account a 25% savings for Transparent Page Sharing, is 657 GB

Based on the design factors, a decision can be made about whether a host should be designed to scale up or scale out. In this case, the following design information provides what is required to size the individual host resources:

▸ Currently, there are 100 physical servers, each hosting a single application. Each application services 10 customers

▸ No more than 20 application servers or 200 customers should be affected by a hardware failure

▸ The business expects to add 50 new customers over the next year

▸ Support growth over the next 5 years

Based on the requirements, the total number of hosts required to support the current workloads, the future workloads, and the redundancy requirements can be calculated as follows:

Total Hosts Required = (100 physical servers / 20 virtual servers per host) + [((50 new customers x 5 years) / 10) / 20] + 2 failover hosts = 8.25 = 9 Physical Hosts Required

Use the following to determine the number of CPU resources required per host (the failover hosts are not included here because these resources are effectively reserved for failovers):

167 GHz / 7 = 23.8 GHz CPU per Host

Use the following to determine the number of memory resources required per host (as with CPU resources, the failover hosts are not included in the calculation):

657 GB / 7 = ~94 GB Memory per Host

Each physical host will need to be sized to support 20 virtual machines and will require 23.8 GHz of CPU resources and 94 GB of memory resources.

There's more...

The requirements from *Chapter 3, The Design Factors*, are very specific about the maximum number of virtual machines that can be run on a host. This simplifies the scale-up or scale-out design decision. The following are a couple of other possible design requirements to work through in order to demonstrate the impact that scaling up and scaling out will have on resources.

- ▶ What if a requirement were to virtualize the environment using three hosts? What resources would be required for each host? If there are 100 virtual machines, how many will be impacted during a host hardware failure?

- ▶ What if the requirement was that each host should be configured with resources to support no more than 10 virtual machines? How will that change the number of resources required for each host? If there are 100 virtual machines, how many will be impacted during a host hardware failure?

Determining the vCPU-to-core ratio

The number of virtual machine vCPUs allocated compared to the number of physical CPU cores available is the vCPU-to-core ratio. Determining this ratio will depend on the CPU utilization of the workloads.

If workloads are CPU-intensive, the vCPU-to-core ratio will need to be smaller; if workloads are not CPU-intensive, the vCPU-to-core ratio can be larger. A typical vCPU-to-core ratio for server workloads is about 4:1—four vCPUs allocated for each available physical core. However, this can be much higher if the workloads are not CPU-intensive.

A vCPU-to-core ratio that is too large can result in high CPU Ready times—the percentage of time that a virtual machine is ready but is unable to be scheduled to run on the physical CPU—which will have a negative impact on the virtual machine's performance.

How to do it...

1. Determine the number of vCPUs required:

   vCPUs per Workload x Number of Workloads Per Host = Number of vCPUs Required

2. Determine the vCPU-to-core ratio based on the CPU utilization of the workloads. If the workloads are CPU-intensive, the vCPU-to-CPU-core ratio will be lower; for less CPU-intensive workloads, the ratio will be higher. The ratio of 4:1 is generally a good starting point for server workloads.

3. Calculate the number of CPU cores required to support the vCPU-to-CPU-core ratio:

   Number of vCPUs / vCPU-to-core ratio = Number of Cores Required

How it works...

The vCPU-to-core ratio is calculated based on the number of vCPUs allocated and the number of physical CPU cores available. For example, if two vCPUs are allocated to each virtual machine, the following is the result:

2 vCPUs allocated to each virtual machine x 20 virtual machines = 40 vCPUs

In a design with 40 vCPUs that requires a 4:1 vCPU-to-core ratio, a minimum of 10 physical cores would be required.

If dual 8-core processors are used, the vCPU-to-core ratio can be calculated as follows:

2 x 8 Cores = 16 Total Cores

40 vCPUs and physical 16 Cores = 2.5 vCPUs to each physical core, or a 2.5:1 vCPU-to-core Ratio

Clustering compute resources

A vSphere cluster is a group of ESXi hosts. The CPU, memory, storage, and network resources of each host are combined to form a logical set of cluster resources. A vSphere cluster is required to facilitate the use of features such as vSphere HA, vSphere DRS, and fault tolerance.

A single vSphere 5.x cluster can contain up to 32 hosts. For vSphere features such as vSphere HA and DRS to work correctly, the configurations must be consistent across all hosts in the cluster. The consistency of shared storage and network configurations is a necessity.

How to do it...

1. Using the vSphere Web Client of vSphere Client, create a new vSphere cluster.
2. Enable vSphere High Availability on the cluster.
3. Enable vSphere Distributed Resource Scheduling on the cluster.

How it works...

A new cluster is created using either the vSphere Web Client or vSphere Client. Right-click on the datacenter object in which you want the cluster to be created and select **New Cluster**. The **New Cluster** dialog will open, as shown in the following screenshot:

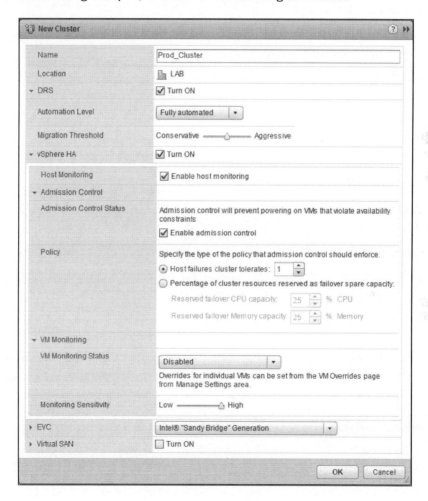

A name must be provided for the cluster. Other cluster options, such as enabling **DRS** and **vSphere HA**, can be configured during the new cluster creation or at a later time by editing the properties of the cluster.

Once the cluster has been created, hosts can be added to the cluster. New hosts are added to the cluster using the **Add Host** wizard by right-clicking on the cluster and selecting **Add Host**. Existing hosts can be added to the cluster by dragging-and-dropping the host inventory object into the new cluster. The cluster's **Summary** tab displays the available cluster resources, the cluster resource usage, and details of vSphere DRS and vSphere HA configurations:

Hosts within a cluster should be configured with similar compute resources. In a cluster where the VMware DRS is enabled, processor compatibility is required. Checking for processor compatibility is covered later in this chapter.

Reserving HA resources to support failover

When vSphere High Availability has been enabled on a vSphere cluster, the virtual machines running on the cluster are protected from a host hardware failure or a virtual machine guest operating system crash.

In the event that a host suffers a hardware failure or if ESXi crashes, the virtual machines are restarted on the surviving hosts in the cluster. Resources must be reserved in the cluster to guarantee that the required resources are available in order to restart the virtual machines.

How to do it...

1. Edit the settings of the vSphere cluster to enable **High Availability**.

2. Enable the HA **Admission Control** policy.

3. Select the HA **Admission Control** policy that should be applied to the cluster.

4. Define the failover settings required based on the HA **Admission Control** policy selected.

How it works...

VMware HA Admission Control ensures that enough physical resources are available to meet the CPU and memory reservation requirements needed to restart the virtual machines on surviving hosts in case there is a host failure:

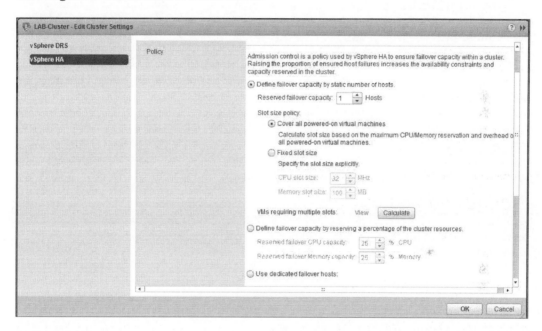

When HA Admission Control is enabled, virtual machines cannot be powered on if there are insufficient resources to meet the reservation requirements for the virtual machines protected in the HA cluster. The resource requirements are calculated based on the HA Admission Control policy selected.

In vSphere 5.x, there are three HA admission control policies:

- Define the failover capacity by the static number of hosts
- Define the failover capacity by reserving a percentage of the cluster resources
- Use dedicated failover hosts

The **Define failover capacity by static number of hosts** policy (for a vSphere client, **Host failures cluster tolerates**) reserves failover resources based on the slot size. The slot size is determined by the largest CPU and memory reservation for a virtual machine that has been powered on. The number of slots available in the cluster and the number of slots to be reserved based on the failover capacity selection are calculated by HA.

A single virtual machine with a large memory or CPU reservation will have an impact on the number of slots available. The value of **Fixed slot size** configured using the vSphere Web Client defines the amount of CPU and memory resources that make up a slot. In the versions of vSphere prior to 5.1, the slot size could be configured with the vSphere Client by setting HA advanced options as `das.slotCPUInMHz` for CPU resources and as `das.slotMeminMB` for memory resources.

Using the **Define failover capacity by reserving a percentage of the cluster resources** policy (for a vSphere client, **Percentage of cluster resources reserved as failover spare capacity**) allows a percentage of the memory and CPU resources to be reserved in order to accommodate a host failure. This reservation is distributed across all hosts in the cluster. To guarantee resource availability in the event of a host failure, the percentage should be set to reserve the CPU and memory resources equal to a single host in a cluster; for example, for a 5-host cluster, 20% of cluster resources should be reserved. This will guarantee that enough resources are available to support a single host failure.

The **Use dedicated failover hosts** policy (for a vSphere client, **Specify failover hosts**) reserves a configured host to be available for failover. The hosts specified as failover hosts will not provide resources to virtual machines during normal operations. The host is a hot spare and virtual machines will only be started on the hosts.

If HA **Admission Control** is disabled, virtual machines can be powered on even if there are not enough resources available to ensure the failover capacity. If surviving hosts are not able to provide the resources with the reservations required to start virtual machines, the virtual machines will not be restarted when a host fails.

Using Distributed Resource Scheduling to balance cluster resources

The vSphere DRS determines the initial placement and balances resources across available host resources in a vSphere cluster. Virtual machine resources can be guaranteed or limited. Rules can be applied to keep virtual machines together on the same host or to ensure that virtual machines run on separate hosts.

How to do it...

1. Edit the settings of the vSphere cluster to enable vSphere DRS.

2. Select a value for the **DRS Automation** level that should be applied to the DRS-enabled cluster.

3. Select a value for **Migration Threshold** that should be applied to the DRS-enabled cluster.

How it works...

vSphere DRS can be enabled when creating a new vSphere cluster or by editing the settings of an existing cluster:

When DRS is enabled, the DRS **Automation Level** and **Migration Threshold** value is set to determine how DRS will place and migrate virtual machines between hosts in the cluster in order to balance the resources across all hosts in the cluster.

If **Automation Level** is set to **Manual**, vCenter will make suggestions for initial virtual machine placement and virtual machine migrations. When a virtual machine is powered on, DRS makes a suggestion for the initial placement of the virtual machine based on the balance of cluster resources, but this must be acknowledged by, or can be changed by, the administrator. Migrations will not be performed unless they are acknowledged by an administrator.

Setting **Automation Level** to **Partially Automated** will make vCenter automatically select a cluster host to place the virtual machine at power-on, but it will only make recommendations for virtual machine migrations. Migrations are not performed unless acknowledged by an administrator.

When **Automation Level** is set to **Fully Automated**, it allows vCenter to automatically determine the initial placement of virtual machines. This setting also causes vCenter to automatically migrate virtual machines between the hosts in the cluster in order to balance resource usage across all cluster hosts. When **Automation Level** is set to **Fully Automated**, virtual machines will also be automatically migrated to other hosts in the cluster when a host is placed in the maintenance mode.

The default DRS migration threshold will typically provide the best balance for most clusters. If cluster resources are not balanced or if too many DRS migrations are invoked, the migration threshold can be adjusted to be either more conservative or more aggressive.

Migration Threshold determines how the cluster will be balanced when **Automation Level** is set to **Fully Automated** or how DRS recommendations will be generated when **Automation Level** is set to **Manual** or **Partially Automated**.

A conservative migration threshold setting will only cause virtual machines to migrate if the migration will result in a significant improvement in the balance of resources. Setting the migration threshold to be more aggressive will cause virtual machines to migrate if any benefit can be realized from the migration. Setting the migration threshold to be too aggressive can result in unnecessary virtual machine migrations or virtual machines constantly migrating in an attempt to aggressively balance the resources.

Ensuring cluster vMotion compatibility

vMotion provides for running virtual machines to be migrated between vSphere hosts. In order to facilitate live vMotion, the processors between hosts must contain the same CPU features and present the same instruction sets. **Enhanced vMotion Compatibility** (**EVC**) masks compatibility issues between the hosts in a cluster.

Enabling EVC on a cluster ensures that hosts added to the cluster in the future will not have vMotion compatibility issues.

Processors must be from the same manufacturer; EVC does not provide vMotion compatibility between Intel and AMD processors. EVC is not required to support HA across different processor types and only supports live vMotion between hosts.

How to do it...

1. Edit the settings of the vSphere cluster.
2. Change the value of **EVC Mode** to **Enable EVC** and select an EVC mode baseline.

How it works...

The EVC mode is enabled on the cluster when the cluster is created or by editing the properties of the cluster. The EVC baseline is selected based on the processor manufacturer (EVC for AMD hosts or EVC for Intel hosts). The selected baseline compatibility is validated against all hosts in the cluster.

The following screenshot shows the EVC mode enabled for Intel hosts and the mode set to **Intel® "Sandy Bridge" Generation**:

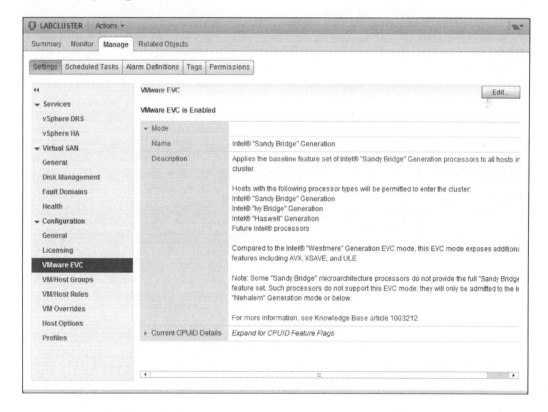

The EVC baseline configuration and the processor supported for each EVC baseline can be found on VMware *Knowledge Base* at http://kb.vmware.com/kb/1003212.

Using resource pools

Resource pools are logical abstractions of resources that can be grouped into hierarchies to reserve or limit CPU and memory resources to virtual machines and subordinate Resource Pools. Shares, limits, and reservations can be applied to a pool and expanded from child pools into parent pools.

How to do it...

1. Understand how resource pool shares, reservations, and limits are applied.

2. Create and configure resource pools to reserve or limit resources to virtual machines. The following screenshot shows how a resource pool is created and configured with **Shares**, **Reservation**, and **Limit** for **CPU** and **Memory** resources:

How it works...

Resource pools are used to define how CPU and memory resources are shared between virtual machines during times of contentions in order to guarantee CPU and memory resources to a group of virtual machines and to limit the amount of resources available to virtual machines.

When creating a resource pool, the following resource allocations can be applied:

► **Shares**: These are used at the time of CPU or memory contention to determine how virtual machines will be scheduled against available CPU and memory resources. Access to resources is relative to the number of shares allocated. Each virtual machine in a resource pool receives a percentage of the shares available to the pool.

► **Reservation**: These include CPU and memory resources guaranteed to the resource pool. Reservations can be set to expandable, which means that if there are not enough resources in the pool to meet the reservation, it can expand into the parent. If resources are not available to meet the reservation, virtual machines cannot be powered on.

► **Limit**: This is about the upper limit of CPU and memory resources available to the resource pool. If a limit is configured, the resource pool will not exceed this limit even when additional resources are available.

Resource pools can be configured in a hierarchy of parents and children. This can be helpful in delegating shares, reservations, and limits to multiple applications or departments. The following figure provides a logical example of how resources pools can be used to allocate available resources between critical virtual machine workloads and DEV/Test environments:

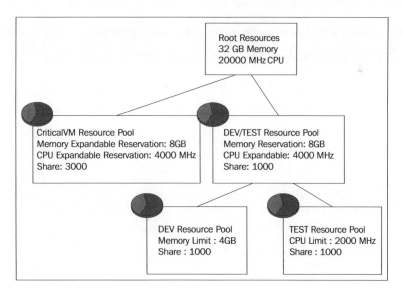

Resources available and consumed by virtual machines in a resource pool can be viewed in a vSphere Web Client, as shown in the following screenshot:

Note that the **Configured Reservation** option of the pool is set to **2.00 GB**, but **Available Reservation** is **43.33 GB**. Since **Reservation Type** is set to **Expandable**, the memory resources in the parent resource pool—in this case, the cluster—are available to this resource pool.

Resource pools add complexity to a design and should be used only if necessary. Do not use resource pools to organize virtual machines.

Providing fault tolerance protection

vSphere **Fault Tolerance** (**FT**) provides protection from a host or storage hardware failure for critical virtual machines by enabling a secondary running copy of the virtual machine running on a separate host and stored on a different datastore. The secondary virtual machine is identical to the primary protected virtual machine, and the failover is instant and transparent:

vSphere **FT Fast Check-Pointing** keeps the primary and secondary virtual machines in sync in order to allow the secondary virtual machine to instantly take over should the primary virtual machine be impacted by a host or storage failure.

How to do it...

1. Identify use cases for vSphere FT.
2. Identify requirements to enable vSphere FT.
3. Enable vSphere FT for a virtual machine.
4. Test vSphere FT for an enabled virtual machine.

How it works...

FT protects critical virtual machines against host and storage hardware failures. Prior to vSphere 6, FT supported only a single vCPU virtual machine. Support for **Symmetric Multi-Processing** (**SMP**) now provides more use cases to utilize FT to protect virtual machines, including the following:

- Protecting critical virtual machines with up to 4 vCPUs and 64 GB memory.
- Reduced complexity of other clustering services.
- Protecting applications sensitive to loss of TCP connections. FT failover maintains TCP connections between clients and to protect the virtual machine.

The requirements to enable FT protection for a virtual machine are as follows:

- 10 GbE network connectivity between hosts when protecting multi-vCPU virtual machines.
- vSphere 6 FT supports virtual disks that are provisioned thin, thick, or eager-zeroed thick.
- Up to 4 FT-protected (primary or secondary) virtual machines with up to 8 vCPUs total per host. For example, across two hosts, four virtual machines with two vCPU each can be protected.
- All virtual machine's allocated memory will be reserved for both primary and secondary virtual machines when FT is enabled.
- NFS v3 and block storage is supported. VSAN, VVOLS, and NFS v4.1 datastores are not supported for primary or secondary FT-protected virtual machines.

FT requires 10 GbE to protect virtual machines with multiple vCPUs. If protecting a single vCPU virtual machine, 1 GbE can be used. The **Fault Tolerance logging** service must be enabled on a VMkernel port, as shown in the following screenshot:

To enable FT for a virtual machine, select the virtual machine in the inventory, right-click on it, and from the **Fault Tolerance** menu, select **Turn On Fault Tolerance**, as shown here:

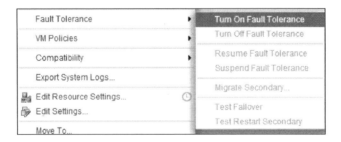

The **Turn On Fault Tolerance** wizard will prompt for a host to run the initial secondary virtual machine and the datastore to store the secondary virtual machine configuration file, vmdk files, and tie breaker file. These should be stored on a separate datastore from the primary virtual machine but can be stored together on the same datastore; this will not provide protection against a storage outage.

When FT is enabled, a secondary virtual machine is created on a different host from the primary virtual machine, and the virtual disk is copied to the selected datastore. Once enabled, the vSphere Web Client displays **Fault Tolerance status**, **Secondary VM location**, and **Log bandwidth usage** for the FT-protected virtual machine on the virtual machines Summary page, as shown here:

Once FT has been enabled on a virtual machine, it can be tested by selecting **Test Failover** from the **Fault Tolerance** menu of the virtual machine, as shown here:

When testing a failover, the secondary virtual machine becomes the primary virtual machine and a new secondary virtual machine is created.

Leveraging host flash

Virtual Flash enables the use of **Solid State Disks** (**SSD**) or PCIe-based flash storage in ESXi hosts in order to accelerate the performance of virtual machines by providing read caching and host swapping.

How to do it...

1. Configure local SSDs or flash devices as Virtual Flash Resource.
2. Configure **vSphere Flash Read Cache** (**vFRC**) for virtual machine disks.
3. Allocate Virtual Flash capacity for the host swap cache.

How it works...

Configuring local SSDs for use as Virtual Flash Resource is done from ESXi host settings, the **Virtual Flash Resource Management** menu. Adding the capacity will display the flash device that is eligible to be used as Virtual Flash Resource, as shown in the following screenshot:

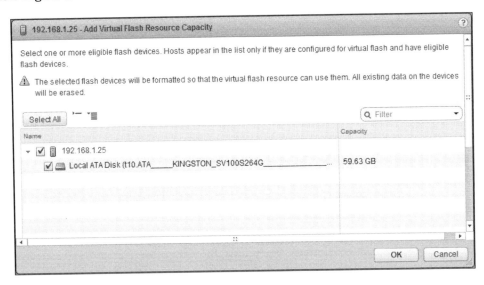

Flash devices selected as virtual flash cache are formatted with **Virtual Flash File System** (**VFFS**), and the capacity can only be used for Virtual Flash Resource.

Once the flash capacity has been added, virtual machines are configured to consume the Virtual Flash Resource as **vSphere Flash Read Cache** (**vFRC**). vFRC is configured per virtual machine disk.

Configuring flash read cache for a virtual machine is done using **Edit Settings**. Select the virtual machine hard disk to configure for vFRC, check the **Enable virtual Flash Read Cache** option and allocate the amount of cache to reserve and **Block Size** for the virtual machine, as shown in the following screenshot:

A portion of Virtual Flash Resource capacity can be reserved for the host swap cache. This cache can be shared by all virtual machines running on the host and provide low-latency caching for virtual machine swap files. Using Virtual Flash Resources for host caching will reduce the performance impact on virtual machines should VMkernel swapping occur.

8

vSphere Physical Design

In this chapter, we will cover the following topics:

- ▸ Using the VMware Hardware Compatibility List
- ▸ Understanding the physical storage design
- ▸ Understanding the physical network design
- ▸ Creating the physical compute design
- ▸ Creating a custom ESXi image
- ▸ Best practices for ESXi host BIOS settings
- ▸ Upgrading an ESXi host

Introduction

The vSphere physical design process (shown in the following diagram) includes choosing and configuring the physical hardware required to support the storage, network, and compute requirements:

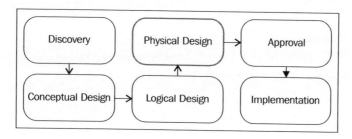

During the physical design process, the hardware and configuration choices should map to the logical design and satisfy the functional and nonfunctional design requirements.

A design architect should answer the following questions about each design decision:

- Does the design meet the requirements of the logical design?
- Does the design satisfy the functional and nonfunctional requirements?
- Is the selected hardware supported?

There will often be more than one physical solution that will meet the design requirements. The job of the architect is to choose the hardware to provide the resources required while meeting the design requirements and constraints.

This chapter contains recipes to check whether or not our hardware is supported by checking VMware's **Hardware Compatibility List** (**HCL**), the physical design of storage, network, and compute resources, creating a custom ESXi image, and best practices for BIOS settings on a server running ESXi. This chapter also provides an overview of methods used to upgrade existing ESXi hosts.

Using the VMware Hardware Compatibility List

VMware's HCL is a database of all tested and supported physical hardware. The physical hardware chosen to support the created design must be checked against the HCL in order to ensure that it will be supported. This includes storage devices, I/O devices, and servers. It is important to not only ensure that the hardware vendor and model is supported, but also check the firmware version of the hardware.

Verifying supportability against the HCL is important for new designs as well as when upgrading a design from one version to another on vSphere. Legacy hardware is often removed from the HCL when new versions of vSphere are released.

How to do it...

To check whether or not a certain hardware device is supported with the current version of vSphere, perform the following process:

1. Visit `http://www.vmware.com/go/hcl/`.
2. Select the type or category of device to determine its compatibility by selecting it using the **What are you looking for** dropdown. For example, if the compatibility of a **Network Interface Card** (**NIC**) is being determined, select **IO Devices**, as shown in the following screenshot:

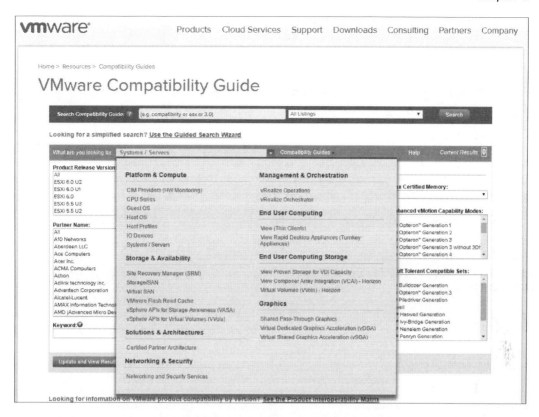

3. Select values for **Product Release Version**, **Brand Name**, and **I/O Device Type**, as shown in the following screenshot:

4. Enter a value for **Keyword**, such as the model number. In this example, the search will be for NC364T, which is an HP quad port 1 Gb server adapter, as shown in the following screenshot:

5. Clicking on the device model will display details about the device, the firmware versions that are supported, and the device driver used by ESXi, as shown in the following screenshot:

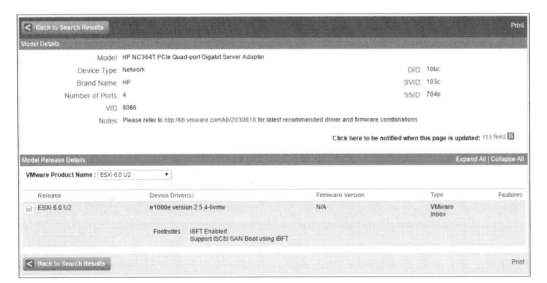

How it works...

The VMware HCL provides an easy-to-search online database of hardware that has been tested and is supported in a vSphere environment.

Hardware that is not listed on VMware's Hardware Compatibility List may still work with vSphere. However, if the hardware is not listed on the HCL, it may cause issues with obtaining support from VMware in the event of issues with the environment. Only hardware found on the HCL should be used in vSphere production environments.

Selecting the hardware type, VMware product and version, hardware vendor, device type, and supported features, allows a design architect to quickly view and select supported hardware. Details about the supported firmware or BIOS versions, the availability of native drivers, and the requirement for third-party drivers can also be quickly viewed for hardware information on the HCL.

There's more...

VMware also provides compatibility guides. The compatibility guides can be accessed through a menu on the HCL page located at http://www.vmware.com/go/hcl. These guides provide details about the features supported by a specific piece of support hardware and can be seen in the following screenshot:

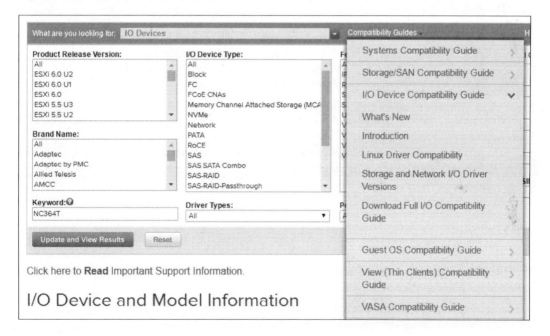

The following screenshot is an excerpt from the **Storage/SAN Compatibility Guide** option, highlighting the support details of the EMC VNX Series arrays:

EMC	VNX5100	FC	VMW_SATP_ALUA_CX / VMW_PSP_FIXED *13, 34, 74 VMW_SATP_ALUA_CX *13, 34, 74, 80, 182, 24, 148, 158, 196, 76, 168, 187, 260, 171, 201, 202, 270, 243, 172, 271, 272, 273, 274, 275	DGC
EMC	VNX5200	FC	VMW_SATP_ALUA_CX *13, 34, 74, 80, 182, 24, 148, 158, 196, 76, 168, 187, 260, 171, 201, 202, 270, 243, 172, 271, 272, 273, 274, 275	RAID5
EMC	VNX5300	FC	VMW_SATP_ALUA_CX / VMW_PSP_FIXED *13, 34, 74 VMW_SATP_ALUA_CX *13, 34, 74, 80, 182, 24, 148, 158, 196, 76, 168, 187, 260, 171, 201, 202, 270, 243, 172, 271, 272, 273, 274, 275	DGC
EMC	VNX5400	FC	VMW_SATP_ALUA_CX *13, 34, 74, 80, 182, 24, 148, 158, 196, 76, 168, 187, 260, 171, 201, 202, 270, 243, 172, 271, 272, 273, 274, 275	RAID5
EMC	VNX5500	FC	VMW_SATP_ALUA_CX *13, 34, 74, 80, 182, 24, 148, 158, 196, 76, 168, 187, 260, 171, 201, 202, 270, 243, 172, 271, 272, 273, 274, 275 VMW_SATP_ALUA_CX / VMW_PSP_FIXED *13, 34, 74, 24	DGC

Another important guide to reference is VMware's *Product Interoperability Matrix*, located at `http://partnerweb.vmware.com/comp_guide2/sim/interop_matrix.php`. This guide provides interoperability information about vSphere products, databases, and host operating systems. If multiple VMware products are to be used in the storage design, their interoperability must be checked against the matrix in order to determine which versions are compatible with which products.

For example, if the VMware **Site Recovery Manager** (**SRM**) is going to be used in a vSphere 6 design, the interoperability matrix is checked to determine which versions of SRM are compatible with that version of ESXi 6 as shown in the following screenshot:

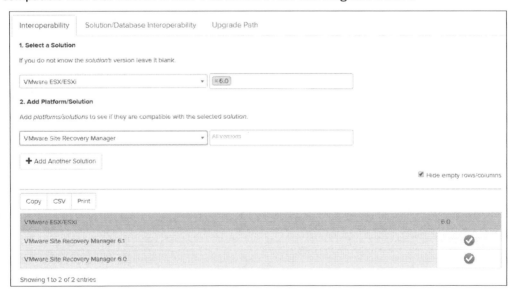

The VMware compatibility guides are also available on the **Product Interoperability Matrixes** page.

Understanding the physical storage design

Storage is the foundation of any vSphere design. Properly designed storage is the key for vSphere features, such as High Availability, Distributed Resource Scheduling, and Fault Tolerance, to operate correctly.

How to do it...

Performance, capacity, availability, and recoverability are all factors that must be taken into account when determining the hardware and configuration of the physical storage. The physical storage design requires the following steps:

1. Select a storage hardware that satisfies the logical storage design. This includes the storage array, storage host bus adapters, and any switching, fiber channel, or Ethernet that may be required to support storage connectivity.

2. Verify the compatibility of each storage hardware component using the VMware HCL.

3. Design the storage configuration to satisfy the design factors related to availability, recoverability, performance, and capacity.

How it works...

The physical storage design must meet the capacity and performance requirements defined by the logical storage design, and these requirements must be mapped back to the design factors.

The logical storage design identifies the capacity, IOPS, and throughput required to support the vSphere design. The design factors identify the functional requirements, such as availability and recoverability, and any constraints that may be placed on the physical design, such as using an array from a specific vendor or using a specific storage protocol.

The logical storage design specifications are as follows:

- **Storage capacity**: 16 TB
- **Storage IOPS**: 6250
- **I/O profile**: 8k
- **I/O size**: 90% read / 10% write
- **Total storage throughput**: 55 MB/s
- **The number of virtual machines per datastore**: 20
- **Datastore size**: 2.5 TB

The factors that influence the physical storage design include the following:

- ▶ Shared or local storage

- ▶ Block storage or file storage

- ▶ Array specifications—such as active/active or active/passive—the number of storage processors, and cache

- ▶ A storage protocol that uses Fiber Channel, iSCSI, NFS, or **Fiber Channel over Ethernet** (**FCoE**) as well as the type and number of disks and the RAID configuration

- ▶ Support for VMware integration such as **vStorage APIs for Array Integration** (**VAAI**) and **vSphere APIs for Storage Awareness** (**VASA**)

- ▶ Support for advanced storage technologies such as de-duplication, tiering, and flash-based cache

- ▶ **Recovery Point Objective** (**RPO**), which is the amount of data that will not be lost in the event of a disaster, and **Recovery Time Objective** (**RTO**), which is the amount of time it takes to recover the system and the data in the event of a disaster

The chief considerations when choosing a storage platform are IOPS, throughput, and support for features such as VAAI, VASA, SRM, and accelerated backups. Physical storage design should focus on both performance and capacity. The physical storage design must be able to meet the performance requirements of the design.

Meeting the design capacity requirements is typically easy to accomplish, but ensuring that the storage will meet the performance requirements takes a bit more work. The I/O profile of the workloads, the number of IOPS required, the types of disks used, and the RAID level selected—all have an impact on the storage performance. It is a good practice to first design the storage to meet the performance requirements and then design to meet the capacity requirements.

Understanding the physical network design

Network connectivity must be provided for both virtual machine network connectivity and VMkernel connectivity. Physical switches, uplinks, virtual switches, and virtual port groups are all components of the physical network design.

How to do it...

Performance, capacity, availability, and recoverability are all factors that must be taken into account when determining the hardware and the configuration of the physical network. The following steps are required in order to successfully complete the physical network design:

1. Select the network hardware that satisfies the logical network design, including physical network switches and network interface cards.

2. Check whether or not the network I/O device hardware, such as network interface cards and **converged network adapters** (**CNA**), is compatible and supported using the VMware HCL.

3. Design the physical network topology and virtual network configuration to satisfy the design factors related to availability, recoverability, performance, and capacity.

How it works...

The physical network design must satisfy the performance and availability requirements defined by the logical network design, which in turn must support the design factors. The logical network design identifies the capacity requirements, and the design factors define the availability and recoverability requirements.

Besides providing virtual machine connectivity, many vSphere features, such as High Availability, vMotion, and Fault Tolerance, have specific virtual and physical network connectivity requirements, which must be taken into account when designing the physical network. If IP-connected storage, iSCSI, or NFS is used, then the physical network connectivity for these must also be included as part of the physical network design.

The logical network design specifications are as follows:

- **The total virtual machine throughput**: 1000 Mbps
- **Virtual machines per host**: 20
- **Virtual machine throughput per host**: 200 Mbps
- **IP storage**: iSCSI
- **Storage throughput**: 55 MB/s
- **vMotion/DRS**: Enabled

The factors that influence the physical network design include the following:

- The number and type of physical switches
- The topology of the existing physical network
- Using either physically or logically separated networks (such as VLANs)
- The number of physical uplinks per host
- The physical adapter type: 1 Gb or 10 Gb
- Teaming and link aggregation
- The network bandwidth and throughput
- Failover and failback policies
- Quality of service and traffic shaping

▸ The type of virtual switches to use: virtual standard switches or virtual distributed switches

▸ Networks required for VMkernels to support management, vMotion, fault tolerance, and IP-connected storage

In the following diagram of an example virtual and physical network design, the VLANs and virtual standard switches have been configured to distinguish traffic types, single points of failure have been minimized using multiple uplinks, and failover policies have been configured to provide redundancy and performance:

Creating the physical compute design

The physical compute design selects the CPU and memory resources to meet the requirements of the design. Besides the CPU and memory resources, the physical compute design also includes the selection of the form factor to support the interface cards required to support the design.

How to do it...

As with other parts of the physical design, the performance, capacity, availability, and recoverability are all factors to consider in the physical compute design. The following steps can be performed to create the physical compute design:

1. Select the server hardware that satisfies the logical compute design.

2. Verify the compatibility of each component of the compute hardware using the VMware HCL.

3. Configure compute resources to satisfy the design factors related to availability, recoverability, performance, and capacity.

How it works...

The logical compute design defines the capacity and performance requirements for CPU and memory resources.

The logical compute design specifications are as follows:

- **Total CPU resources**: 167 GHz
- **Total memory resources (25% TPS savings)**: 657 GB
- **The number of virtual machines per host**: 20
- **The number of hosts required (_N+2_)**: 9
- **CPU resources per host**: 23.8 GHz
- **Memory resources per host**: 94 GB

The hardware selected for the physical compute design must satisfy the resource requirements of the logical compute design. These resources include the CPU and memory resources. The physical hardware selected must also be able to support the network and storage connectivity resources defined in the logical network and storage design.

Along with the design requirements and constraints, the factors that influence the physical compute design include the following:

- The required CPU resources
- The required memory resources
- The vCPU-to-CPU-core ratio
- The processor manufacturer and model
- The number of hosts required: scale up or scale out
- The host form factor: rack or blade
- The number of PCI slots
- The number and type of network uplinks
- The number and type of **Host Bus Adapters** (**HBA**)
- Power, space, and cooling requirements

The following diagram is an example of a physical compute design using the Cisco UCS blade platform; the blades have been configured to support the logical requirements and multiple chassis have been chosen to eliminate single points of failure:

The following diagram is the rear view of the Cisco UCS blade solution, showing the supporting components, including the connectivity of the chassis to the fabric interconnects. The diagram also shows connectivity between the fabric interconnects and the network and storage. Multiple links to the chassis, network, and storage not only provide the capacity and performance required, but also eliminate single points of failure, as shown in the following diagram:

Creating a custom ESXi image

Drivers for some supported hardware devices are not included as part of the base ESXi image. These devices require a driver be installed before the hardware can be used in vSphere.

How to do it...

Third-party drivers are packaged as **vSphere Installation Bundles** (**VIBs**). A VIB file is similar to a ZIP archive in that it is a single file that includes an archive of the driver files, an XML descriptor file, and a signature file. VIB files have the `.vib` file extension.

The required drives can be installed after ESXi has been installed, using the `esxcli` command:

```
esxcli software vib install -v <path to vib package>
```

When installing from a bundle or ZIP, the following `esxcli` command is used:

```
esxcli software vib install –d <path to vib zip bundle>
```

A custom ESXi image can also be created using the Image Builder tools included with PowerCLI. PowerCLI can be downloaded from `https://www.vmware.com/support/developer/PowerCLI/`. Custom ESXi images can be used when deploying hosts using VMware Auto Deploy, or custom images can be exported to an ISO to be used for installation or upgrades. Perform the following steps to create a custom EXSi image:

1. Download **ESXi Offline Bundle** from the My VMware portal. The following screenshot displays the **ESXi Offline Bundle** download link on the My VMware portal:

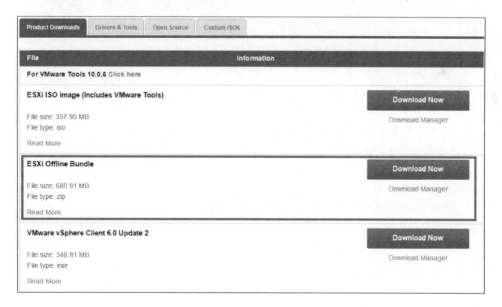

2. Download the required third-party VIBs. This example uses the drivers of QLogic FC-FCoE downloaded from the My VMware portal, as shown in the following screenshot:

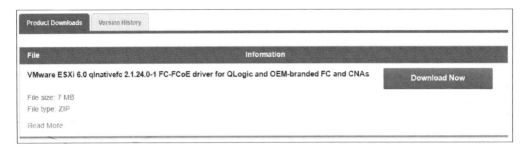

3. Use Image Builder PowerCLI to add **ESXi Offline Bundle** and third-party VIBs as software depots, as follows:

```
Add-EsxSoftwareDepot <pathtoESXiOfflineBundel.zip>

Add-EsxSoftwareDepot <pathto3rdPartyVIB.zip>
```

4. The following screenshot illustrates how to add **Offline ESXi Bundle** and third-party software bundles using the `Add-EsxSoftwareDepot` Image Builder PowerCLI command:

```
VMware vSphere PowerCLI 6.3 Release 1                              —  □  ×

PowerCLI C:\temp> Add-EsxSoftwareDepot C:\vSphere6\update-from-esxi6.0-6.0_updat
e02.zip

Depot Url
---------
zip:C:\vSphere6\update-from-esxi6.0-6.0_update02.zip?index.xml


PowerCLI C:\temp> Add-EsxSoftwareDepot C:\vSphere6\VMW-ESX-6.0.0-qlnativefc-2.1.
20.0-offline_bundle-2731168.zip

Depot Url
---------
zip:C:\vSphere6\VMW-ESX-6.0.0-qlnativefc-2.1.20.0-offline_bundle-2731168.zip...


PowerCLI C:\temp>
```

5. List the available software packages required to locate the Qlogic drivers and note the package names:

```
Get-EsxSoftwarePackage | where {$_.Vendor -eq "Qlogic"}
```

The following screenshot illustrates the use of the `Get-EsxSoftwarePackage` PowerCLI command to locate the package name of the third-party package that will be added to the new ESXi image:

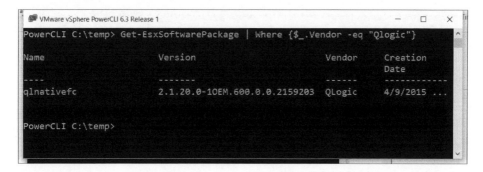

6. List the available image profiles using the following command:

   `Get-EsxImageProfile`

   The following screenshot illustrates the output of the `Get-EsxImageProfile` PowerCLI command that lists the available profiles:

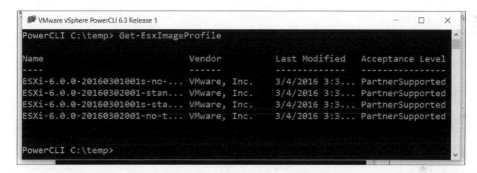

7. Create a clone of an image profile to apply customizations to. The clone will allow the profile to be manipulated without making changes to the original profile:

   `New-EsxImageProfile -CloneProfile <ProfiletoClone> -Name <CustomProfileName> -Vendor Custom -AcceptanceLevel PartnerSupported`

The following screenshot illustrates the output of the `New-EsxImageProfile` PowerCLI command that creates a clone of an existing profile:

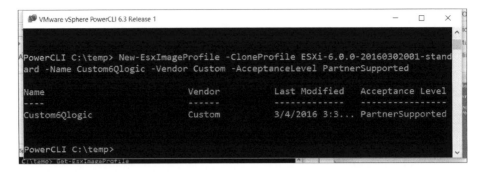

8. Add the software packages to the cloned image profile; this step is repeated for each package to be added to the new image profile:

```
Add-EsxSoftwarePackage -ImageProfile <CustomProfileName> -
SoftwarePackage <SoftwarePackagetoAdd>
```

The following screenshot displays the output of the `Add-EsxSoftwarePackage` PowerCLI command when the third-party software package is added to the new ESXi image:

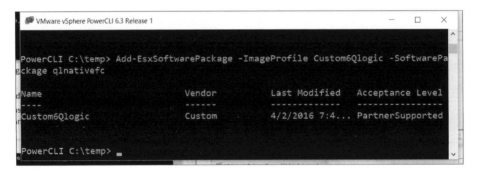

9. Create an ISO from the cloned image profile using the following command; the ISO will include the additional software packages:

```
Export-EsxImageProfile -ImageProfile <CustomProfileName> -
ExportToIso -filepath <Pathtonew.iso>
```

The following screenshot shows the `Export-EsxImageProfile` PowerCLI command. There will be no message output from the command if it completes successfully, but the ESXi image ISO will be created and made available in the provided path:

```
VMware vSphere PowerCLI 6.3 Release 1                          —   □   ×

PowerCLI C:\temp> Export-EsxImageProfile -ImageProfile Custom6Qlogic -ExportToIs
o -filepath C:\vSphere6\CustomESX6.0-Qlogic.iso
PowerCLI C:\temp> dir C:\vSphere6\*.iso


    Directory: C:\vSphere6


Mode                LastWriteTime         Length Name
----                -------------         ------ ----
-a----        4/2/2016     7:43 AM      375396352 CustomESX6.0-Qlogic.iso


PowerCLI C:\temp>
```

The new ISO image includes the third-party VIBs and can be used to install ESXi.

How it works...

The Image Builder PowerCLI commands are used to create a custom image from ESXi Offline Bundle and the vendor-provided bundle. In order to maintain the smallest footprint possible, not all supported hardware drivers are included with the native ESXi installation package.

ESXi Offline Bundle contains multiple profiles: one that includes VMware tools—the standard profile—and one without VMware tools—the no-tools profile. A clone of the profile is created and the vendor software is added to it. When all of the required software has been added to the profile, it is exported to an ISO image that can be used to deploy ESXi hosts.

> Custom image profiles created using the Image Builder PowerCLI commands are also used when using Auto Deploy to deploy stateless or stateful hosts. The procedure to create a custom image profile to be used by Auto Deploy is the same, with the exception of the profile being exported to the custom ISO.

There's more...

Custom ESXi ISOs are also provided by manufacturers. Cisco, HP, Hitachi, Fujitsu, and other hardware manufacturers provide these custom ESXi ISO images, which can be downloaded from the My VMware portal using the **Custom ISOs** tab, as illustrated in the following screenshot:

These custom ISOs are preconfigured to include the drivers required for manufacturer-specific hardware.

Best practices for ESXi host BIOS settings

The BIOS settings will vary depending on the hardware manufacturer and the BIOS version. Supported BIOS versions should be verified on the VMware HCL for the hardware selected. The following screenshot shows the HCL details of a Dell PowerEdge R620 with the supported BIOS versions:

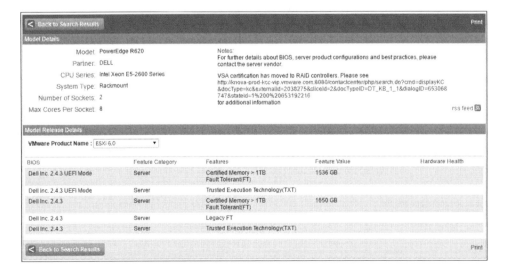

If the hardware is supported but the running BIOS version is not supported, the BIOS should be upgraded to a supported version.

How to do it...

The BIOS settings will vary depending on the hardware manufacturer and the BIOS version. The settings available along with the layout and access will vary depending on the BIOS manufacturer and the BIOS version. The following screenshot is an example of a BIOS setup utility:

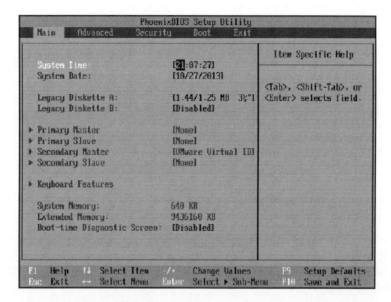

The following settings are provided as guidelines to optimize the BIOS for an ESXi installation. Ask the hardware vendor for recommendations on settings specific to the hardware and BIOS versions:

1. Enable Intel VTx or AMD-V.
2. Enable **Intel Extended Page Tables** (**EPT**) or AMD **Rapid Virtualization Indexing** (**RVI**).
3. Disable node interleaving if the system supports **non-uniform memory architecture** (**NUMA**).
4. Enable **Turbo Boost** if the processor supports it.
5. Enable **Hyper-Threading (HT)** if supported by the processor.
6. Set **Intel Execute Disable (XD)** or **AMD No Execute (NX)** to **Yes**.
7. Set power-saving features to **OS Control Mode**.
8. Enable the C1E halt state.

9.   Disable any unnecessary hardware or features (floppy controllers, serial ports, USB controllers, and so on).

How it works...

Intel VTx, Intel EPT, AMD-V, and AMD RVI are hardware-based virtualization technologies that provide extensions to perform tasks that are normally handled by software to improve resource usage and enhance virtual machine performance. Enabling Intel VTx or AMD-V is required if the host is running 64-bit guests.

If the design calls for the disabling of large memory pages in order to realize the advantages of **Transparent Page Sharing** (**TPS**) at times other than when there is memory contention, the Intel EPT or AMD RVI must be disabled. Enabling EPT or RVI will enforce large pages, even if they have been disabled in ESXi. This is not recommended for production environments, but it can provide sufficient memory savings in lab or test environments.

If the system is NUMA-capable, the option to enable node interleaving, which will disable NUMA, may be available. Enabling NUMA, by disabling node interleaving, will provide the best performance. This ensures that the memory accessed by a processor is local to that processor or in the same NUMA node as that processor.

Enabling Turbo Boost will increase efficiency by balancing CPU workloads over unused cores.

Intel Hyper-Threading allows multiple threads to run on each core. When HT is enabled, the number of logical processors available is doubled. Each core is able to accept two concurrent threads of instructions.

Setting the power-saving features to **OS Control Mode** will allow ESXi to manage power saving on the host. If **OS Control Mode** is not available or supported, power-saving features should be disabled. Enabling the C1E halt state increases the power saving.

Upgrading an ESXi host

Many environments have already adopted some level of virtualization. A datacenter design will most likely have to include the upgrading of the current infrastructure in order to leverage new features and functionality. Upgrading ESXi is a simple process, but it requires planning in order to ensure compatibility and support ability. *Chapter 4, vSphere Management Design,* provides details on upgrading vCenter Server; this recipe provides details on planning an upgrade of ESXi hosts.

ESXi 5.0, ESX 5.1, and ESXi 5.5 can be upgraded directly to ESXi 6. Earlier versions of ESX/ESXi must first be upgraded to 5.x before upgrading to ESXi 6.

How to do it...

When preparing to upgrade ESXi hosts, use the following steps:

1. Identify the methods available to upgrade ESXi.

2. Verify hardware and firmware compatibility using the VMware Hardware Compatibility List at `http://www.vmware.com/go/hcl`.

How it works...

The following methods are available to upgrade ESXi:

▶ **Interactive upgrade**: An interactive upgrade can be performed from the ESXi console to upgrade ESXi from an ESXi image on a CD/DVDROM or USB drive. To perform an interactive upgrade, boot to the image on the CDROM or USB drive and follow the onscreen wizard to upgrade ESXi.

▶ **Scripted upgrade**: ESXi upgrades can be scripted using a kickstart file. The default kickstart file is located at `/etc/vmware/ks.cfg`. The `ks.cfg` file allows the upgrade to be performed from a CD/DVDROM, USB, FTP server, NFS server, or HTTP/HTTPS server. Details on creating a `ks.cfg` file and automating the ESXi upgrade can be found in the VMware vSphere documentation, *Installing or Upgrading Hosts by Using a Script*, located at `http://pubs.vmware.com/vsphere-60/topic/com.vmware.vsphere.upgrade.doc/GUID-870A07BC-F8B4-47AF-9476-D542BA53F1F5.html`.

▶ **Command line using esxcli**: The `esxcli` command can be used to upgrade ESXi from a depot or bundle using this command:

```
esxcli software vib install -d <pathtoupgradedepot>
```

▶ **vSphere Update Manager**: Using **vSphere Update Manager** (**VUM**), an ESXi is uploaded and the upgrade baseline is created, the baseline is applied to hosts, and the hosts are remediated against the baseline. The *Designing a vSphere Update Manager deployment* recipe in *Chapter 4, vSphere Management Design*, provides details on installing and using VUM to upgrade ESXi hosts.

▶ **vSphere Auto Deploy**: Hosts deployed using vSphere Auto Deploy can be reprovisioned using a new image profile. Creating an ESXi 6 image profile is covered in the *Creating a custom ESXi image* recipe discussed earlier in this chapter.

Anytime an ESXi upgrade is performed, it is important to verify compatibility on the VMware Hardware Compatibility List. The host hardware and BIOS and the installed adapters should be verified on the list in order to ensure the stability of the host and the support of the environment. Verifying compatibility using HCL is covered in the *Using the VMware Hardware Compatibility List* recipe earlier in this chapter.

9

Virtual Machine Design

In this chapter, we will cover the following topics:

- ▸ Right-sizing virtual machines
- ▸ Enabling CPU Hot Add and Memory Hot Plug
- ▸ Using paravirtualized VM hardware
- ▸ Creating virtual machine templates
- ▸ Upgrading and installing VMware Tools
- ▸ Upgrading VM virtual hardware
- ▸ Using vApps to organize virtualized applications
- ▸ Using VM affinity and anti-affinity rules
- ▸ Using a VM to host affinity and anti-affinity rules
- ▸ Converting physical servers with vCenter Converter Standalone

Introduction

Virtual machine (**VM**) design is just as important as physical hardware design and should be part of the physical design process. Correctly designing and configuring virtual machines with proper resource allocation will help increase consolidation in the virtual environment and ensure that a virtual machine has access to the resources that it requires in order to run the workloads efficiently.

A few questions that should be answered as part of the virtual machine design are as follows:

- ▸ What resources will be assigned to individual virtual machines?
- ▸ What virtual hardware will be allocated to virtual machines?

- ► How will new virtual machines be deployed?

- ► How will multiple virtual machines supporting an application be grouped based on dependencies?

- ► How will virtual machines be placed on host resources in order to ensure the efficient use of resources and availability?

- ► How will physical servers be converted to virtual machines?

This chapter will cover right-sizing virtual machines to ensure that they have the resources they require without overallocating resources. It will cover the allocation of virtual hardware to virtual machines and how to create a virtual machine template and quickly deploy a virtual machine.

Configuring the ability to add CPU and memory resources without taking the virtual machine out of production will also be covered, along with how to group virtual machines into applications or vApps. We'll also discuss using affinity and anti-affinity rules on a DRS cluster in order to reduce the demand on a physical network or to provide application availability in the event of a host failure. Finally, the chapter will demonstrate how to convert a physical server to a virtual machine.

Right-sizing virtual machines

Right-sizing a virtual machine means allocating the correct amount of CPU, memory, and storage resources required to support a virtual machine's workload. Optimal performance of the virtual machine and efficient use of the underlying hardware are both obtained through right-sizing virtual machine resources.

In a physical server environment, it is difficult to add resources. Because of this, physical servers are often configured with more resources than actually required in order to ensure that there are sufficient resources available if the need for resources increases. Typically, physical servers only use a small percentage of the resources available to them; this means that a great deal of resources are constantly kept idle or wasted. Adding resources to a physical server also typically requires the server to be powered off and, possibly, even removed from the rack, which takes even more time and impacts the production.

In a virtual environment, it becomes much easier to add CPU, memory, and disk resources to a virtual machine. This eliminates the need to overallocate resources. Virtual machines are configured with the resources they require, and more resources can be added as the demand increases. If a virtual machine has been configured to use CPU Hot Add and Memory Hot Plug, additional resources can be added without taking the virtual machine out of production.

How to do it...

Perform the following steps to right-size virtual machines:

1. Determine the CPU, memory, and storage resources required by the virtual machine.

> When sizing virtual machine resources, start with the minimum requirements and add additional resources to the virtual machine as required.

2. Adjust the virtual machine CPU, memory, and storage resource allocation to meet the requirements of the workload without overallocating.

How it works...

Tools such as VMware Capacity Planner or Windows Perfmon can be used to determine the actual resources required by an application running on a physical server. Resources used by a virtual machine can be examined using the vSphere Client program. From the **Summary** tab on the summary page of a virtual machine, it is easy to determine what CPU, memory, and disk resources have been allocated to the virtual machine, along with the current usage of each of these resources, as shown in the following screenshot:

Performance charts can also be used to provide information about CPU and memory usage over time. The real-time advanced memory performance chart shown in the following screenshot shows the memory metrics of the Win7Client virtual machine:

K..	Object	Measurement	1 ▲ Rollup	Units	Latest	Maximum	Minim...	Avera
■	Win7Client	Active	Avera...	KB	335544	608172	251...	372.
■	Win7Client	Balloon	Avera...	KB	0	0	0	0

The chart options can be adjusted to show metrics for the last day, week, month, or even the last year. These metrics can be used to determine whether a virtual machine has been allocated more memory than required.

Once the resource requirements have been identified, the virtual machine resources can be modified or right-sized in order to ensure that a virtual machine has not been allocated more resources than required for the workload running on it.

vRealize Operations Manager (**vROPs**) is a separate VMware product that can be used to monitor the resources used by a virtual machine and has capacity planning and efficiency monitoring specific to right-sizing virtual machines. More information on vROPs can be found at `http://www.vmware.com/products/vcenter-operations-management/`.

Enabling CPU Hot Add and Memory Hot Plug

Adding CPU and memory resources to a virtual machine is a simple process. The process of adding resources to a virtual machine is to power down the virtual machine, increase the number of vCPUs or the amount of memory, and power on the virtual machine again.

In vSphere 4.0, two new features, CPU Hot Add and Memory Hot Plug, were introduced to allow virtual machine vCPUs and the virtual machine memory to be increased without requiring the virtual machine to be powered off. CPU Hot Add and Memory Hot Plug must first be enabled on the virtual machine, which requires it to be powered off. Once enabled, however, CPU and memory resources may be added dynamically; powering off the virtual machine is not necessary.

How to do it...

Perform the following steps to enable vCPU Hot Add and Memory Hot Plug for virtual machines:

1. Check the VMware *Guest OS Compatibility Guide*, which can be found at `http://partnerweb.vmware.com/comp_guide2/pdf/VMware_GOS_Compatibility_Guide.pdf` to identify whether vCPU and memory hot-adding is supported for the virtual machine guest operating system. The following screenshot is from the VMware *Guest OS Compatibility Guide* and shows the **Hot Add Memory** and **Hot Add vCPU** support for Windows Server 2012 Datacenter Edition R2:

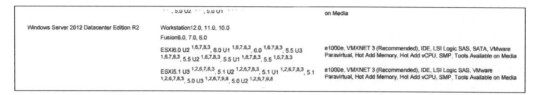

2. To configure CPU Hot Add or Memory Hot Plug for a virtual machine, it must be powered off first.

3. To enable CPU Hot Add on the virtual machine, edit the virtual machine settings and expand the **CPU** settings. Select the **Enable CPU Hot Add** checkbox, as shown in the following screenshot:

4. To enable Memory Hot Plug, expand the **Memory** settings and select the **Enable** checkbox for **Memory Hot Plug (*)**, as shown in the following screenshot:

5. Once CPU Hot Add and Memory Hot Plug have been enabled for a virtual machine, the virtual machine can be powered back on.

6. vCPUs or memory can now be added to the running virtual machine without having to shut it down.

How it works...

Once CPU Hot Add and Memory Hot Plug have been enabled on a virtual machine, it will not be necessary to power off the virtual machine to add additional vCPUs or additional memory.

 Though vCPUs and memory can be added while the virtual machine is running, once Hot Add/Hot Plug has been enabled, some operating systems may require the guest to be rebooted before the added vCPUs or memory are recognized by the operating system.

Enabling the CPU Hot Add and Memory Hot Plug features increases the virtual machine overhead reservation slightly. Also, remember that when a virtual machine's memory is increased, the virtual machine swap file (.vswp) also increases to the size of the allocated memory (minus any memory reservations). The swap file grows automatically when the virtual machine's memory is increased.

CPU resources do not have to be added in "twos". If a virtual machine requires the resources associated with three CPUs, three vCPUs can be assigned to the virtual machine. It is also not necessary to allocate the virtual machine memory in GB increments; a virtual machine can be allocated 1,256 MB of memory if that is what is necessary to meet resource requirements.

With CPU Hot Add and Memory Hot Plug enabled, the removal of vCPUs and memory from a virtual machine may still require that the virtual machine be powered off or the operating system be rebooted before the resources are removed or before the removal of resources is recognized by the guest operating system.

Using paravirtualized VM hardware

Paravirtualization provides a direct communication path between the guest OS within the virtual machine and the ESXi hypervisor. Paravirtualized virtual hardware and the corresponding drivers installed with VMware Tools are optimized to provide improved performance and efficiency. This hardware includes the VMXNET network adapter and the PVSCSI storage adapter.

How to do it...

Adding paravirtualized hardware adapters to a virtual machine is done using the following steps:

1. Access the **Guest OS** compatibility section of the VMware HCL at `http://www.vmware.com/go/hcl` in order to determine the guest OS support for paravirtual adapters. A screenshot of the **Guest OS** compatibility HCL with the **Networking** and **Storage** adapters in highlighted red boxes is shown in the following screenshot:

2. Install VMware Tools in the virtual machine.

3. To install the paravirtualized network adapter, edit the virtual machines' **Virtual Hardware**, add **New Network adapter**, and select **VMXNET3** for **Adapter Type**, as shown in the following screenshot:

4. To install the paravirtualized SCSI adapter, edit the virtual machines' **Virtual Hardware** option, add **New SCSI controller**, and select **VMware Paravirtual** for adapter type, as shown in the following screenshot:

How it works...

Once the adapter is configured, the optimized virtual hardware is presented to the virtual machine guest. The drivers for the paravirtualized hardware adapters are included with VMware Tools. The paravirtualized hardware can be added to a virtual machine before VMware Tools is installed, but the hardware will not be available for use by the guest OS until VMware Tools is installed.

The VMXNET3 adapter should be used anytime it is supported, and it will provide higher network throughput with less host CPU overhead.

The PVSCSI adapter is suitable for IO-intensive applications. As with the VMXNET3 adapter, the PVSCSI adapter increases the storage throughput with minimal host CPU overhead.

Creating virtual machine templates

Virtual machines can be deployed quickly from prebuilt templates. Virtual machine templates are configured with minimum CPU, memory, and storage resources. The guest operating system and any prerequisite applications are installed in the template. Instead of taking hours (or even days in some cases) to install the operating system and prepare the server, once a template has been created, a new virtual machine can be deployed within minutes. Virtual machine templates not only allow for quick deployment, but they also help maintain consistency across virtual machines deployed in the environment.

How to do it...

The following steps are required in order to create a virtual machine template:

1. Create a virtual machine; configure the vCPU, memory, and storage resources; install the guest operating system; install the required applications; and apply any application or operating system updates or patches.

2. The virtual machine can be cloned to a template using the **Clone to Template...** wizard, as shown in the following screenshot:

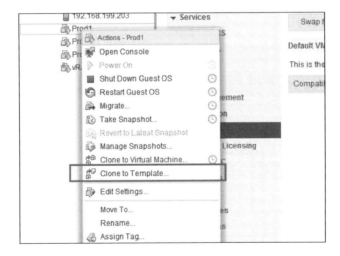

3. The virtual machine can also be converted to a template using the **Convert to Template** wizard, as shown in the following screenshot:

4. Once the virtual machine template has been created, new virtual machines can be deployed from the template using the **Deploy VM from this Template...** wizard, as shown in the following screenshot:

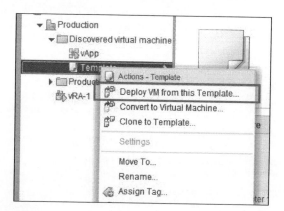

How it works...

When cloning a virtual machine to a template, the **Clone to Template** wizard allows the administrator to choose the datacenter, cluster, and storage to create the new virtual machine template. Cloning a virtual machine to a template can be done while the source virtual machine is powered on.

When a virtual machine is converted to a template, the virtual machine is converted locally; the template will have the same inventory properties (the datacenter, cluster, and storage) as the virtual machine that has been converted. The virtual machine configuration file (.vmx) is changed to a template configuration file (.vmtx) when a virtual machine is converted. The virtual machine needs to be powered off in order to be converted to a virtual machine template.

The following screenshot shows the virtual machine template files on a datastore (the virtual machine template configuration file has been highlighted in red):

The virtual machine template file is similar to the .vmx file and contains configuration information about the virtual hardware presented to the virtual machine or template.

There's more...

A guest customization specification can be applied to a virtual machine that is being deployed from a template. The customization specification allows settings unique to the deployed virtual machine to be applied during the deployment process. These custom specifications include information such as the computer's name, licensing, IP address, and domain membership. The **New VM Guest Customization Spec** wizard is displayed in the following screenshot:

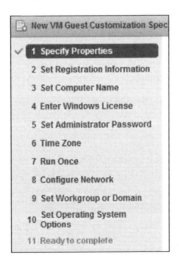

The customization specification can be saved so that it can be applied to future virtual machines deployed from templates. Guest customization specifications can also be applied when cloning a virtual machine.

Upgrading and installing VMware Tools

VMware Tools enhances performance and improves the management of virtual machines by loading optimized drivers for virtual hardware and installing utilities to access virtual machine configurations and metrics. VMware Tools is not required, but for optimal virtual machine performance, it should be installed on all virtual machines in the environment. The status of VMware Tools is displayed on the virtual machines **Summary** page, as shown in the following screenshot:

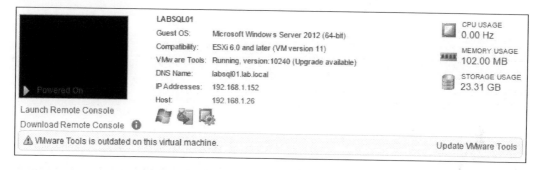

The drivers for the optimized paravirtual hardware, such as the VMXNET3 adapter and the PVSCSI adapter, are included in VMware Tools, and VMware Tools must be installed before the hardware is available for use with in the guest. VMware Tools should be installed and kept up to date on every guest operating system.

How to do it...

There are multiple options available for the upgrading of VMware Tools:

1. If VMware Tools is out of date, a warning is displayed in the vSphere Client, and VMware Tools can be updated from the VM's **Summary** page using the **Update VMware Tools** link, as shown in the following screenshot:

> ⚠ VMware Tools is outdated on this virtual machine.　　　　　　　　Update VMware Tools

2. Right-clicking on the virtual machine and selecting the **Guest OS** menu will allow you to install or select **Upgrade VMware Tools**, as shown in the following screenshot:

3. If VMware Tools is not installed, the **Install VMware Tools** option will be available.

4. Update or install VMware Tools as required.

How it works...

When upgrading or installing VMware Tools on a virtual machine, a VMware Tools ISO image is connected to the virtual machine. If VMware Tools is already installed, the upgrader runs automatically and updates VMware Tools to the current version. If VMware Tools is not already installed, the installer must be run manually in order to install VMware Tools; a reboot of the virtual machine will be required once the VMware Tools installation has completed.

There's more...

Virtual machines can be configured to automatically upgrade VMware Tools to the current version. This is done by editing the virtual machine settings and selecting **Check and upgrade VMware Tools before each power on** in **VM Options**, as shown in the following screenshot:

Upgrading VM virtual hardware

The virtual machine hardware version or virtual machine compatibility specifies the version of virtual machine hardware presented to the virtual machines and the ESXi versions that the virtual machine is then compatible to run on. Updating the virtual machine hardware exposes new features available to virtual machines—for example, the ability to provision vmdks up to 62 TB—and ensures that the virtual hardware is optimized to the version of ESXi.

How to do it...

To upgrade the virtual hardware of a virtual machine, perform the following steps:

1. Install or update VMware Tools in the virtual machine.

2. Edit the settings of a virtual machine and access the **Virtual Hardware** tab.

3. If a virtual hardware upgrade is available, the **Upgrade** option will be available. Select **Schedule VM Compatibility Upgrade**, as shown in the following screenshot:

4. Set the compatibility level the virtual hardware should be upgraded to, as shown here:

5. Shut down and power on the virtual machine to upgrade the virtual machine hardware.

How it works...

The hardware compatibility maps to a virtual hardware version. The following table shows the relationship between compatibility and the virtual machine hardware version:

Virtual machine hardware version	Compatibility
VM version 11 (vmx-11)	ESXi 6.0 and higher
VM version 10 (vmx-10)	ESXi 5.5 and higher
VM version 9 (vmx-9)	ESXi 5.1 and higher
VM version 8 (vmx-8)	ESXi 5.0 and higher
VM version 7 (vmx-7)	ESX/ESXi 4.0 and higher
VM version 4 (vmx-4)	ESX/ESXi 3.5 and higher

When a virtual hardware upgrade is scheduled, the virtual hardware of the virtual machine is upgraded the next time the virtual machine is rebooted.

The virtual machine hardware version should be set to the compatibility of the lowest version of ESXi in the environment in order to ensure that the virtual machine can run on any host in the environment. If a design includes both 5.5 and 6.0 hosts and a virtual machine's hardware is upgraded to vmx-11, the VM will no longer run on ESXi 5.5 hosts.

There's more...

The default VM compatibility can be set on a vSphere datacenter or cluster. Setting the default virtual machine compatibility is done with the **Edit Default VM Compatibility** dialog, which can be accessed by right-clicking on the **Datacenter or Cluster** option in **vCenter Inventory**. The **Edit Default VM Compatibility** dialog is shown in the following screenshot:

Once a default VM Compatibility value is set on a **Datacenter or Cluster** option, virtual machines will be deployed in the datacenter and cluster will be deployed with the default virtual machine hardware based on the compatibility setting.

Using vApps to organize virtualized applications

vApps can be used to group individual virtual machines with interdependencies into a single application. A common use case for this would be a multitier web application that requires a web server frontend, an application server, and a supporting database server. The application can then be managed as a single inventory object.

How to do it...

The following steps can to be performed to use vApps to organize virtual machine workloads:

1. Create a new vApp by launching the **New vApp** wizard, as shown in the following screenshot:

2. The method to create the vApp (either creating a new vApp or cloning an existing vApp), the vApp name, the folder location, and the resource allocation settings are configured in the **New vApp** wizard, as shown in the following screenshot:

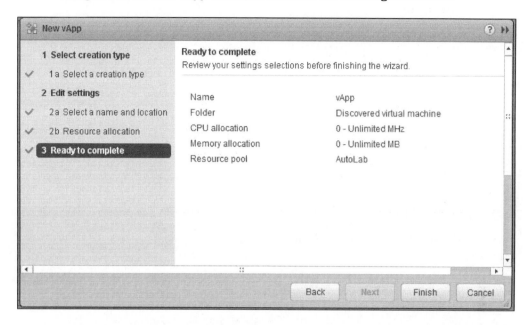

3. Once the vApp has been created, you can add virtual machines to the new vApp by dragging them into the vApp. The following screenshot shows a vApp containing the **Prod1** and **Prod2** virtual machines:

4. The settings of the vApp can be edited. In the following screenshot, **Start order** is configured to start virtual machines in the vApp in a specific order. **Start order** ensures that virtual machines are started in the order of their dependency when the vApp is powered on:

How it works...

A vApp is a container of virtual machines that support an application. Once placed in a vApp, startup and shutdown can be configured based on application dependencies, resources can be reserved or limited, and the entire vApp can be exported in the OVA or OVF format. A vApp can also be cloned to duplicate the application.

Using VM affinity and anti-affinity rules

When virtual machines are powered on in a DRS cluster, vCenter determines where the virtual machines should be placed in order to balance resource usage across the cluster. The DRS scheduler runs periodically to migrate virtual machines using vMotion in order to maintain a balance of resource usage across the cluster. Affinity or anti-affinity rules can be used to control where VMs are placed within a cluster. Affinity rules keep VMs on the same physical host, reducing the load on the physical network by keeping traffic between them from leaving the host. Anti-affinity rules keep VMs separated on different physical hosts, ensuring higher availability.

One case of an affinity rule would be to keep all of the virtual machines supporting an application on the same host. This would ensure that network communications between the virtual machines supporting the application do not traverse the physical network.

An example use case of an anti-affinity rule would be to keep multiple virtual Active Directory domain controllers running on separate hosts in order to ensure that all of the domain controllers are not affected by a single host failure.

How to do it...

The following steps are required in order to use VM affinity and anti-affinity rules:

1. DRS rules are created on the **Settings** page of a DRS-enabled cluster, as shown in the following screenshot:

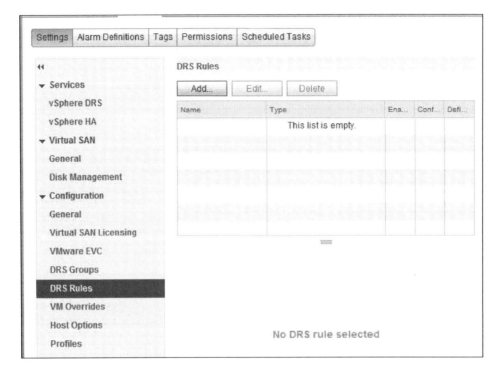

2. DRS rules can be created for three purposes: to keep virtual machines together on the same host, to separate virtual machines across different hosts, or to assign virtual machines to hosts, as shown in the following screenshot:

How it works...

With the DRS rules configured, the distributed resource scheduler will apply the rules when determining the placement of virtual machines when they are powered on or when migrating virtual machines to other hosts in order to balance the cluster resource usage.

When an affinity rule has been configured to keep several virtual machines together, if DRS migrates one of the virtual machines in the rule, all the virtual machines configured will also be migrated to the new host. When an anti-affinity rule has been configured to keep virtual machines separated, DRS will not migrate a virtual machine to a host running another virtual machine configured in the rule.

Using a VM to host affinity and anti-affinity rules

Virtual Machine to Hosts rules can be created to keep virtual machines on or off specific hosts or groups of hosts. These types of DRS rules are useful in order to keep management virtual machines, such as vCenter Server, on specific hosts to make these virtual machines easier to locate in the event of a failure. This also allows virtual machines to be separated across different hosts in a rack or blade chassis in order to ensure that the loss of a rack or chassis does not impact all virtual machines, for example, to split members of a Microsoft SQL always on availability group across chassis.

How to do it...

The following process is used to create **Virtual Machine to Hosts** affinity or anti-affinity rules:

1. From the cluster **Settings** page, access the **VM/Host Groups** section to manage virtual machine and host groups, as shown in the following screenshot:

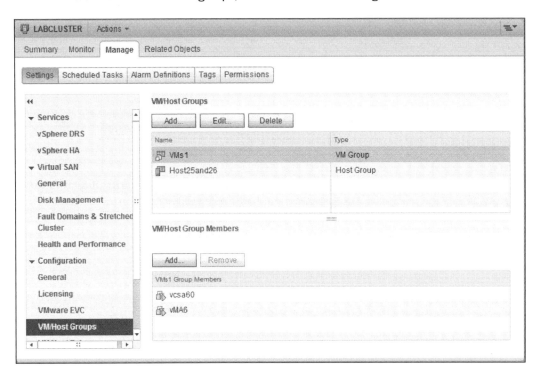

2. Select **Add** to create a new host group and select hosts to add to the group, as shown in the following screenshot:

3. Select **Add** to create a new VM group and select virtual machines to add to the group, as shown in the following screenshot:

4. From the **DRS Rules** menu, create **VM/Host Rule** by providing a rule name, setting **Type** to **Virtual Machines to Hosts**, and selecting **VM Group** and **Host Group** to include in the rule, and selecting required or preferential affinity/anti-affinity, as shown in the following screenshot:

5. Click on **OK** to create the Virtual Machines to Hosts rule.

How it works...

When creating the Virtual Machine to Hosts rule, the affinity or anti-affinity can be set to be required or preferential, as shown in this screenshot of the drop-down box from the **Create VM/Host Rule** wizard:

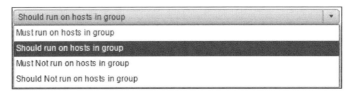

The Virtual Machines to Host affinity and anti-affinity rules include the following:

▸ **Must run on hosts in group**: This is a required Virtual Machines to Host affinity rule, and the virtual machines must run on the specified hosts. This rule will not be violated even in an HA event.

▸ **Should run on hosts in group**: This is a preferential Virtual Machines to Host affinity rule, and the virtual machines will run on the selected host when possible. The virtual machines can run on hosts outside the group if required, for example, in an HA event.

▸ **Must Not run on hosts in group**: This is a required Virtual Machines to Host anti-affinity, rule and the virtual machines will not run on hosts within the group. This rule will not be violated even in an HA event.

▸ **Should Not run on hosts in group**: This is a preferential Virtual Machines to Host anti-affinity rule, and the virtual machines can run on hosts within the group if required, for example, in an HA or maintenance event.

Once the VM/Host rules are created, vSphere DRS will apply the rules when managing the virtual machine placement and resource balancing within the vSphere Cluster.

Converting physical servers with vCenter Converter Standalone

There are two methods to virtualize workloads running on physical servers. The workloads can be migrated into the virtual environment by creating new virtual machines, loading a guest operating system, installing applications, and migrating the application data to the new virtual machines; or, physical servers can directly be converted to virtual machines using VMware vCenter Converter Standalone.

How to do it...

The following steps are required to use VMware vCenter Converter Standalone:

1. Download VMware Converter from `http://www.vmware.com/web/vmware/downloads`.

   VMware Converter can be installed either as a local installation or as a client-server installation. More information on installing VMware Converter is available in the VMware vCenter Converter Standalone guide, which can be found at `http://www.vmware.com/support/pubs/converter_pubs.html`.

> The local installation is used to convert the physical machine that the converter is installed on.
>
> When installed using the client-server installation, the local machine becomes a server that can be managed remotely using the Converter Standalone client to convert physical servers.

2. Once VMware Converter has been installed, the VMware vCenter Converter Standalone client is used to connect to the Converter server, either locally or through the one installed on a remote machine. The **VMware vCenter Converter Standalone** login dialog is shown in the following screenshot:

3. To convert a machine, select **Convert machine** to start the conversion wizard, as shown in the following screenshot:

4. The first step of the conversion is to select the **Source System** type. This is the type of system that will be converted to the virtual environment. The source type can be **Powered-on machine** (physical or virtual), **VMware Infrastructure virtual machine**, **Backup image or third-party virtual machine**, or **Hyper-V Server**.

5. Once the source type has been selected, specify the powered-on virtual machine's information. This is the machine that will be converted, and it can either be the local machine or a remote machine. To convert a remote machine, the **IP address or name** field must be filled in along with administrator credentials and the **OS Family** field. If converting the local machine, the user running the converter must have administrator access to the local machine. The following screenshot shows a sample **Source System** configuration to convert a remote powered-on machine:

6. Once the source system information has been provided, **Converter Standalone agent** will be installed on the source system. Once the conversion is finished, the agent can be uninstalled automatically or manually:

7. Once **Converter Standalone agent** has been successfully installed, the destination system where the source system will be converted is configured. The destination type, the destination IP address, and the destination credentials are configured. The following screenshot shows the configuration of a vCenter Server as **Destination System**:

8. Information on **Destination Virtual Machine**, such as the name and the virtual machine inventory placement, is then configured. The following screenshot shows the name and inventory placement for a physical-to-virtual conversion:

9. **Destination Location** is then selected, as shown in the following screenshot. This location is the datacenter, cluster, or host that the converted machine will be deployed to. The datastore where the converted machine configuration file (.vmx) will reside and the virtual machine version to use is also configured here:

10. A number of options can be configured for the converted machine, including what
virtual machine network to connect to, what datastore to deploy the converted disk to
and in what format, and the device configuration. The following screenshot shows the
Options configuration screen with the volume configuration for the machine that is
being converted:

11. The **Summary** screen is displayed where the conversion options can be reviewed before starting the conversion process. An example **Summary** dialog is shown in the following screenshot:

12. Once the conversion starts, the progress can be monitored in the **VMware vCenter Converter Standalone** client, as shown in the following screenshot. The client allows multiple conversions to be configured and run simultaneously:

How it works...

When a physical server is converted using vCenter Converter Standalone, the physical server is cloned into the virtual environment. This creates a copy of the physical server as a virtual machine containing a duplicate of the operating system, applications, and data from the physical server.

When the physical server is converted, new virtual hardware is presented to the virtual machine. The physical hardware that was associated with the virtual machines is no longer present, and references to it should be removed. In Windows, this is done using the **Device Manager** option.

> During the physical-to-virtual conversion, the physical hardware is replaced with the virtual hardware. During the conversion, references to the physical hardware and the associated drivers are not removed from the operating system. To remove nonpresent hardware from a Windows server, set an environment variable, `devmgr_show_nonpresent_devices`, to 1. This will enable nonpresent devices to be visible in **Device Manager**.

The conversion can be verified by booting the new virtual machine while it is disconnected from the virtual switch and checking whether the operating system and applications were converted correctly. Once verified, the physical server can be powered off or removed from the network, and the newly converted virtual machine can be connected to the network.

The migration of servers and applications can be time-consuming, and vCenter Converter Standalone provides a way to quickly convert physical servers to virtual machines.

10

vSphere Security Design

In this chapter, we will cover the following topics:

- ▸ Managing Single Sign-On Password Policy
- ▸ Managing Single Sign-On Identity Sources
- ▸ Using Active Directory for ESXi host authentication
- ▸ ESXi Firewall configuration
- ▸ The ESXi Lockdown mode
- ▸ Configuring role-based access control
- ▸ Virtual network security
- ▸ Using the VMware vSphere 6.0 Hardening Guide

Introduction

Security requirements of the virtual environment are a critical part of the vSphere design. If components of the virtual datacenter are compromised, a great deal of damage can be done, from powering off virtual machines to accessing sensitive data and impacting business process by disrupting or deleting virtual resources. To identify security requirements, there are a few questions the datacenter architect should ask, and these include the following:

- ▸ What users require access? What resources should be available to users? Administrators, users, auditors, and so on.
- ▸ Do resources require physical separation to ensure security?

▶ Which resources should be separated? For example, separating DMZ resources from internal production resources: is it okay to share storage between DMZ and internal production resources? What about compute?

▶ Are there compliance policies, for example, **Health Insurance Portability and Accountability Act (HIPAA)** or **Payment Card Industry (PCI)** policies, which the design must adhere to?

In this chapter, we will take a look at some of the security features of vSphere that can be incorporated into a datacenter design to satisfy the security requirements for authentication and access.

Beyond the security features available in vSphere, there are a few simple security best practices that should be applied as part of any datacenter design. These security best practices include the following:

▶ Using multiple layers of security to protect systems and services

▶ Physical or logical separation of systems and services based on security domains

▶ Unnecessary services should be removed or disabled

▶ Controlling access to resources within the environment based on user roles

▶ Configuring firewalls, software, and hardware to allow and deny access to services

▶ Keeping security updates and patches up to date

Managing the Single Sign-On Password Policy

When installing the vCenter **Platform Service Controller (PSC)**, a default **Single Sign-On (SSO)** domain is created. By default, this domain is vsphere.local, but with vSphere 6.0, this domain can be defined by the user during the installation.

The vsphere.local domain becomes an identity source for SSO. Users within this identity source can be configured to administer SSO. These users can also be assigned permissions within vCenter. Each user authenticates using a password. Password lifetime, complexity, and how to handle failed login attempts are configured by the policy in SSO. These policies should be configured to maintain compliance with the security requirements of the design.

How to do it...

To configure SSO password policies, perform the following steps:

1. Use the vSphere Web Client to access the SSO configuration and policies. **Password Policy** is shown in the following screenshot:

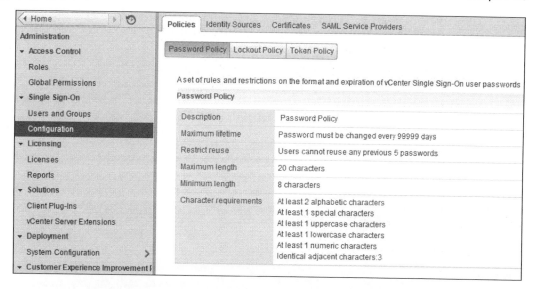

2. Edit **Password Policy** to set the password expiration and complexity requirements. The **Edit Password Policies** dialog is shown in the following screenshot:

3. Using the **Edit Lockout Policy** wizard, configure the policies on how failed login attempts will be handled, as shown here:

How it works

Passwords are one of the first levels of security. The policies should be configured to meet the security requirements of the design.

The SSO Password Policy defines when a password will expire and when a password can be reused. The password format and complexity is also configured as part of the Password Policy. When an SSO user's password has expired, the user will not be able to access the environment until the password has been changed. When the user creates or updates their password, it must meet the password format defined in the policy.

The SSO Lockout Policy is configured to protect the environment from a brute-force type password attack. When a user attempts to log in with an incorrect password, the user's account is locked after the maximum number of attempts is reached. The interval between failures defines the time period in which the attempts occur to set the lockout. When an account is locked, the user will not be granted access, even if the correct password is used, until after unlock time has passed.

Managing Single Sign-On Identity Sources

Single Sign-On Identity Sources integrate authentication databases that can be used by SSO to provide access to vSphere components. An identity source provides user and group authentication information. Users and groups within the identity source can be assigned permissions within the vSphere environment. The default identity source is the vsphere.local domain.

How to do it...

Perform the following steps to create, edit, or remove SSO Identity Sources:

1. Access the vSphere Web Client to view the configured **Identity Sources** tab, as shown in the following screenshot:

2. Identity sources are created using **Add Identity source**. The following screenshot is an example of creating an **Active Directory (Integrated Windows Authentication)**:

How it works...

Identity sources can be configured from the following types:

▶ **Active Directory (Integrated Windows Authentication)**

▶ **Active Directory as an LDAP Server**

▶ **Open LDAP**

▶ **Local OS**

Once an identity source is configured, it is available to provide users and groups in order to create permissions in the vSphere environment. The following screenshot shows the three domains associated with configured identity sources that are available when creating permissions:

Using Active Directory for ESXi host authentication

The default administrator user for ESXi is root. The root user can be used to manage the ESXi host directory using either the vSphere Client or the CLI. As a security best practice, access to the vSphere hosts using root should be limited. For authentication on the ESXi host, local users can be created or the host can be joined to Active Directory.

How to do it...

To use Active Directory for host authentication, perform the following steps:

1. Use the vSphere Client or the vSphere Web Client to access the **Authentication Services** configuration for the ESXi host. The following screenshot shows the **Authentication Services** configuration in the vSphere Web Client:

2. Select **Join Domain** and provide the domain and credentials to join the ESXi host to a domain, as shown in the following screenshot:

3. Select **OK** to join the ESXi host to the domain.

How it works...

The ESXi host is joined to the Active Directory domain and becomes a member server within the domain. Once the ESXi host is joined to the domain, domain users and groups can be used to create permissions to manage the ESXi hosts.

The following screenshot of the **Select Users and Groups** dialog shows access to the LAB domain to configured permissions after the host has joined:

Once permissions are applied for active directory users on the host, the users can access the host using the vSphere Client or the CLI. User actions are logged and auditable when logging directly into a host.

ESXi Firewall configuration

The ESXi Firewall can be configured to control access to and from services within the vSphere environment. The ESXi Firewall can be configured to block incoming or outgoing network traffic or to limit traffic to or from a specific host or network.

How to do it...

Perform the following steps to configure and manage the ESXi Firewall:

1. The ESXi Firewall configuration is accessed through the **Security Profile** section of the host configuration, as shown in the following screenshot:

2. Select **Edit** to configure the ESXi Firewall.

3. Inbound access to a service or outbound access from a service can be enabled. Access can be configured to/from any IP address, or it can be limited to specific hosts or networks, as shown in the following screenshot:

4. Click on **OK** to apply changes to the ESXi Firewall.

How it works...

By default, the ESXi Firewall opens the firewall port required for a service when the service is started. The ESXi Firewall can be configured to only allow connections from specific IP addresses in order to increase security.

The ESXi Lockdown mode

Environment security is greatly increased by limiting the ability to directly access ESXi hosts. The Lockdown mode can be enabled when first adding a host to the vCenter inventory, or it can be configured using the vSphere Web Client. The Lockdown mode can be easily disabled and enabled at any time in order to directly access a host, if required, for support or troubleshooting.

How to do it...

Perform the following steps to enable the **Lockdown Mode** option on an ESXi host:

1. Access the **Security Profile** menu of the ESXi host using the vSphere Web Client. The following screenshot displays the **Lockdown Mode** host configuration in the vSphere Web Client:

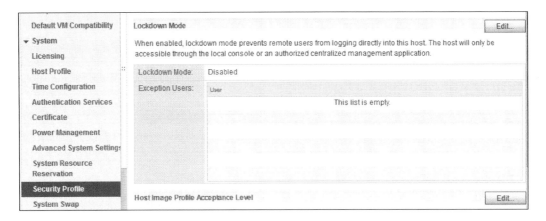

2. Select **Lockdown Mode** for the ESXi host, as shown in the following screenshot:

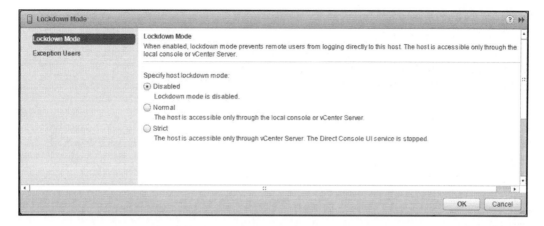

3. Configure **Exception Users**, as shown in the following screenshot:

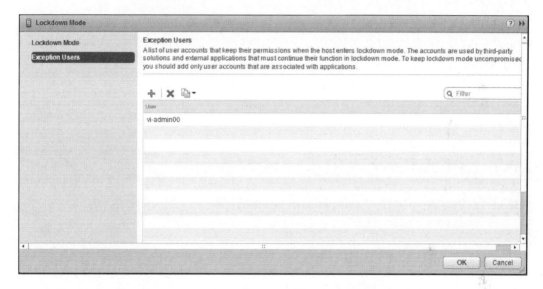

4. Click on **OK** to complete the **Lockdown Mode** configuration.

How it works...

When the lockdown mode is enabled, the host is managed using the vSphere Client connected to the managing vCenter Server, VMware PowerCLI, or VMware **vSphere Command-Line Interface** (**vCLI**). The only difference is that access is authenticated through the vCenter Server instead of using a local account on the ESXi host. When the lockdown mode is enabled, access to the host through SSH is unavailable except to configured exception users.

There are three lockdown modes that can be configured for the ESXi host:

- ▶ **Disabled**: The Lockdown mode is disabled. The host can be accessed normally.
- ▶ **Normal**: The Lockdown mode is enabled, and the host can only be accessed through vCenter or the local console.
- ▶ **Strict**: The Lockdown mode is enabled and the local console is disabled.

When the Lockdown mode is enabled on a host any attempts to access the host directly will result in an error. The following screenshot shows an attempt to access a host in the Lockdown mode using the vSphere Client:

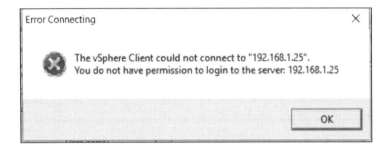

Exception users can continue to access a host in the Lockdown mode. Exception users can be used for emergency troubleshooting or for third-party applications that require direct access to a host.

Configuring role-based access control

vSphere environments use **role-based access control** (**RBAC**) to provide access and permissions on vCenter inventory objects. Not everyone who accesses the vCenter Server should be set up as an administrator. Use roles and permissions to assign only the required permissions that a user, or group of users, needs in order to perform actions in the vSphere environment.

How to do it...

To configure RBAC in a vSphere environment, perform the following steps:

1. Create a role with the privilege required. Preconfigured roles include **Administrator**, **Read-Only**, and **No Access**. Several sample roles are included, which can be cloned or edited.

2. Create or edit roles to provide only the necessary privileges required to perform the roles' function, for example, a role that only provides console access to a virtual machine.

3. Add permissions to vSphere inventory objects by assigning a user and role to the object, for example, allowing a specific user to access the console of a single virtual machine or a group of virtual machines.

How it works...

Privileges define access and actions that can be performed. A role is simply a collection of privileges. Roles can be created, edited, or deleted. The following screenshot displays the **Roles** administration with **Privileges** listed for the **Administrator** role:

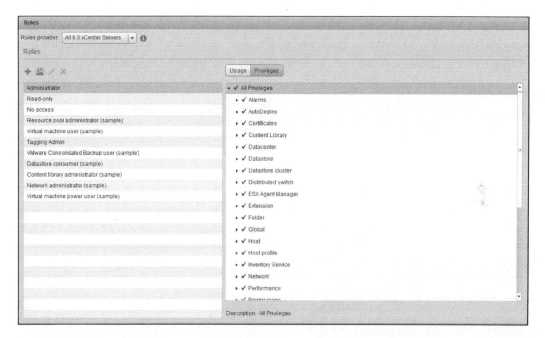

New roles can be created or existing roles can be edited. The available sample roles can be cloned and edited to meet the requirements.

A permission is created by assigning a user or a group of users to a role and applying it to an object, such as a vCenter, datacenter, cluster, folder, or virtual machine, in the inventory. Permissions are managed from the vSphere Web Client and accessed by navigating to **Manage | Permissions** for the object.

When adding a permission, a user or a group is selected, as shown in the following screenshot:

A role is assigned to the user or group, as shown in the following screenshot:

The permission can be propagated to children. This will apply the permissions to child objects in the inventory, for example, all virtual machines in a specific folder or all objects in a datacenter. The **View Children** link will display all the subordinate objects the permission will be applied to.

When creating roles and assigning permissions, it is important to ensure that users are limited to the privileges required to access only the objects they require. Limit the use of complete administrator privileges and discourage the use of shared logins.

Virtual network security

Security is an important factor that must be considered when designing virtual networks. Many of the same network practices that are used in the physical network can be applied to the virtual network. The virtual network provides several advantages to security, but it also introduces some challenges.

The security of virtual machine network traffic is critical along with the security of the VMkernel traffic in order to prevent attacks that may compromise the management, vMotion, Fault Tolerance, and IP storage networks.

How to do it...

1. Identify the available virtual switch security options.

2. Select a virtual switch security configuration based on the design requirements.

3. Apply security best practices to create a virtual network design, separating virtual machine services and the network traffic into security zones based on the design requirements.

How it works...

Separate the virtual machine network traffic based on the services and security zones. Use separate vSwitches or VLAN tagging on port groups to separate nonproduction, DMZ, Test/ Dev, management, vMotion, IP storage, and production virtual machine network traffic. The following are some things that need to be taken care of:

▶ The vSphere management network should be separated from other network traffic using a management VLAN or a physically separate network.

▶ vMotion network traffic is transmitted unencrypted. It could be possible for an attacker to obtain the memory contents of a virtual machine during the vMotion migration. The recommended practice is for the vMotion network to be on a separate VLAN or physically separated nonroutable network from other production traffic.

▶ iSCSI and NFS IP storage traffic is also typically unencrypted. IP-based storage should be logically separated on its own VLAN or on a separate physical nonroutable network segment.

The following screenshot shows the **Security** settings that can be applied to a virtual standard switch:

Virtual switch security settings are as follows:

- **Promiscuous mode**: This policy is set to **Reject** by default. Setting it to **Accept** allows for guest network adapters connected to the virtual switch to detect all network frames passed on the virtual switch.

- **MAC address changes**: If this policy is set to **Reject** and the guest operating system changes the MAC address to a MAC address other than what is defined in the virtual machine configuration file, inbound network frames are dropped.

- **Forged transmits**: Setting this policy to **Reject** will drop any outbound network frame with a source MAC address different from the one currently set on the adapter.

Using the VMware vSphere 6.0 Hardening Guide

The VMware *vSphere 6.0 Hardening Guide* provides configuration guidance in order to secure a vSphere environment. The guide includes recommended security settings for ESXi hosts, virtual machines, and virtual networks.

How to do it...

1. Download the VMware *vSphere 6.0 Hardening Guide* from `https://www.vmware.com/security/hardening-guides`.

2. Use the guide to apply security settings based on the design security requirements.

How it works...

The *vSphere 6.0 Hardening Guide* is an Excel spreadsheet with security settings for ESXi hosts, virtual machine configurations, and virtual networks. Each guideline includes information such as a **Guideline ID**, **Description**, **Risk Profile**, **Vulnerability Discussion** (the reason for the guideline), **Configuration Parameter**, **Default Setting**, and the desired setting for **Risk Profile**.

The following screenshot provides an example of the information available in the **vSphere 6.0 Hardening Guide** file:

Guidelines are categorized into three Risk Profiles: Risk Profile 3 should be implemented in all environments, Risk Profile 2 should be implemented in more security-sensitive environments, and Risk Profile 1 should be implemented in environments that require the highest level of security setting.

A section for each guideline documents any potential negative effects that may be produced as a result of a specific setting. The guide also includes examples on how to check and remediate settings using the vSphere Web Client, the vSphere API, esxcli, vCLI, and PowerCLI.

11
Disaster Recovery and Business Continuity

In this chapter, we will cover the following recipes:

- ► Backing up ESXi host configurations
- ► Configuring ESXi host logging
- ► Backing up virtual distributed switch configurations
- ► Deploying VMware Data Protection
- ► Using VMware Data Protection to back up virtual machines
- ► Replicating virtual machines with vSphere Replication
- ► Protecting the virtual datacenter with Site Recovery Manager

Introduction

The factors that influence the design of the backup and recovery of the virtual datacenter are **Recovery Point Objective** (**RPO**) and **Recovery Time Objective** (**RTO**). RPO defines the amount of data loss that is acceptable. RTO is the amount of time it should take to restore an application or service a workload after an outage.

The acceptable RPO and RTO should be defined for each workload. It is important to consider the application's dependencies when determining the RPO and RTO. Specifically, the RTO of an application will depend on the RTO of all of the application's dependencies. For example, if an application depends on a database server and the RTO of the database server is determined to be 2 hours, then the RTO of the application itself cannot be less than 2 hours if the outage affects both the server running the application and the database server that supports the application.

vSphere provides many options that provide the continued operation of the virtual machines and the workloads they run in the event of an outage. These solutions do not replace the need for virtual machine backups.

The following are two different methods used for the backing up of virtual machine workloads:

- ▶ Traditional backup using in-guest backup agents
- ▶ Agentless backup using the vSphere Storage APIs—Data Protection

The backup and recovery design should not only include virtual machines, but also the backups of the virtual infrastructure configuration containing the management, network, and other configurations. This ensures that the virtual infrastructure can be restored after a failure within the infrastructure, such as a host failure or a vCenter failure.

This chapter will cover the backing up of vSphere infrastructure components. This includes backing up the ESXi host and the virtual distributed switch configurations in order to ensure that the infrastructure can be restored in the event of an outage.

VMware provides several products to protect virtual machines and recover them in the event of a virtual machine or infrastructure failure. This chapter demonstrates many of these options, including the deployment and basic configurations for the protection and recovery of virtual machines. The backup and recovery solution that will be selected will depend on the design factors.

Backing up ESXi host configurations

A complete backup of an ESXi host is not necessary because the installation of ESXi is a quick and simple process. Host configurations should be backed up in order to quickly restore the configuration of a host in case ESXi needs to be reinstalled.

If hosts are deployed using auto deploy or the host configurations are stored in a host profile, the individual backups of host configurations may not be required but are a good way to ensure that a backup of the host configuration is available in case there is an issue with vCenter or a configured host profile.

How to do it...

The simplest way to back up ESXi host configurations is to use the `vicfg-cfgbackup` vCLI command, as shown in the following steps:

1. Use the `vicfg-cfgbackup` vCLI command to create a backup of an ESXi host configuration:

   ```
   vicfg-cfgbackup -server <esxihostname> -s <pathtobackupfile>
   ```

2. Use the `vicfg-cfgbackup` vCLI command to restore an ESXi host configuration from a backup:

```
vicfg-cfgbackup -server <esxihostname> -l <pathtobackupfile>
```

How it works...

The **vSphere Command-line Interface** (**vCLI**) can be downloaded from the VMware site at `http://www.vmware.com/support/developer/vcli/`, and it can be installed on a Windows PC or Linux workstation. vCLI is also included as part of the **vSphere Management Assistant** (**vMA**), which can be deployed in the vSphere environment.

The ESXi backup is saved to the specified file. This file is not human-readable but contains the configuration information of the ESXi host and can be used to restore the configuration in the event that the host is lost and has to be reinstalled. The backup can also be used to return the host to a known good configuration if a configuration change that negatively impacts the host is made.

A configuration backup should be made before upgrading hosts or before making configuration changes to a host.

Restoring a host configuration using `vicfg-cfgbackup` will require the host to be rebooted once the restoration has been completed. This will cause any virtual machines on the host to be shut down. The host should be placed in the maintenance mode, and all running virtual machines should be migrated to other hosts if possible.

> Complete documentation on the `vicfg-cfgbackup` vCLI command can be found in the vSphere documentation at `http://pubs.vmware.com/vsphere-60/topic/com.vmware.vcli.ref.doc/vicfg-cfgbackup.html`.

There's more...

An ESXi host configuration backup can also be performed using PowerCLI with the `Get-VMHostFirmware` PowerCLI cmdlet, as shown in the following command line:

```
Get-VMHostFirmware -vmhost <hostname or IP Address> -
BackupConfiguration -DestinationPath<PathtoBackupLocation>
```

The following screenshot demonstrates a host configuration backup using PowerCLI and the `Get-VMHostFirmware` cmdlet:

```
PowerCLI C:\>
PowerCLI C:\>
PowerCLI C:\> Get-VMHostFirmware -vmhost 192.168.1.25 -BackupConfiguration -Dest
inationPath C:\Temp\

Host            Data
----            ----
192.168.1.25    C:\Temp\configBundle-192.168.1.25.tgz


PowerCLI C:\> _
```

To restore the ESXi host configuration, the `Set-VMHostFirmware` PowerCLI cmdlet is used:

```
Set-VMHostFirmware -vmhost <hostname or IP Address> -Restore -
SourcePath<PathtoBackupLocation>
```

As with restoring the ESXi configuration using `vicfg-cfgbackup`, the host will be rebooted once the configuration is restored. The `Set-VMHostFirmware` cmdlet will not run against an ESXi host that has not been placed in the maintenance mode.

Configuring ESXi host logging

Having access to the ESXi host logs is required in order to troubleshoot or determine the root cause of an ESXi host failure. Redirecting host logs to persistent storage or to a Syslog server is especially important when a host has not been installed to persistent storage, for example, a stateless host deployed using vSphere Auto Deploy or a host that has been installed to a USB stick.

Logging may not seem to be a key component in disaster recovery. Having a proper backup of the host configuration allows a host to be quickly returned to a service. However, if the root cause of the failure cannot be determined, preventing the failure from happening again cannot be guaranteed. Logs are the best source to perform analyses in order to determine the root cause of a failure and determine the best course of action required to prevent future failures.

How to do it...

ESXi logs should be redirected to the persistent storage or sent to a central Syslog server in order to ensure that the logs are available for analysis after a host failure. The following process details how to configure ESXi logging:

1. To redirect host logs, select the host and edit **Advanced System Settings** on the **Manage** tab. Use the **Filter** box to display the **Syslog** settings, as shown in the following screenshot:

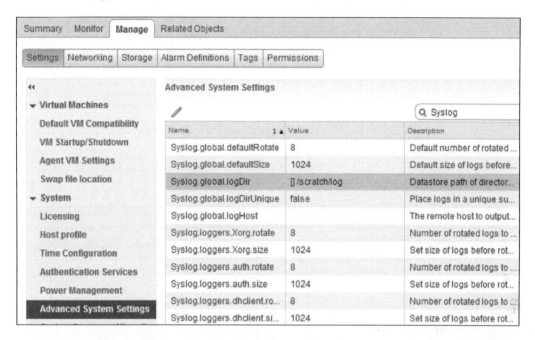

2. Edit the **Syslog.global.logDir** setting in order to set the datastore path to output the logs to. This can be set to a VMFS or NFS datastore which has been configured on the host, as shown in the following screenshot:

3. Edit the **Syslog.global.logDirUnique** setting to create a unique subdirectory for each host under **Syslog.global.logDir**. This setting is useful if logs from multiple hosts are being stored in the same directory. The following screenshot displays the enabling of the **Syslog.global.logDirUnique** setting by selecting the **Yes** option:

4. If the host logs are set to a central Syslog server, edit the **Syslog.global.logHost** setting and enter the FQDN or IP address of the Syslog server. The following screenshot shows the advanced configuration option required to set **Syslog.global.logHost**:

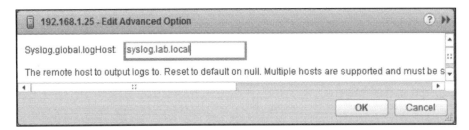

How it works...

When **Syslog.global.logDir** is configured, host log files will be stored in the configured path. The following screenshot shows an example of a host configured with **Syslog.global.logDir** set to **[datastore1] scratch/log** and **Syslog.global.logDirUnique** set to **Yes**:

[esxi2_local] scratch/log/esxi2

Name	Size	Type	Path	Mc
ddecomd.log	0.00 KB	Virtual Machine ...	[esxi2_local] scratch/log/esxi2	6/:
vprobe.log	0.00 KB	Virtual Machine ...	[esxi2_local] scratch/log/esxi2	6/:
iofiltervpd.log	0.00 KB	Virtual Machine ...	[esxi2_local] scratch/log/esxi2	6/:
vmkdevmgr.log	0.00 KB	Virtual Machine ...	[esxi2_local] scratch/log/esxi2	6/:
vmauthd.log	0.00 KB	Virtual Machine ...	[esxi2_local] scratch/log/esxi2	6/:
esxupdate.log	0.00 KB	Virtual Machine ...	[esxi2_local] scratch/log/esxi2	6/:
rabbitmqproxy.log	0.00 KB	Virtual Machine ...	[esxi2_local] scratch/log/esxi2	6/:
vmsyslogd-dropped.log	0.00 KB	Virtual Machine ...	[esxi2_local] scratch/log/esxi2	6/:
usb.log	0.00 KB	Virtual Machine ...	[esxi2_local] scratch/log/esxi2	6/:
osfsd.log	0.00 KB	Virtual Machine ...	[esxi2_local] scratch/log/esxi2	6/:
vsanvpd.log	0.00 KB	Virtual Machine ...	[esxi2_local] scratch/log/esxi2	6/:
syslog.log	0.49 KB	Virtual Machine ...	[esxi2_local] scratch/log/esxi2	6/:
shell.log	0.00 KB	Virtual Machine ...	[esxi2_local] scratch/log/esxi2	6/:
vsantraceUrgent.log	0.00 KB	Virtual Machine ...	[esxi2_local] scratch/log/esxi2	6/:

With **Syslog.global.logDirUnique** set to **Yes**, a subdirectory with the FQDN of the host is created to store the log files. If **Syslog.global.logHost** has been configured, the host logs are sent to a centralized Syslog server. The host logs can be sent to multiple Syslog servers by separating the servers with a comma. The ESXi host logs can be configured to be stored on persistent storage and to also be sent to a central Syslog server.

Backing up virtual distributed switch configurations

Virtual distributed switch configurations can be exported to a file. The file contains the switch configuration settings and can also contain information about the dvPortGroup configurations. This file can then be used to restore the virtual distributed switch configuration or import the configuration to a different deployment.

 Virtual distributed switch import, export, and restore operations are available in the vSphere Web Client.

Virtual distributed switch configurations should be exported before making changes to the distributed virtual switches in a production environment in order to ensure that the switch can be restored to an operational state in the event of a configuration error.

How to do it...

Perform the following procedure to create a backup of the VDS configuration:

1. In the vSphere Web Client, right-click on the VDS to be exported. Navigate to **Settings | Export Configuration...**, as shown in the following screenshot:

2. Select an option depending on whether you want to export the distributed switch and all of the port groups or the distributed switch only. Selecting the **Distributed switch only** option exports only the virtual distributed switch configuration and does not include any configurations for the port groups associated with the dvSwitch. Give the exported configurations a short description, as illustrated in the following screenshot:

3. Select **Yes** when the **Confirm Configuration Export** dialog is displayed. The **Confirm Configuration Export** dialog box is shown in the following screenshot:

4. Select the local path to which you want to save the configuration, and specify a filename for the exported configuration.

How it works...

Once exported, the configuration file will contain all of the settings for VDS and the dvPortgroup configurations. This file can then be used to restore the VDS configurations of an existing distributed switch or import the configurations in case VDS is accidently deleted or lost.

Restoring the VDS configuration from the exported configuration file is a simple process. Right-click on the VDS to be restored, and navigate to **Settings | Restore Configuration...**, as shown in the following screenshot:

When restoring or importing a VDS from an exported configuration file, we can use one of the following two options: **Restore distributed switch and all port groups** or **Restore distributed switch only**, as shown in the following screenshot:

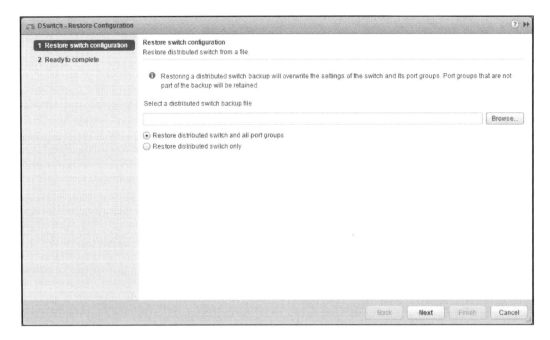

When using the **Restore distributed switch only** option, only the distributed switch configuration is restored. The dvPortGroups and their associated configurations are not restored. If the **Restore distributed switch and all port groups** option is selected, the virtual distributed switch configuration and the associated dvPortgroups are restored. Note that during the restoration process, the current settings of the distributed virtual switch and the associated dvPortgroups will be overwritten.

Deploying VMware Data Protection

vSphere Data Protection (**VDP**) is an easy-to-deploy, Linux-based virtual appliance that leverages **EMC Avamar** to provide the backup and recovery of virtual machines. Before the release of vSphere 6, VDP was available in two versions: VDP and VDP Advance. VDP Advance required a separate license to enable advanced features. In VDP 6, these have been combined and VDP 6 includes all the capabilities, with no requirement for additional licensing. VDP 6 provides the following capabilities:

- ▶ 8TB of deduplicated capacity per VDP appliance
- ▶ An application-aware agent for Microsoft Exchange, Microsoft SQL, and Microsoft Sharepoint

▶ Backup replication to another VDP appliance

▶ Automated backup verification

▶ Backup to an EMC Data Domain appliance

How to do it...

In order to deploy VDP, perform the following steps:

1. Download the VMware Data Protection appliance from `http://www.vmware.com/go/download-vsphere`.

2. Deploy the vSphere Data Protection Appliance from the OVA. Enter the appliance's network configuration information during the OVA deployment, as shown in the following screenshot:

3. When the OVA deployment is complete and the VDP appliance is powered on, visit `https://<vdp-ip-address>:8543/vdp-configure` to complete the appliance's configuration. Log in to the appliance for the first time using the username, `root`, and the default password, `changeme`.

4. Once you are logged in, the initial configuration wizard starts to configure the VDP appliance.

5. The first step performed by the wizard is verifying the network settings, as shown in the following screenshot:

 The wizard verifies that the appliance's hostname can be resolved in DNS. Forward and reverse DNS entries will need to be configured before the network settings can be saved successfully.

6. The configuration wizard will then prompt you to choose the time zone.

7. The default VDP password must be changed. Enter the VDP password, taking note of the password requirements. The wizard will place green checks next to the rules that the password meets. The password must meet all the password rules.

8. The VDP appliance is then registered with vCenter. Enter values for **vCenter username**, **vCenter password**, **vCenter FQDN or IP**, and **vCenter port**, as shown in the following screenshot:

9. Create a new storage for the VDP backups. This can be configured from 0.5 TB to 2 TB per VDP appliance. The **Create Storage** dialog is displayed in the following screenshot:

10. Choose where you want the VDP storage disks to be allocated. They can be stored with the appliance or on a specified datastore. The provisioning method for the storage disk can be configured as well, as shown in the following screenshot:

11. On completion of the VDP configuration, the following screen is shown:

12. Select the **Run performance analysis on storage configuration** and **Restart the appliance if successful** checkboxes.

13. When you are prompted to start the storage configuration, select **Yes** to begin the process. A status window is displayed as the configuration is applied. The configuration will take some time to complete—30 minutes or more—and the appliance will reboot once the configuration process has been completed successfully. The following screenshot shows the configuration status window:

14. Once the configuration has been completed and the VDP appliance restarts, the **vSphere Data Protection** management option will be available in the vSphere Web Client. The following screenshot shows the VDP connection screen in the vSphere Web Client:

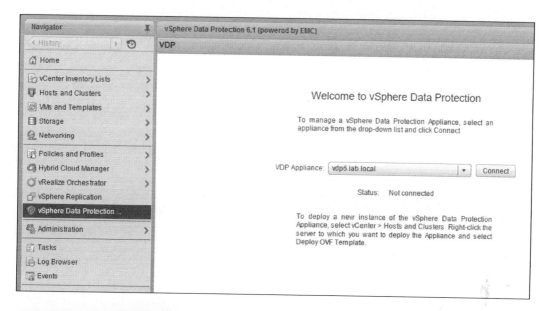

How it works...

During the VDP appliance OVA deployment, the initial network settings are configured, which includes the network address of the appliance, the subnet mask, the default gateway, and the primary DNS.

Once the appliance has been deployed and powered on, the VDP configuration wizard is used to verify the network configurations, configure the hostname and domain, set the root password of the appliance, configure the time zone, and register the appliance with a vCenter server. The configuration of the storage for the virtual machine backups is configured as well.

After the initial configuration and analysis has completed, the appliance will reboot and can then be managed using the vSphere Web Client. Backup jobs to protect virtual machines can then be created through the vSphere Web Client.

Using VMware Data Protection to back up virtual machines

Virtual machine backups using the VDP appliance are created and managed using the vSphere Web Client connected to vCenter, where the VDP appliance has been registered.

How to do it...

Perform the following steps to create a backup job in order to protect virtual machines using VDP:

1. In the vSphere Web Client, select **vSphere Data Protection** and connect to the VDP appliance.

2. Select the **Backup** tab, and from the **Backup job actions** menu, select **New**, as shown in the following screenshot:

3. Select the type of backup to be performed—either **Full Image**, which is a complete backup of the virtual machine, including all the disks and configurations—or **Individual Disks**, which are individual **virtual machine disks** (**VMDKs**), as shown in the following screenshot:

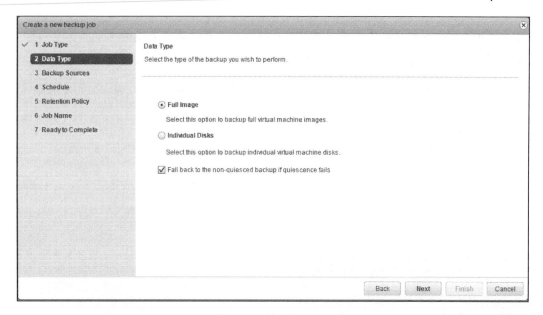

4. Select the backup targets. Targets can be vCenter inventory objects, including datacenters, clusters, resource pools, or individual virtual machines. The following screenshot illustrates the selection of two individual virtual machines to be a part of this backup job:

5. Create a schedule of the backup job. **Schedule** determines how often and when the backup job will run. The following screenshot demonstrates a daily schedule with the start time of **8:00 P.M**:

6. Set a retention policy for the backup job. **Retention Policy** determines for how long the backups are retained. In the following screenshot, the retention policy has been set to 30 days:

7. Set a job name for the backup job. It would be helpful if the name is a short description of the backup job, as shown in the following screenshot:

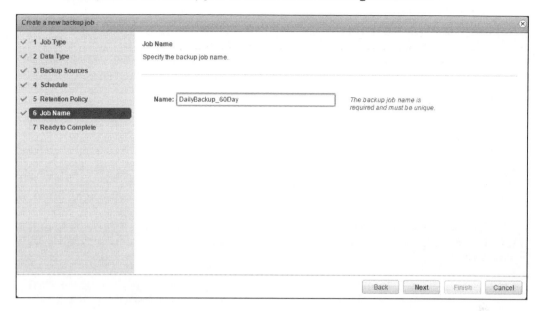

8. A **Ready to Complete** screen is shown in order to allow the configuration settings to be reviewed, as shown in the following screenshot:

9. Once completed, the backup job is created and will run according to the configured schedule.

How it works...

Backup jobs are created in order to back up virtual machines or groups of virtual machines. Backup jobs include the backup targets, the backup schedule, and the backup retention policy.

The best RPO that can be obtained for a single backup job is 24 hours because only a single daily backup can be configured. If the RPO for a specific virtual machine or a group of virtual machines is less than 24 hours, multiple backup jobs will need to be created. For example, if the RPO for a virtual machine is 6 hours, four daily backup jobs configured to start at 12:00 A.M., 6:00 A.M., 12:00 P.M., and 6:00 P.M. would need to be created in order to meet the RPO.

Once the backup jobs have run, the virtual machines can be restored to their original location or a different location. Restoring to a different location provides a way to test the virtual machine backups without impacting the running virtual machine.

File-level restores can also be performed by connecting to the VDP appliance from the backup target. To access file-level restores, visit `https://vdp-appliance-ip:8543/flr` from the virtual machine that has been backed up. The file-level restore client is shown in the following screenshot:

The health of the appliance, the current usage, and the status of the backup jobs can be monitored using the **Reports** tab, as shown in the following screenshot:

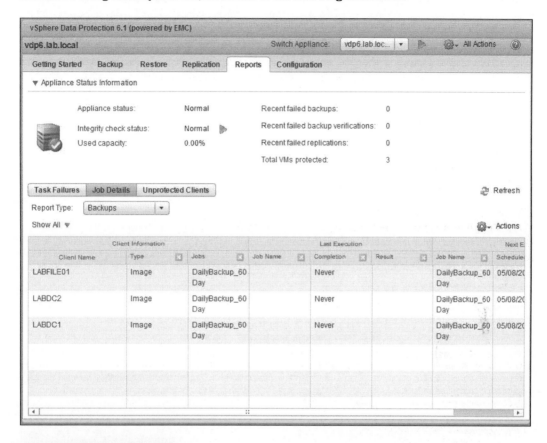

There's more...

VDP 6 includes application-aware protection for Microsoft SQL, Microsoft Exchange, and Microsoft SharePoint. This requires an agent to be installed in the guest OS. The agents can be downloaded from the VDP management interface in the vSphere Web Client, as shown in the following screenshot:

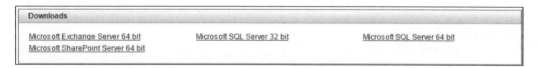

Once the agent has been installed in the guest OS, application backup jobs can be created in VDP to perform application-aware backups.

Replicating virtual machines with vSphere Replication

vSphere Replication is included for free with vSphere Essentials Plus or higher. vSphere Replication allows virtual machines to be replicated between sites or between datastores on the same site. It leverages **Change Block Tracking** (**CBT**) to replicate changes only between the source virtual machines and the replication target.

vSphere Replication appliances are deployed at each site participating in the replication. Multiple vSphere Replication appliances can be deployed in order to improve the replication performance.

How to do it...

To deploy vSphere Replication and configure a virtual machine for replication, perform the following steps:

1. Download the vSphere Replication appliance from `http://www.vmware.com/go/ download-vsphere`.

2. The vSphere Replication appliance is deployed from an OVA. During OVA deployment, the initial configuration of the administrator password, the database, and the management network IP address are configured, as shown in the following screenshot:

3. Once the vSphere Replication appliance has been deployed, it can be managed from the vSphere Web Client, as shown in the following screenshot:

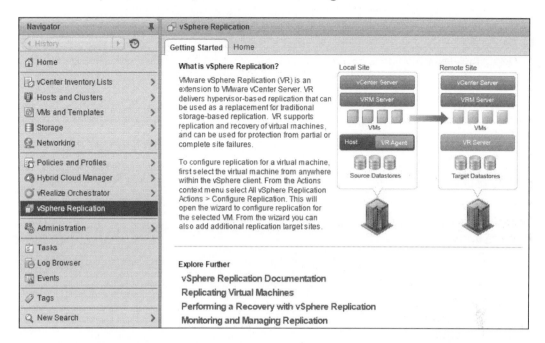

4. Replication can now be configured for virtual machines. To enable replication, right-click on the virtual machine to be replicated. Then, navigate to **All vSphere Replication Actions | Configure Replication...** from the menu, as shown in the following screenshot:

5. The replication wizard walks through the configuration of **Target site**, **Replication server**, **Target location**, and **Replication options**. The following screenshot displays the **Configure Replication for CA** wizard for a virtual machine:

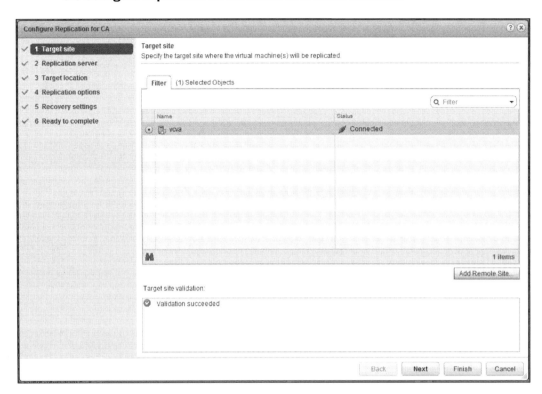

6. The **Recovery settings** menu allows you to configure **Recovery Point Objective (RPO)**, the time between replications, and the number of **Point in time instances** to keep track of the replicated virtual machine. The best RPO that can be realized with vSphere Replication is 15 minutes. The following screenshot shows the configuration of an RPO of 15 minutes for the selected virtual machine:

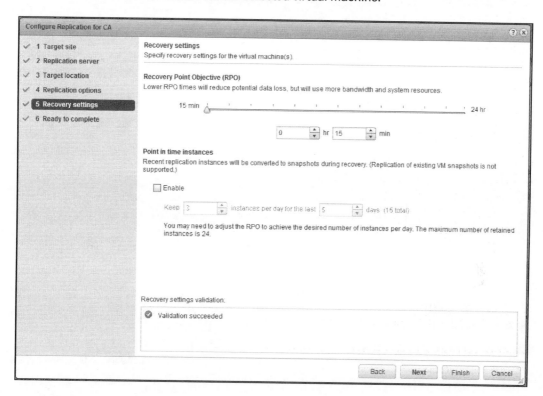

7. Once the replication for a virtual machine has been configured, the replication can be monitored in the vSphere Web Client. The following screenshot shows the status of **Initial Full Sync** on a virtual machine that has been configured for replication:

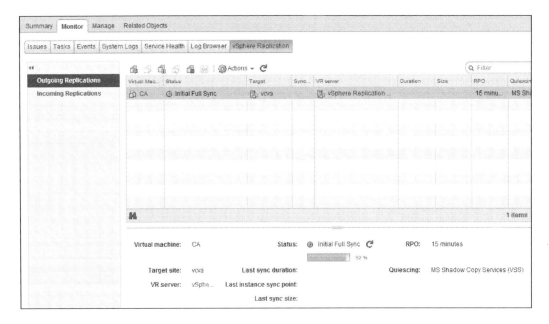

How it works...

After the initial synchronization has been completed, the vSphere kernel tracks the writes to the protected virtual machine and transfers only the blocks that have changed. The following diagram illustrates the traffic flow for a virtual machine replicated with vSphere Replication:

Here, VM1 has been configured for replication. Changed blocks are tracked and transferred to the target vSphere Replication appliance.

Once a replication has been set up, it can be recovered from the **vSphere Replication** management by selecting the replicated virtual machine and choosing **Recover...**, as shown in the following screenshot:

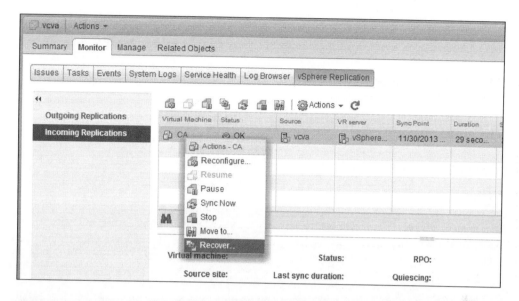

Protecting the virtual datacenter with Site Recovery Manager

Site Recovery Manager (**SRM**) is a VMware product that provides a framework to automate the protection and failover between VMware-virtualized datacenters. SRM is licensed as a separate product. Licensing is per-VM protected, and there are two license editions: Standard and Enterprise. The Standard edition provides protection for up to 75 virtual machines, and the Enterprise edition can protect an unlimited number of virtual machines.

A complete book can be dedicated to the implementation and use of SRM. This book is just meant to be a quick overview of the configuration and capabilities of SRM. More information on the implementation and use of SRM can be found in the SRM documentation at http://www.vmware.com/support/pubs/srm_pubs.html.

How to do it...

Protecting the datacenter using SRM is accomplished through the following process:

1. Identify the requirements of Site Recovery Manager.
2. Deploy Site Recovery Manager at the protected and recovery sites.
3. Configure connections between the protected and recovery sites.

4. Establish virtual machine replication between the protected and recovery sites.

5. Create resource mapping between the protected and recovery sites.

6. Create protection groups containing the virtual machines to be protected.

7. Configure recovery plans to automate the recovery of virtual machines.

8. Test the recovery plan to ensure that it will operate as expected.

How it works...

SRM does not provide the replication of virtual machines. It provides a framework to easily automate and manage the protection and failover of virtual machines. The SRM service runs on a Windows server and requires a supported database. Supported databases for the deployed SRM version can be found on the product and solution interoperability matrix at `http://partnerweb.vmware.com/comp_guide2/sim/interop_matrix.php`.

Virtual machines can be replicated between sites using either vSphere Replication or array-based replication. If array-based replication is used, a supported **Storage Replication Adapter** (**SRA**) is installed on the SRM servers at each site. SRA communicates with the array to control the replication flow during normal, failover, and failback operations.

vSphere Replication can be deployed independently, or it can be deployed as part of the SRM installation. vSphere Replication connectivity between sites can be configured and managed from within SRM.

 SRM configuration and management can only be done using the thick vSphere Client. It cannot be managed using the vSphere Web Client.

The following diagram illustrates a basic SRM architecture using both vSphere Replication and array-based replication between the protected and recovery sites:

Compute resources (datacenters, clusters, and resource pools) and network resources on the protected site are mapped to the resources at the recovery site. For example, the port group named *Production VM Network* at the protected site is mapped to a port group named *Failover VM Network* at the recovery site. The resource must exist at the recovery site before they can be mapped. A placeholder datastore is configured to hold the protected virtual machine configuration files at the recovery site.

Protection groups are created and contain virtual machines that are protected. When virtual machines are added to a protection group, a placeholder configuration file is created at the recovery site on the placeholder datastore. Protection groups can be used to group virtual machines that should be recovered together in order to ensure that workload dependencies are met. For example, an application that includes a virtual machine running a web frontend and another virtual machine running the support database can be placed in a protection group in order to ensure that all of the workload dependencies are recovered when a failover is initiated.

Recovery plans contain protection groups. Multiple recovery plans can be created, and a protection group can be included in more than one recovery plan. For example, a recovery plan can be created for a single protection group in order to facilitate recovery, or a single application and another recovery plan can be created to include all the configured protection groups in order to facilitate the recovery of the entire site.

As part of the recovery plan, the virtual machine startup order can be configured with virtual machine network options. If the virtual machine network configuration (the IP address or DNS servers) needs to be changed during the recovery, the virtual machine network options are set on the individual virtual machines in the recovery plan. VMware Tools must be installed on the virtual machines if network changes are required.

A recovery plan can be tested without impacting the protected virtual machines by running a recovery test. During the test, an isolated vSwitch—a vSwitch with no uplinks—will be created at the recovery site. When virtual machines are recovered during the test, they are connected to this isolated switch. Once the test recovery has been completed, the virtual machine can be verified at the recovery site. Once the test has been completed and verified, the cleanup operation can be run to return the virtual machines to a protected state.

12

Design Documentation

In this chapter, we will cover the following topics:

- ▸ Creating the architecture design document
- ▸ Writing an implementation plan
- ▸ Developing an installation guide
- ▸ Creating a validation test plan
- ▸ Writing operational procedures
- ▸ Presenting the design
- ▸ Implementing the design

Introduction

The design documentation provides written documentation of the design factors and the choices the architect has made in the design in order to satisfy the business and technical requirements.

The design documentation also aids in the implementation of the design. In many cases where the design architect is not responsible for the implementation, the design documents ensure the successful implementation of the design by the implementation engineer.

 Once you have created the documentation for a few designs, you will be able to develop standard processes and templates to aid in the creation of design documentations.

Documentations can vary from project to project. Many consulting companies and resellers have standard documentation templates that they use when designing solutions. A properly documented design should include a minimum of the following information:

- ▶ The architecture design
- ▶ The implementation plan
- ▶ The installation guide
- ▶ The validation test plan
- ▶ Operational procedures

This information can be included in a single document or separated into different documents.

VMware provides Service Delivery Kits to VMware partners. These kits can be found on the VMware Partner University portal at `http://www.vmware.com/go/partneruniversity`, which provides documentation templates that can be used as a foundation to create design documents. If you do not have access to these templates, example outlines are provided in this chapter to assist you in developing your own design documentation templates.

The final steps of the design process include gaining customer approval in order to begin the implementation of the design.

Creating the architecture design document

The architecture design document is a technical document that describes the components and specifications required to support the solution and ensure that the specific business and technical requirements of the design are satisfied.

> An excellent example of an architecture design document is the *VMware Cloud Infrastructure Architecture Case Study* white paper article, which can be found at `http://www.vmware.com/files/pdf/techpaper/cloud-infrastructure-achitecture-case-study.pdf`.

The architect creates the architecture design document to document the design factors and the specific choices that have been made to satisfy those factors. The document serves as a way for the architect to show their work when making design decisions. It includes the conceptual, logical, and physical designs.

How to do it...

The architecture design document should include the following information:

- ▸ The purpose and the overview
    - ❑ The executive summary
    - ❑ The design methodology

- ▸ Conceptual design: requirements, constraints, assumptions, and risks
- ▸ Logical management, storage, compute, and network design
- ▸ Physical management, storage, compute, and network design

How it works...

The *Purpose and Overview* section of the architecture design includes the *Executive Summary* section. The *Executive Summary* section provides a high-level overview of the design and the goals the design will accomplish, and it defines the purpose and scope of the architecture design document.

The following is an example executive summary in the *VMware Cloud Infrastucture Architecture Case Study* white paper:

> *This architecture design was developed to support a virtualization project to consolidate 100 existing physical servers on to a VMware vSphere 6.x virtual infrastructure. The primary goals this design will accomplish are to increase operational efficiency and to provide high availability of customer-facing applications.*
>
> *This document details the recommended implementation of a VMware virtualization architecture based on specific business requirements and VMware recommended practices. The document provides both logical and physical design considerations for all related infrastructure components including servers, storage, networking, management, and virtual machines.*
>
> *The scope of this document is specific to the design of the virtual infrastructure and the supporting components.*

The purpose and overview section should also include details of the design methodology the architect has used in creating the architecture design. This should include the processes followed to determine the business and technical requirements along with definitions of the infrastructure qualities that influenced the design decisions.

Design factors, requirements, constraints, and assumptions are documented as part of the conceptual design. *Chapter 3, The Design Factors*, provides details on the key factors included as part of the conceptual design. In order to document the design factors, use a table to organize them and associate them with an ID that can be referenced easily.

The following table illustrates an example of how to document the design requirements:

ID	Requirement
R001	Consolidate the existing 100 physical application servers down to five servers
R002	Provide the capacity to support growth for 25 additional application servers over the next 5 years
R003	Server hardware maintenance should not affect the application uptime
R004	Provide *N+2* redundancy to support a hardware failure during normal and maintenance operations

The conceptual design should also include tables documenting any constraints and assumptions. A high-level diagram of the conceptual design can be included as well.

Details of the logical design are documented in the architecture design document. The logical design of management, storage, network, and compute resources, should be included. When documenting the logical design document, any recommended practices that were followed should be included. Also include references to the requirements, constraints, and assumptions that influenced the design decisions.

 When documenting the logical design, show your work to support your design decisions. Include any formulas used for resource calculations and provide detailed explanations on why design decisions were made.

An example table outlining the logical design of compute resource requirements is as follows:

Parameter	Specification
Current CPU resources required	100 GHz
*CPU growth	25 GHz
CPU required (75% utilization)	157 GHz
Current memory resources required	525 GB
*Memory growth	131 GB
Memory required (75% utilization)	821 GB
Memory required (25% TPS savings)	616 GB
*CPU and memory growth of 25 additional application servers (R002)	

Similar tables will be created to document the logical design for storage, network, and management resources.

The physical design documents have the details of the physical hardware chosen along with the configurations of both the physical and virtual hardware. Details of vendors and hardware models chosen and the reasons for the decisions made should be included as part of the physical design. The configuration of the physical hardware is documented along with the details of why specific configuration options were chosen. The physical design should also include diagrams that document the configuration of physical resources, such as physical network connectivity and storage layout.

A sample outline of the architecture design document is as follows:

- **Cover page**: This includes the customer and project names
- **Document version log**: This contains the log of authors and changes made to the document
- **Document contacts**: This includes the subject matter experts involved in the creation of the design
- **Table of contents**: This is the index of the document sections for quick reference
- **List of tables**: This is the index of tables included in the document for quick reference
- **List of figures**: This is the index of figures included in the document for quick reference
- **Purpose and overview**: This section consists of an executive summary to provide an overview of the design and the design methodology followed in creating the design
- **Conceptual design**: This is the documentation of the design factors: requirements, constraints, and assumptions
- **Logical design**: This has the details of the logical management, storage, network, and compute design
- **Physical design**: This contains the details of the selected hardware and the configuration of the physical and virtual hardware

Writing an implementation plan

The implementation plan documents the requirements necessary to complete the implementation of the design.

The implementation plan defines the project roles and what is expected of the customer and what they can expect during the implementation of the design.

This document is sometimes referred to as the statement of work. It defines the key points of contact, the requirements that must be satisfied to start the implementation, any project documentation deliverables, and how changes to the design and implementation will be handled.

How to do it...

The implementation plan should include the following information:

- ▶ The purpose statement
- ▶ Project contacts
- ▶ Implementation requirements
- ▶ An overview of the implementation steps
- ▶ The definition of the project documentation deliverables
- ▶ The implementation of change management

How it works...

The purpose statement defines the purpose and scope of the document. The purpose statement of the implementation plan should define what is included in the document and provide a brief overview of the goals of the project. It is simply an introduction so that someone reading the document can gain a quick understanding of what the document contains.

The following is an example purpose statement:

This document serves as the implementation plan and defines the scope of the virtualization project. This document identifies points of contact for the project, lists implementation requirements, provides a brief description of each of the document deliverables, and provides an overview of the implementation process for the data-center virtualization project.

The scope of this document is specific to the implementation of the virtual data-center implementation and the supporting components as defined in the Architecture Design.

Key project contacts, their roles, and their contact information should be included as part of the implementation plan document. These contacts include customer stakeholders, project managers, project architects, and implementation engineers.

The following is a sample table that can be used to document project contacts for the implementation plan:

Role	Name	Contact information
The customer's project sponsor		
The customer's technical resource		
The project manager		
The design architect		

Role	Name	Contact information
The implementation engineer		
The QA engineer		

Support contacts for the hardware and software used in the implementation plan may also be included in the table, for example, contact numbers for VMware support or other vendor support.

Implementation requirements contain the implementation dependencies required to include the access and facility requirements. Any hardware, software, and licensing that must be available to implement the design are also documented here.

Access requirements include the following:

- ▶ Physical access to the site.
- ▶ Credentials required for access to resources. These include active directory credentials and VPN credentials (if remote access is required).

Facility requirements include the following:

- ▶ Power and cooling to support the equipment that will be deployed as part of the design
- ▶ Rack space requirements

Hardware, software, and licensing requirements include the following:

- ▶ vSphere licensing
- ▶ Windows or other operating system licensing
- ▶ Other third-party application licensing
- ▶ Software (ISO, physical media, and so on)
- ▶ Physical hardware (hosts, arrays, network switches, cables, and so on)

A high-level overview of the steps required to complete the implementation is also documented. The details of each step are not a part of this document; only the steps that need to be performed will be included. For example, take a look at the following:

1. Procure the hardware, software, and licensing.
2. Schedule engineering resources.
3. Verify access and facility requirements.
4. Perform an inventory check for the required hardware, software, and licensing.
5. Install and configure the storage array.

6. Rack, cable, and burn-in of physical server hardware.

7. Install ESXi on physical servers.

8. Install vCenter Server.

9. Configure ESXi and vCenter.

10. Test and verify the implementation plan.

11. Migrate physical workloads to virtual machines.

12. Perform the operational verification of the implementation plan.

The implementation overview may also include an implementation timeline documenting the time required to complete each of the steps.

The project documentation deliverables are defined as part of the implementation plan. Any documentation that will be delivered to the customer once the implementation has been completed should be detailed here. Details include the name of the document and a brief description of the purpose of the document.

The following table provides example descriptions of the project documentation deliverables:

Document	Description
The architecture design	This is a technical document that describes the vSphere components and specifications required to achieve a solution that addresses the specific business and technical requirements of the design.
The implementation plan	This identifies implementation roles and requirements. It provides a high-level map of the implementation and deliverables detailed in the design. It documents change management procedures.
The installation guide	This document provides detailed, step-by-step instructions on how to install and configure the products specified in the architecture design document.
The validation test plan	This document provides an overview of the procedures to be executed post installation in order to verify whether or not the infrastructure is installed correctly. It can also be used at any point subsequent to the installation to check whether or not the infrastructure continues to function correctly.
Operational procedures	This document provides detailed, step-by-step instructions on how to perform common operational tasks after the design has been implemented.

How changes are made to the design, specifically changes made to the design factors, must be well documented. Even a simple change to a requirement or an assumption that cannot be verified can have a tremendous effect on the design and implementation. The process to submit a change, research the impact of the change, and approve the change should be documented in detail.

The following is an example outline for an implementation plan:

▶ **Cover page**: This includes the customer and project names

▶ **Document version log**: This contains the log of authors and the changes made to the document

▶ **Document contacts**: This includes the subject matter experts involved in the creation of the design

▶ **Table of contents**: This is the index of the document sections for quick reference

▶ **List of tables**: This is the index of the tables included in the document for quick reference

▶ **List of figures**: This is the index of the figures included in the document for quick reference

▶ **Purpose statement**: This defines the purpose of the document

▶ **Project contacts**: This is the documentation of key project points of contact

▶ **Implementation requirements**: This provides the access, facilities, hardware, software, and licensing required to complete the implementation

▶ **Implementation overview**: This is the overview of the steps required to complete the implementation

▶ **Project deliverables**: This consists of the documents that will be provided as deliverables once the implementation has been completed

Developing an installation guide

The installation guide provides step-by-step instructions for the implementation of the architecture design. This guide should include detailed information on how to implement and configure all the resources associated with the virtual datacenter project.

In many projects, the person creating the design is not the person responsible for implementing it. The installation guide outlines the steps required to implement the physical design outlined in the architecture design document.

The installation guide should provide details about the installation of all components, including the storage and network configurations required to support the design. In a complex design, multiple installation guides can be created to document the installation of the various components required to support the design. For example, separate installation guides may be created for the storage, network, and vSphere installation and configuration.

How to do it...

The installation guide should include the following information:

- The purpose statement
- The assumption statement
- Step-by-step instructions on implementing the design

How it works...

The purpose statement simply states the purpose of the document. The assumption statement describes any assumptions the document's author has made. Commonly, an assumption statement simply states that the document has been written, assuming that the reader is familiar with virtualization concepts and the architecture design.

The following is an example of a basic purpose and assumption statement that can be used for an installation guide:

Purpose: *This document provides a guide to install and configure the virtual infrastructure design defined in the Architecture Design.*

Assumptions: *This guide is written for an implementation engineer or administrator who is familiar with vSphere concepts and terminologies. The guide is not intended for administrators who have no prior knowledge of vSphere concepts and terminologies.*

The installation guide should include details on implementing all areas of the design. It should include the configuration of the storage array, physical servers, physical network components, and vSphere components. The following are just a few examples of the installation tasks to include instructions for the following:

- Storage array configurations
- Physical network configurations
- Physical host configurations
- The ESXi installation
- The vCenter Server installation and configuration
- The virtual network configuration
- The datastore configuration
- High availability, distributed resource scheduler, storage DRS, and other vSphere components' installation and configuration

The installation guide should provide as much detail as possible. Along with the step-by-step procedures, screenshots can be used to provide installation guidance.

The following screenshot is an example taken from an installation guide that details the enabling and configuration of the Software iSCSI adapter:

The following is an example outline for an installation guide:

- ▸ **Cover page**: This includes the customer and project names
- ▸ **Document version log**: This contains the log of authors and the changes made to the document
- ▸ **Document contacts**: This includes the subject matter experts involved in the creation of the design
- ▸ **Table of contents**: This is the index of document sections for quick reference
- ▸ **List of tables**: This is the index of tables included in the document for quick reference
- ▸ **List of figures**: This is the index of figures included in the document for quick reference
- ▸ **Purpose statement**: This defines the purpose of the document
- ▸ **Assumption statement**: This defines any assumptions made in creating the document
- ▸ **Installation guide**: This provides the step-by-step installation instructions to be followed when implementing the design

Creating a validation test plan

The validation test plan documents how the implementation will be verified. It documents the criteria that must be met in order to determine the success of the implementation and the test procedures that should be followed when validating the environment. The criteria and procedures defined in the validation test plan determine whether or not the design requirements have been successfully met.

How to do it...

The validation test plan should include the following information:

- ▸ The purpose statement
- ▸ The assumption statement
- ▸ The success criteria
- ▸ The test procedures

How it works...

The purpose statement defines the purpose of the validation test plan, and the assumption statement documents any assumptions the author of the plan has made in developing the test plan. Typically, the assumptions are that the testing and validation will be performed by someone who is familiar with the concepts and the design.

The following is an example of a purpose and assumption statement for a validation test plan:

> **Purpose**: *This document contains testing procedures to verify that the implemented configurations specified in the Architecture Design document successfully address the customer requirements.*

> **Assumptions**: *This document assumes that the person performing these tests has a basic understanding of VMware vSphere and is familiar with the accompanying design documentation. This document is not intended for administrators or testers who have no prior knowledge of vSphere concepts and terminologies.*

The success criteria determines whether or not the implemented design is operating as expected. More importantly, these criteria determine whether or not the design requirements have been met. Success is measured based on whether or not the criteria satisfies the design requirements.

The following table shows some examples of the success criteria defined in the validation test plan:

Description	Measurement
Members of the active directory group vSphere administrators are able to access vCenter as administrators	Yes/No
Access is denied to users outside the vSphere administrators active directory group	Yes/No
Access to a host using the vSphere Client is permitted when the lockdown mode is disabled	Yes/No
Access to a host using the vSphere Client is denied when the lockdown mode is enabled	Yes/No
Cluster resource utilization is less than 75%	Yes/No

If the success criteria are not met, the design does not satisfy the design factors. This can be due to a misconfiguration or an error in the design. Troubleshooting will need to be done in order to identify the issue, or modifications to the design may need to be made.

Test procedures are performed in order to determine whether or not the success criteria have been met. Test procedures should include the testing of usability, performance, and recoverability. They should also include the test description, the tasks required to perform the test, and the expected results of the test.

The following table provides some examples of usability testing procedures:

The test description	Tasks required to perform the test	The expected result
vCenter administrator access	Use the vSphere Web Client to access the vCenter Server. Log in as a user who is a member of the vSphere administrators AD group.	Administrator access to the inventory of the vCenter Server
vCenter access: No permissions	Use the vSphere Web Client to access the vCenter Server. Log in as a user who is not a member of the vSphere administrators AD group.	Access is denied
Host access: lockdown mode disabled	Disable the lockdown mode through the DCUI. Use the vSphere Client to access the host and log in as `root`.	Direct access to the host using the vSphere Client is successful
Host access: lockdown mode enabled	Re-enable the lockdown mode through the DCUI. Use the vSphere Client to access the host and log in as `root`.	Direct access to the host using the vSphere Client is denied

The following table provides some examples of reliability testing procedures:

The test description	Tasks required to perform the test	The expected result
Host storage path failure	Disconnect a vmnic providing IP storage connectivity from the host	The disconnected path fails, but IO continues to be processed on the surviving paths. A network connectivity alarm should be triggered and an e-mail should be sent to the configured e-mail address.
Host storage path restore	Reconnect the vmnic providing IP storage connectivity	The failed path should become active and begin processing the IO. Network connectivity alarms should get cleared.
Array storage path failure	Disconnect one network connection from the active SP	The disconnected paths fail on all hosts, but IO continues to be processed on the surviving paths.
Management network redundancy	Disconnect the active management network vmnic	The standby adapter becomes active. Management access to the host is not interrupted. A loss-of-network redundancy alarm should be triggered, and an e-mail should be sent to the configured e-mail address.

These are just a few examples of test procedures. The actual test procedures will depend on the requirements defined in the conceptual design.

The following is an example outline of a validation test plan:

- ▶ **Cover page**: This includes the customer and project names
- ▶ **Document version log**: This contains the log of authors and the changes made to the document
- ▶ **Document contacts**: This includes the subject matter experts involved in the creation of the design
- ▶ **Table of contents**: This is the index of document sections for quick reference
- ▶ **List of tables**: This is the index of tables included in the document for quick reference
- ▶ **List of figures**: This is the index of figures included in the document for quick reference
- ▶ **Purpose statement**: This defines the purpose of the document
- ▶ **Assumption statement**: This defines any assumptions made in creating the document
- ▶ **Success criteria**: This is a list of the criteria that must be met in order to validate the successful implementation of the design
- ▶ **Test Procedures**: This is a list of the test procedures to be followed, including the steps to follow and the expected results

Writing operational procedures

The operational procedure document provides the detailed, step-by-step procedures required for the successful operation of the implemented virtual datacenter design. These procedures should include monitoring and troubleshooting, virtual machine deployment, environment startup and shutdown, patching and updating, and any other details that may be required for the successful operation of the implemented design.

How to do it...

The operational procedures should include the following information:

- The purpose statement
- The assumption statement
- Step-by-step procedures for daily operations
- Troubleshooting and recovery procedures

How it works...

As with other design documents, the purpose statement defines the purpose of the operational procedures document. The assumption statement details any assumptions the author of the plan made in developing the procedures.

> **Purpose**: *This document contains detailed step-by-step instructions on how to perform common operational tasks. It provides a guide to performing common tasks associated with management, monitoring, troubleshooting, virtual machine deployment, updating, and recovery.*

> **Assumptions**: *This document assumes that an administrator who uses these procedures is familiar with VMware vSphere concepts and terminologies.*

The operational procedure document provides step-by-step procedures for common tasks that will need to be performed by the administrator of the environment. Examples of the procedures to include are as follows:

- Accessing the environment
- Monitoring the resource usage and performance
- Deploying new virtual machines
- Patching ESXi hosts
- Updating VMware tools and virtual machine hardware

The operational procedure document should also describe troubleshooting and recovery. Examples of these procedures include the following:

▸ Monitoring alarms

▸ Exporting log bundles

▸ Restoring a virtual machine from a backup

▸ Environment shutdown and startup

The following screenshot is an example taken from an operational-procedures document that details the process to export a log bundle:

5. Exporting a vCenter Log Bundle

When a service request is submitted to VMware for support, VMware Support may require the system logs to troubleshoot the reported issue.

1. To export system logs right-click the vCenter Server inventory object and select **All vCenter Actions -> Export System Logs**.
2. Select the hosts and vCenter logs to include in the log bundle.

3. Select the logs to export. In most cases the default selections will be used unless otherwise stated by VMware Support. Click **Generate Log Bundle** to begin the log export.

4. After the log bundle has been generated click **Download Log Bundle** to download the logs.
5. Choose a location to save the log export. A zipped archive containing the exported logs will be downloaded to location selected.

The following is an example outline of an operational procedure document:

- ▸ **Cover page**: This includes the customer and project names
- ▸ **Document version log**: This contains the log of authors and the changes made to the document
- ▸ **Document contacts**: This includes the subject matter experts involved in the creation of the design
- ▸ **Table of contents**: This is the index of document sections for quick reference
- ▸ **List of tables**: This is the index of tables included in the document for quick reference
- ▸ **List of figures**: This is the index of figures included in the document for quick reference
- ▸ **Purpose statement**: This defines the purpose of the document
- ▸ **Assumption statement**: This defines any assumptions made when creating the document
- ▸ **Operational procedures**: These are the step-by-step procedures for the day-to-day access, monitoring, and operation of the environment
- ▸ **Troubleshooting and recovery procedures**: These are the step-by-step procedures for the troubleshooting of issues and recovering from a failure

Presenting the design

Typically, once the design has been completed, it is presented to the customer for approval before the implementation as shown in the following design process diagram:

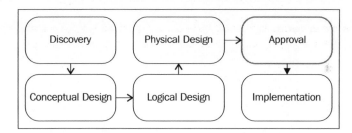

In order to obtain the customer approval, typically, a high-level presentation is provided to the project stakeholders in order to provide details on how the design satisfies the requirements along with the benefits associated with the design.

 If you are not comfortable giving presentations, check out `http://www.toastmasters.org/`. Toastmasters can help you develop presentation skills and build confidence when speaking in front of people.

How to do it...

Presenting the design to stakeholders is a simple, but important, part of the design process:

1. Develop a presentation.
2. Present the design to the customer.

How it works...

The presentation should include the following information:

▸ An overview of the design methodology

▸ An overview of the discovery process

▸ The design factors: requirements, constraints, and assumptions

▸ A high-level overview of the logical and physical design

Remember to tailor your presentation to your audience. Keep the presentation at a high level, but be ready to provide details about the technical and business decisions made to support the design.

When presenting the design, explain the key design decisions and how they satisfy the requirements. Cover the entire design, but keep the presentation brief. Be ready to answer questions about the design and the reasons behind the design decisions.

Implementing the design

The final step of the design process is the implementation of the design as shown in the following design process diagram:

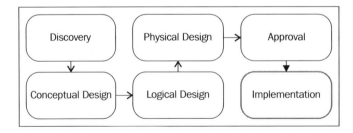

Implementation takes the design from paper and puts it into practice. If time has been taken to create and correctly document a solid design, its implementation will be the easiest part of the process.

How to do it...

The following steps are part of the design implementation:

1. Implement the documented design.
2. Perform the validation and testing.
3. Perform the review and delivery.

How it works...

Implement the design as documented in the architecture design. The implementation plan provides a guide to the implementation process, while the installation guide provides the details about performing the installation. The validation test plan is then used to test and validate the implementation against the design requirements.

Once the design has been implemented successfully, it should be reviewed by the customer in order to identify any lessons learned for the next steps. The documented deliverables are then provided to the customer.

Good luck.

Index

Printed in Great Britain
by Amazon